Following God

LEARNING LIFE PRINCIPLES
FROM THE NEW TESTAMENT
MEN OF FAITH

P9-BJV-605

LEARNING LIFE PRINCIPLES
FROM THE NEW TESTAMENT
MEN OF FAITH

A Bible Study by

Wayne Barber
Eddie Rasnake
Richard Shepherd

AMG *Publishers*™

Chattanooga, TN 37422

Following God

LEARNING LIFE PRINCIPLES FROM THE NEW TESTAMENT MEN OF FAITH

© 1999 by Wayne A. Barber, Eddie Rasnake, and Richard L. Shepherd

Eighth Printing, 2012

Published by AMG Publishers
All Rights Reserved.

ISBN: 0-89957-304-5

Unless otherwise noted,
Scripture is taken from the *New American Standard Bible*®.
Copyright © 1960, 1962, 1963, 1968, 1971, 1972, 1973, 1975, 1977
by The Lockman Foundation.
Used by permission.

Printed in the United States of America
17 16 15 14 13 12 —W— 12 11 10 9

This book is dedicated to:

Roy Hession (1908-1992)

Through his writing and preaching he faithfully showed each of us the Calvary road and taught us what it means to live, *"Not I, but Christ."*

"Remember those who led you, who spoke the word of God to you; and considering the results of their conduct, imitate their faith" Hebrews 13:7.

Acknowledgements

This work goes forth to those who have encouraged us in the publication of the first four books in this series: *Life Principles from the Old Testament, Life Principles from the Kings of the Old Testament, Life Principles from the Women of the Bible,* and *Life Principles from the Prophets of the Old Testament.* This series has been a labor of love, and through our study we have made friends with many saints of days gone by. We look forward to getting to know them even better in heaven. We are especially grateful to the body of believers at Woodland Park Baptist Church in Chattanooga, Tennessee, who have walked through many of these studies with us and have been a continual source of encouragement as the writing of new studies progresses. Thanks to the folks at AMG, especially Warren Baker and Rick Steele, Trevor Overcash and Dale Anderson, and to Phillip Rodgers. Thanks to Robin Currier for her invaluable help in proofreading. Most of all, we remain grateful to the Lord Jesus, who continues to teach us and lead us in what it means to follow Him with a whole heart.

THE AUTHORS

Wayne Barber

WAYNE BARBER has recently become Senior Pastor of Hoffmantown Church, Albuquerque, New Mexico. A renowned national and international conference ministry speaker, the primary goal of Wayne's ministry is in spreading the message of "the sufficiency of Christ." People around the world connect with Wayne's unique ability to make God's Word come alive through his honest and open "real-life" experiences. Wayne has authored or co-authored several books, and his most recent book, *The Rest of Grace*, was published in 1998. He also authors a regular column in AMG's *Pulpit Helps* monthly magazine. For more than twenty years he has served as Senior Pastor-Teacher of Woodland Park Baptist Church, in Chattanooga, Tennessee, and for many of those years in Chattanooga, Wayne co-taught with noted author Kay Arthur of Precept Ministries and had studied under the late Dr. Spiros Zodhiates, who was one of the world's leading Greek scholars. Wayne and his wife Diana have two grown children and make their home in Chattanooga, Tennessee.

Rick Shepherd

Richard L. Shepherd has been engaged in some form of ministry for more than twenty years, focusing on areas of teaching, discipleship, and prayer. He has served in churches in Alabama, Florida, Texas, and Tennessee and now serves as Director of Prayer and Spiritual Awakening with the Florida Baptist Convention. For nearly seventeen years (1983–2000), Rick served as an associate pastor at Woodland Park Baptist Church in Chattanooga, Tennessee. The Lord's ministry has taken him to several countries, including Haiti, Romania, Ukraine, Moldova, Italy, Israel, England, and Greece, where he has been involved in training pastors, church leaders, and congregations. Rick has also lectured on college and seminary campuses. He graduated with honors from the University of Mobile and holds a Master of Divinity and a Ph.D. from Southwestern Baptist Theological Seminary in Fort Worth, Texas. He and his wife Linda Gail have four children and make their home in Jacksonville, Florida.

Eddie Rasnake

EDDIE RASNAKE met Christ in 1976 as a freshman in college. He graduated with honors from East Tennessee State University in 1980. He worked in business for two years following graduation, during which he married his wife Michele. Together they joined the staff of Campus Crusade for Christ. While on staff they served two and one-half years at the University of Virginia and started a Campus Crusade ministry at James Madison University. Eddie then served for four years as campus director of the Campus Crusade ministry at the University of Tennessee. In 1989 Eddie left Campus Crusade to serve with Wayne Barber at Woodland Park Baptist Church as the Associate Pastor of Discipleship and Training. He has been ministering in Eastern Europe in the role of equipping local believers for the past ten years and has published materials in Albanian, Italian, Romanian, and Russian. Eddie is also the author of numerous books, including *What Should I Do, Lord?*. Eddie and Michele live in Chattanooga, Tennessee, where they enjoy the adventure of home schooling their four children.

AMG
INTERNATIONAL

With operations of ministry in over 50 countries, AMG stands for Advancing the Ministries of the Gospel. Since 1942, AMG International has operated on the premise that God works primarily through the local church and through individual Christians. Therefore AMG is dedicated to helping advance the gospel both locally and worldwide. Some areas of AMG's worldwide ministry include: missionary outreach, child care facilities, hospitals and clinics devoted to helping the poor, orphanages, church planting, training national workers, and Christian publishing.

Further information concerning AMG International can be obtained by calling 1-800-251-7206, or by writing us at: AMG International, 6815 Shallowford Road, Chattanooga, TN, 37421.

Our internet address is:
www.amgpublishers.com

Preface

Following by faith . . . "*Without faith it is impossible to please* [God], *for u   mes to God must believe that He is, and that He is a rewarder of those who seek Him.*" So reads the exhortation of Hebrews 11:6. The writer of Hebrews goes on to exhort his readers to fix their "*eyes on Jesus, the author and perfecter of faith, who for the joy set before Him endured the cross, despising the shame, and has sat down at the right hand of the throne of God*" (Hebrews 12:2). From His throne through the power of His Spirit our Lord Jesus calls each of us to follow Him by faith. "*If anyone wishes to come after Me, let him deny himself, and take up his cross daily, and follow Me*" (Luke 9:23). The life Jesus desires from us is a life that consistently follows by faith—abiding in Him and letting His Word abide in us (see John 15), dying to ourselves and living unto Him (see 2 Corinthians 5:15), forgetting what lies behind and pressing on to what lies ahead (see Philippians 3:13–14).

Real faith is marked by faith actions not "religious" outward show. There is a Greek word in the New Testament for someone who merely imitates outward actions. It is the word "hypocrite" from the Greek word "*hupocrites,*" meaning an actor on a stage playing a part. Those who merely imitate righteousness have no heart. Their acting is a facade like a drama set with only appearances and no substance—all religious smoke and mirrors. Hebrews 11 tells us that genuine faith has substance. Genuine faith is built on something that is real, something upon which one can stand. Those that have faith today have heart and soul like the believers of Hebrews 11 or the leaders of Hebrews 13:7. Hebrews 13:7 calls us to real faith, tested faith—"*Remember those who led you, who spoke the word of God to you; and considering the result of their conduct, imitate their faith.*" This verse does not say "imitate their conduct." That could lead to more empty show and no substance. It says "*imitate their faith.*" In other words, look at how they look to Jesus, how they follow Him in faith, and then imitate that faith.

As we walk through the lives of the New Testament believers presented here, we are called to real faith that acts on the revealed Word of God. What we will see in the pages of Scripture are people who heard the call of Jesus to come and follow. These were not perfect people who followed Him—far from it—but they proved to be faithful people. They can show us many things about a faithful (full of faith) walk. Some of the principles they can teach us are found in their battles with unanswered questions, in the reality of their doubts along the way, in the joy of their surrender to a faithful Lord, as well as in their growth in faith. Jesus is still calling, "Come and follow Me"—follow like these New Testament men of faith. Remember them, and imitate their faith.

May your journey with these men of faith lead you to **follow Him** more faithfully.

Following Christ,

WAYNE A. BARBER

Wayne A. Barber

RICHARD L. SHEPHERD

Richard L. Shepherd

EDDIE RASNAKE

Eddie Rasnake

Table of Contents

Palestine in the Time of Jesus

- Extent of Herod's kingdom
- Herodian fortress city
- Decapolis city (time of Herod)
- Other city
- Mountain

ABILENE

Abila

ITUREA

Abana R.

Damascus

SYRIA

Sidon

▲ Mt. Hermon

Pharpar R.

Leontes R.

Caesarea-Philippi

PHOENICIA

Tyre

TRACHONITIS

Raphana

J. Jarmuk ▲ Hazor

GALILEE

GAULANITIS

TETRARCHY
OF PHILIP

Chorazin

Ptolemais
(Acco)

Capernaum Bethsaida
Gennesaret Gergesa

*Sea
of Galilee*

BATANEA

Mt. Carmel ▲

Magdala
Cana Tiberias

Hippos

AURANITIS

Kishon

Nazareth

▲ Mt. Tabor
Nain

Jarmuk R.

Gadara Abila

*Mediterranean
Sea*

Dor

Megiddo

Bethany
beyond Jordan

Caesarea
(Strato's Tower)

Scythopolis

Pella

SAMARIA

Dion

DECAPOLIS

Sebaste
(Samaria)

Salim?

Gerasa

▲ Mt. Ebal

Amathus

Mt. Gerizim ▲ Sychar

Joppa

Antipatris
(Aphek)

Alexandrium

PEREA

Philadelphia
(Amman)

(SEMI-INDEPENDENT
MUNICIPALITY)

Jamnia

Azotus
(Ashdod)

Emmaus

Cyprus Jericho

Esbus (Heshbon)

▲ Mt. Olivet

Jerusalem Bethany

Medeba

Bethlehem

■ Hyrcania

Ashkelon

JUDEA

■ Herodium

■ Machaerus

Hebron

*Dead
Sea*

Arnon R.

Gaza

Adora

IDUMEA

Masada
Arad ■

N
A
B
A
T
E
A

Beersheba

Malatha

0   10   20   30 miles

0 10 20 30 kilometers

Zered Br.

© 1999 MapQuest.com, Inc

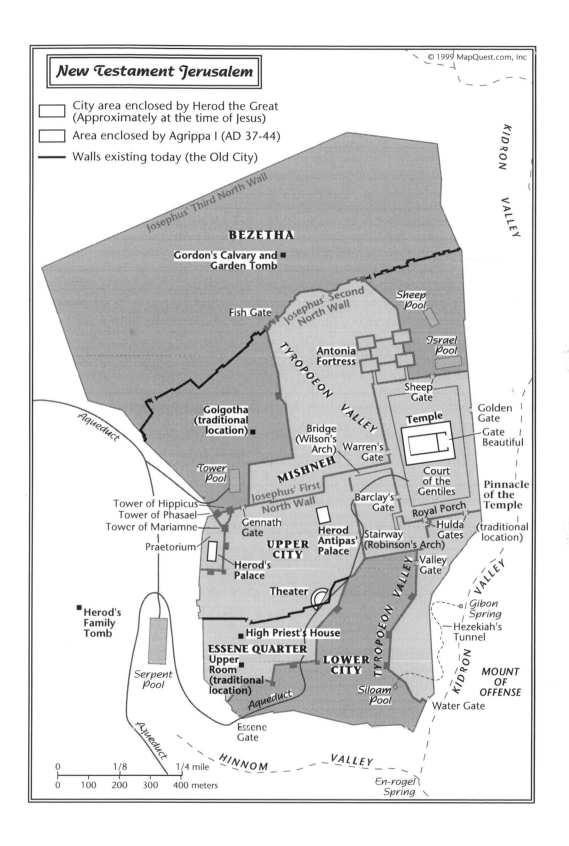

© 1999 MapQuest.com, Inc

New Testament Jerusalem

City area enclosed by Herod the Great
(Approximately at the time of Jesus)

Area enclosed by Agrippa I (AD 37-44)

Walls existing today (the Old City)

Josephus' Third North Wall

BEZETHA

Gordon's Calvary and Garden Tomb ▪

Sheep Pool

Fish Gate

Josephus' Second North Wall

Israel Pool

Antonia Fortress

TYROPOEON VALLEY

Sheep Gate

Golden Gate

Temple

Gate Beautiful

Aqueduct

Golgotha (traditional location) ▪

Bridge (Wilson's Arch)

Warren's Gate

Court of the Gentiles

Pinnacle of the Temple

Tower Pool

MISHNEH

Josephus' First North Wall

Barclay's Gate

Royal Porch

Tower of Hippicus
Tower of Phasael
Tower of Mariamne

Gennath Gate

Herod Antipas' Palace

Hulda Gates

Stairway (Robinson's Arch)

(traditional location)

Praetorium

UPPER CITY

Valley Gate

Valley

Herod's Palace

Gibon Spring

KIDRON

▪ **Herod's Family Tomb**

Theater

Hezekiah's Tunnel

High Priest's House ▪

ESSENE QUARTER
Upper Room (traditional location)

LOWER CITY

TYROPOEON VALLEY

KIDRON

MOUNT OF OFFENSE

Serpent Pool

Aqueduct

Siloam Pool

Water Gate

Essene Gate

Aqueduct

HINNOM *VALLEY*

| 0 | 1/8 | 1/4 mile |

| 0 | 100 | 200 | 300 | 400 meters |

En-rogel Spring

John the Baptist

LEARNING TO TRUST GOD'S WAYS

*J*ohn the Baptist was certainly unique! Wearing garments of camel's hair, living on a diet of locusts and wild honey, and lodging in the wilderness hardly sounds like an ideal lifestyle to most people today. But that was what surrendering to God's ways meant for John. Surrendering to God's ways may be the hardest part of following God. Many times we are eager to know and do God's will until we discover God's way of doing His will. It is when we are puzzled by God's methods that we must move to a new level of surrender, and we must make a more decisive choice to promptly obey God without questioning the wisdom or ways that God uses to accomplish his will. In other words, we must choose to surrender our ways, our agendas, and our timing to God and accept His ways and His timing.

JOHN THE BAPTIST

John the Baptist served as the bridge between the Old Testament prophets and the coming of the Messiah (Christ), the Lord Jesus. He was born around 5 BC (six months before Jesus) and began ministering around the spring of AD 26. He died around January AD 29.

THE LIFE OF JOHN THE BAPTIST

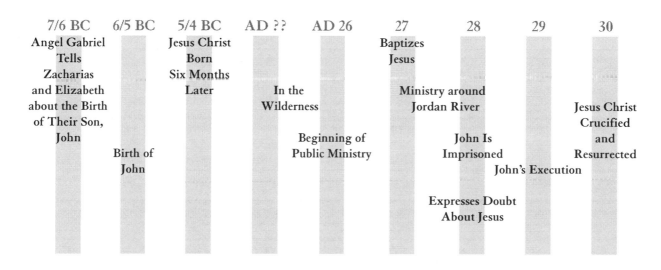

7/6 BC	6/5 BC	5/4 BC	AD ??	AD 26	27	28	29	30
Angel Gabriel Tells Zacharias and Elizabeth about the Birth of Their Son, John		Jesus Christ Born Six Months Later	In the Wilderness		Baptizes Jesus	Ministry around Jordan River		Jesus Christ Crucified and Resurrected
	Birth of John			Beginning of Public Ministry		John Is Imprisoned	John's Execution	
						Expresses Doubt About Jesus		

As we look at the life and ministry of John the Baptist we will find the issues of surrender and trust coming up over and over again. His father Zacharias, and his mother Elizabeth had to deal with some of the surprising ways of God pertaining to their perception of God's plan for them. In learning the ways of God, John and his parents also learned some new truths about surrender, truths that we also can learn. As you study this lesson, ask the Lord to make you sensitive to the surrender He wants in your life. Being sensitive to the idea of surrender will result in you discovering a new dimension of knowing God and a new adventure in following Him.

John the Baptist DAY ONE

JOHN THE BAPTIST—"MY MESSENGER"

Many prophets of the Old Testament spoke of the advent of the Messiah and the salvation He would bring. On the subject of Christ's redemptive plan, the apostle Peter had this to say:

> *"As to this salvation, the prophets who prophesied of the grace that would come to you made careful search and inquiry, seeking to know what person or time the Spirit of Christ within them was indicating as He predicted the sufferings of Christ and the glories to follow. It was revealed to them that they were not serving themselves, but you, in these things which now have been announced to you through those who preached the gospel to you by the Holy Spirit sent from heaven—things into which angels long to look."*—1 Peter 1:10–12

The Old Testament closes with the prophecies of Malachi where the promise is given of a messenger to come, a messenger who would announce this long-awaited Messiah.

What do you discover about that messenger in Malachi 3:1?

_____

_____

_____

Who was this messenger according to Jesus' words in Matthew 11:7–10?

_____

_____

_____

When Malachi spoke of a messenger who would come, he described him as *"My messenger,"* referring to **the Lord's** messenger, who would come to *"prepare the way before Me."* When Jesus came He applied those words to John the Baptist, calling him a prophet and *"one who is more than a prophet."*

The first chapter of Luke provides an introduction to Zacharias and Elizabeth, the parents of John the Baptist. In this account valuable truths can be gathered from the walk of this couple. Through them we can learn much about the ways of God in dealing with His people and what it means to follow Him throughout life.

"Behold, I am going to send My messenger, and he will clear the way before Me...."

Malachi 3:1

📖 Read Luke 1:5–7. List the facts about Zacharias and Elizabeth. Note any insights about how they followed God.

_____

_____

_____

_____

_____

ABIJAH AND THE PRIESTHOOD

Zacharias was a part of the division of Abijah, one of twenty-four divisions in the priesthood. These were organized by King David so that they might function more effectively in the Temple to be built under his son, Solomon. First Chronicles 24:1–19 explains these divisions and their various responsibilities. Verse 10 speaks of Abijah, the division from which Zacharias descended.

Zacharias and Elizabeth lived in the days of Herod (Herod the Great ruled from 37 to 4 BC). Zacharias served as a priest of the division of Abijah. (See sidenote concerning Abijah on this page.) His wife, Elizabeth, was a descendant of Aaron the priest, and they both walked righteously in God's sight, observing _"all the commandments and requirements of the Lord."_ Their righteous walk, however, did not make them sinless. This verse simply means that, as part of the nation of Israel, they followed all the regulations and participated in all the offerings, feasts, and so forth. Something of great importance is noted in verse 7—they had no children because Elizabeth was barren. They were both very old and, understandably, expected no children, yet they followed God with a whole heart.

Although Zacharias and Elizabeth were obedient in their service for the Lord, they faced some struggles with their childless condition. In their culture and time people considered children to be one of the blessings God gave to the obedient—but they had no children and were not getting any younger.

📖 Read Luke 1:8–17. Look carefully. What is the meaning of the angel's statement in verse 13?

_____

_____

_____

When would Zacharias have prayed for a son? Would it have been a recent occurrence?

_____

_____

Beyond Zacharias' prayers, what had God promised in Malachi 4:6? (This is repeated in Luke 1:17.)

_____

_____

_____

What was to be the ministry of this messenger (1:16–17)?

_____

_____

_____

_____

Did You Know?

INCENSE IN THE TEMPLE

As a member of one of the twenty-four divisions of the priesthood (see 1 Chronicles 24:1–19), Zacharias was chosen by lot to offer incense at the Altar of Incense in the inner court of the Temple, a privilege that came to a priest only once in a lifetime because of the large number of priests in Israel at this time.

We often must wait on the wise timing of God before we see His answer to our prayers.

Extra Mile
THE MESSAGE OF JOHN THE BAPTIST

Read Luke 1:68–79. What do you find about God, about His salvation, and about John the Baptist?

The angel Gabriel came both in answer to the prayers of Zacharias and in fulfillment of the prophecies given in the Old Testament, specifically the prophecy mentioned in Malachi 4:6. Certainly it had been a long while since Zacharias had last prayed for a son. God had heard the earlier petitions of Zacharias and Elizabeth for a child, but He waited for His timing to bring His answer to them. God's plans and ways go beyond our understanding or our desires. The wait they endured was part of God's eternal plan. God's plan would bring them joy, and many others would experience joy as well (1:14). Zacharias and Elizabeth would experience the birth of the forerunner of the Messiah! This forerunner would prepare the people for Christ's coming. What an awesome privilege!

John's ministry was one of preparing hearts to be open and receptive to the Messiah and His message. John certainly convinced many in Israel to turn back to the Lord from whom they had strayed. He dealt with the wicked and the rebellious, calling them to repent before a holy God and begin obeying His Word. Those who listened intently to John's message would also be receptive to the message of the Messiah.

Read Luke 1:18–25. What was Zacharias' response to the angel's announcement of the approaching arrival of his long-awaited son?

_____

_____

_____

What was Elizabeth's response (1:24–25)?

_____

_____

_____

_____

Zacharias responded with doubt, questions, and unbelief. He looked at his circumstances (being an older man with a wife far beyond child-bearing age) rather than at the Lord and His promises. Because of his blatant disbelief of God's promise, God (through the angel Gabriel) made Zacharias unable to speak. Gabriel told Zacharias that this inability to speak would last through the duration of Elizabeth's pregnancy. In contrast, Elizabeth knew God had *"looked with favor upon"* her—He had seen her and completely understood her condition. He looked at all her circumstances and acted in grace and mercy. He saw everything clearly and acted in line with His perfect understanding and perfect love for Zacharias and Elizabeth. By giving her a child He had taken away her reproach in the sight of men (that is, among her acquaintances, neighbors, friends and family members) as well as all who would come after her and hear the story of how God favored her.

Read Luke 1:39–45. What did John do while yet in the womb?

_____

_____

_____

_____

Do you see any connection to Luke 1:15?

_____

_____

_____

Extra Mile
"SENT FROM GOD"

For further study, look at the use of "send" or "sent" in the Gospel of John. Those words are used over 50 times in John's Gospel. See what God says about how He uses people and events to accomplish His purposes.

When Mary entered the room and greeted Elizabeth, the baby John leaped in Elizabeth's womb at the sound of Mary's voice. Elizabeth said it was *"for joy"* that the baby leaped. Verse 41 says Elizabeth was filled with the Holy Spirit when she heard Mary's voice. Elizabeth must have been elated to witness this event, for as Galatians 5:22 relates, *"the fruit of the Spirit is . . . joy."* Luke 1:15 says, *"he [John] will be filled with the Holy Spirit while yet in his mother's womb."* It is likely that the coming of Mary to Elizabeth provided the setting for the fulfillment of that promise from the angel Gabriel. God's ways were very unique in the life of John as well as in the lives of Elizabeth, Zacharias, and Mary.

Zacharias learned much in his nine months of silence. When the day came for the parents to give their son a name, Zacharias acted in faith, having come to believe what Gabriel spoke to Him. In Luke 1:57–80, God opened Zacharias' mouth after those long months of silence. Zacharias' song of praise reveals a heart taught of God through His Word, for in this song Zacharias speaks of the ways of God in bringing salvation and redemption and of His showing of mercy and forgiveness. The song is filled with praise for the character and ways of God. The light in the darkness and peace that are mentioned in this song were all part of what God would accomplish in bringing redemption.

 We have covered a lot of material today, yet this lesson has just begun. As you study the life of John the Baptist, ask the Lord to make you keenly aware of His ways with His messenger (John) who was *"more than a prophet."* In what you have seen thus far, can you pinpoint some surprising ways in which God has worked in your life? Talk to Him about these things.

JOHN THE BAPTIST—"SENT FROM GOD"

 **DAY TWO**

What does it mean to be "sent"? How do we cooperate with God's design of sending in "ministry," whether on the job, in the neighborhood, at home, or in the church? What does it take to follow God wherever He sends us? Hopefully, we will discover the answers to these questions as we look at the life of John the Baptist, *"a man, sent from God"* (John 1:6).

Luke 1:80 gives a summary of the early life of John; he continued to grow and became *"strong in spirit."* At some point he began living in the *"deserts,"* that is, the deserted wilderness region of Israel, until he appeared publicly. Since John was about six months older than Jesus, and since Jesus was *"about thirty"* when He began His ministry (Luke 3:23), John was also approximately thirty years old when he came preaching in the wilderness of Judea in the region around the Jordan River (Matthew 3:1; Luke 3:3).

📖 Read John 1:6–8. Who sent John?

_____

_____

What was John's primary task?

_____

_____

God sent John. God initiated the ministry of John, and John recognized that fact. He knew that God raised him up to bear witness to the Light, Jesus Christ, the Word of God, the Word made flesh. If we are to understand God's ways with John, it is vital at this point to see and understand that it is God who **sends** a person to fulfill His ministry. He sends **who** He wants, **when** He wants, **where** He wants, **why** He wants, **how** He wants, to do **what** He wants.

📖 What did John do to be "sent," to gain the honor to have this ministry? Read Luke 1:15–17, 41, 44.

_____

_____

_____

_____

> ## "A voice is calling, 'Clear the way for the LORD in the wilderness; make smooth in the desert a highway for our God.'"
>
> ### Isaiah 40:3

The grace of God is evident in the life of John. John did nothing to merit being "sent." His position and ministry were unearned and undeserved. It was only by God's gracious and loving kindness that John was chosen for this ministry of forerunner to Christ. The concept of God's grace must capture our hearts if we are to walk with God in the way He desires. The apostle Paul said his ambition was to be pleasing to Christ (2 Corinthians 5:9), yet he knew that anything he did that was worthwhile for the kingdom or in any way pleasing to God was always by the grace of God. In 1 Corinthians 15:10 Paul speaks of how much he labored as an apostle, _"I labored even more than all of them"_ (the other apostles), but then he quickly adds, _"yet not I, but the grace of God with me."_

📖 Read John 1:19–28. What did John understand about himself (20–23)?

_____

_____

_____

What was his attitude toward Jesus (1:27)?

_____

_____

_____

John knew he was not the Christ (Messiah), nor Elijah, nor "the Prophet." He was simply a voice _"calling,"_ as Isaiah alluded to in Isaiah 40:3. John's job was to _"clear the way for LORD in the Wilderness,"_ a phrase that referred to the practice of servants going before a king as he prepared to enter a city. They repaired and leveled the roads and arranged for all the people to greet the king, so that the king would have easy access to the country or city to which he was traveling and an honorable welcome once he arrived. This was John's task in preparation for the coming of the Messiah. John honored Jesus as that Messiah. His attitude toward Jesus was that of a servant to a master, though John did not even feel worthy to do one of the most menial chores, that of unloosing the thong of the Master's sandal so that he might wash the dust from the feet of his travel-weary Lord. John truly walked into his public ministry with an attitude of humility and awe at God's ways in bringing His Messiah.

📖 Read John 1:29–36. What did John understand about Jesus (1:29–30)?

_____

_____

_____

_____

In his time in the wilderness, what did God teach John about the Messiah (1:32–34)?

_____

_____

_____

_____

_____

John understood that this Messiah was the sacrificial *"Lamb of God who takes away the sin of the world."* It had been revealed to John that Jesus actually existed before him, although John was born several months before Christ came to earth—clear evidence of Christ's deity. John further declared that Jesus was indeed *"the Son of God."* In all likelihood the Father taught John these things in his wilderness schooling. We know that the Father spoke specifically about how to recognize this Messiah when He came, for John would *"see the Spirit descending and remaining upon Him"* (1:33).

What kind of attitude did John the Baptist have toward following God? What heart-felt attitudes and actions do we see in John toward the Messiah as he announced His ministry (Luke 3:16)?

_____

_____

_____

_____

What do you see in John when Jesus came to be baptized (Matthew 3:13–15)?

_____

_____

_____

_____

_____

"He must increase, but I must decrease."
John 3:30

Doctrine
THE FRIEND OF THE BRIDEGROOM

In Jewish custom, the friend of the bridegroom negotiated the details of a marriage including the betrothal ceremony and the communication between the bride and bridegroom during the interval prior to the actual wedding. This friend also made preparations for the wedding feast. John the Baptist served as the friend of the Bridegroom, the Lord Jesus.

What did John reveal later as Jesus' ministry progressed (John 3:28–30)? How did John see himself, and how did he see Christ?

_____

_____

_____

_____

Word Study
"PURPOSE"

John came to declare the purpose of God for His people. The word translated "purpose" (*boulen*) in Luke 7:30 refers to the will and intention of God. God's purpose is His desire, or His counsel which He desires to see followed. In Modern Greece the parliament is called the *boule*, the body of lawmakers who present the counsel (legislation) which they desire the country to follow. John presented the Lord's righteous counsel. Some received it. Others rejected God's purpose for selfish reasons.

As John announced the imminent arrival of the Messiah, he made it clear that he considered himself unworthy even to untie His sandal, bringing great honor to Christ. In Matthew 3, John exhibits a clear attitude of submission toward Jesus and to His ways as He comes to be baptized by John. There is a definite humility in John's attitude. He knew he had been sent, but he also knew that he was not his own boss. God directed, and he simply followed. He was the *"friend of the Bridegroom,"* who brings together the Bride and the Bridegroom. He cooperated with the Father in His designs for His Son and rejoiced to do so. With joy John decreased so that Jesus might increase all the more (John 3:30)!

 Think about John's attitude of humility. Consider your attitude. Are you walking with a bit of pride or even living the motto, "I must increase some, too"? Or do the qualities of submission and humility mark your life?

_____

_____

_____

John the Baptist **DAY THREE**

WHEN OTHERS DON'T UNDERSTAND GOD'S WAYS

John the Baptist followed God with a whole heart. As a result many people listened and gladly heeded John's message. Many regarded him as a prophet of God (see Matthew 3:5–6, Mark 11:30–32, Matthew 21:26, 32 and John 1:35–37), but there were some who did not understand John, nor the ministry God gave him, nor how he fit into God's design. Think through today's questions and Scriptures carefully. As you meditate upon these questions and verses, think of those who don't understand you when you follow the Lord.

John's clothing (compare 2 Kings 1:8), diet, and where he lived were very out of the ordinary. What do you discover in Mark 1:6 and Luke 1:15?

_____

_____

_____

_____

What do you discover in Luke 1:80; 3:2?

_____

_____

_____

_____

_____

📖 Read Luke 7:31–33 (note v. 33) How did many of the people view John?

_____

_____

_____

John had a unique lifestyle with a unique diet. He ate locusts and wild honey, and he refused to eat bread or drink wine. His clothing, a garment woven from camel's hair and girded with a leather belt, also made him look unusual, although this may have been the apparel of a prophet, similar to Elijah's clothing (2 Kings 1:8). He also lived away from people in the wilderness region where God had led him and taught him. Many people thought he was so strange that they said he must be demon possessed. They accused him of wickedness because of what he did not eat. These accusers did not understand the ways of God in John's life.

What was the attitude of the **religious leaders** toward John (see Matthew 21:23–32)? What insights can you glean from Matthew 3:7–10 and Luke 7:29–30?

_____

_____

_____

_____

HEROD'S WICKEDNESS

Matthew 14:3–12, Mark 6:17–29 and Luke 3:19–20 record the condemnation of Herod's adultery by John and his subsequent arrest of John. After John had spent some time in jail, the wicked hearts of Herod's household had their way, and John was slain—beheaded at the request of Herod's unlawful wife, Herodias, and her daughter, Salome.

The religious leaders also did not understand, neither did they accept John or the message he brought. He did not fit into their religious mold. Matthew clearly states that the Pharisees and Sadducees heard the messages and the warnings of judgment to all who would not repent of their wickedness, their viper-like nature (Matthew 3:7; Luke 3:7). They would not turn to God to follow Him in all He said. Luke 7 reveals that the Pharisees and lawyers *"rejected God's purpose* [God's righteous will and desire] *for themselves."* They refused to be baptized by John and rejected the message God had given John. Their disdain for John's message was also a rejection of Jesus as their Messiah and Lord.

📖 Read Luke 3:3–20. What was John's message? How did the **political leaders** respond to John and his message? Did they understand or accept him?

_____

_____

_____

_____

Did You Know?

? JOHN IN PRISON

According to the Jewish historian, Josephus, John was imprisoned in Herod's palace-fortress in Machaerus in the arid wilderness of Perea about 5 miles east of the Dead Sea and 15 miles south of its northern tip. Archaeological findings identify this prison with one of two dark, underground dungeons that are very deep and hot. These two archaeological sites have been proven to have served as prisons as evidenced by iron staples found in the walls to which prisoners were chained. John was imprisoned around a year and was allowed to receive visits from his disciples. It was there that he was beheaded by order of Herod Antipas probably around January of AD 29.

John the Baptist **DAY FOUR**

The best question to ask in times of trouble is not "Why, Lord?" but "What next, Lord?—What is the next step for me to take?"

John faithfully proclaimed a message of repentance for the forgiveness of sins. Baptism was the outward symbol of a change of heart toward sin and toward God. John warned of a false, "just-for-show" kind of "repentance." God wanted a genuine change with genuine fruit, and He gave people specific applications of what a righteous walk entailed.

Among those in political power, few responded positively to John's message. When John reproved Herod the Tetrarch for his adultery and other wicked things he had done, Herod locked John in prison. Mark 6:20 reveals that Herod knew he was wrong, and he knew John was *"a righteous and holy man."* At his birthday banquet he entertained several *"lords and military commanders and the leading men of Galilee."* None of them followed God or listened to John's message. None of them objected to Herodias' request for John to be beheaded.

APPLY Many times others will not understand what we say or do, or why we choose to follow God. We must remain faithful to God and His Word. Ask yourself: "Am I faithfully listening to God through His Word? Am I faithfully speaking His word as He gives me opportunities? Am I following God in what He wants, even if others do not understand God's message or how I fit into His plans?" Prayerfully consider these questions.

WHEN WE DON'T UNDERSTAND GOD'S WAYS

Often God's ways are far beyond our limited understanding. That we do not understand what God is doing does not mean He is not at work. Today we will explore how John faced that very truth and see ways in which we can apply God's Word and God's ways in our lives.

Remember that John went to prison. He was rejected by the religious and political elite and imprisoned because he proclaimed the righteous standard of God and confronted the sin, the hypocrisy, and the unrighteousness that he saw. During his incarceration John the Baptist faced a struggle. Matthew 11:2–3 tells us that John began to question whether or not Jesus was truly the Messiah, *"the Expected One," "the Coming One,"* the One whom he had said would come after him. This doubt that John experienced almost seems inexplicable when you consider all the amazing things about the Messiah that John had witnessed in his lifetime.

Think about all that had happened in John's life, all he had seen and heard. Look over your notes and the Scriptures we have studied. Write out all the things that John had seen or heard that pointed to Jesus as the Messiah.

_____

_____

_____

_____

_____

_____

_____

_____

_____

Let's review the main events in John's life that pointed to his being the forerunner of the Messiah, and to his acknowledgment that **Jesus** was indeed this prophesied Messiah.

1) John's birth was miraculous in the following areas:
- in its announcement
- in the age of his parents
- in the prophecies about his life and ministry
- in the silence of Zacharias
- in the joy and filling of the Holy Spirit that Elizabeth experienced
- in the return of Zacharias' voice and his prophecy concerning John
- in the amazement of all those who heard and saw these things

2) John's upbringing and growth into manhood—his diet, his clothes, his life in the wilderness—were unique to God's call on his life.

3) The Word of God came to John in the wilderness. God revealed Himself and His plan for John as the forerunner of the Messiah, the Coming One. God taught John the meaning of the prophecies of Isaiah (40:3–5) and Malachi (3:1; 4:5–6).

4) God "sent" John into this ministry, and John knew it. He knew God had brought him forth at exactly the right time to announce the coming of the Messiah.

5) John knew that the Messiah was *"the Lamb of God who takes away the sin of the world"* (John 1:29), Who had a much higher rank than he could ever attain, and Who existed before him (though physically John was born six months earlier).

6) John did not consider himself worthy to stoop down and untie the thong of Jesus' sandal.

7) John knew that Jesus would baptize people in the Holy Spirit and fire—not in water.

8) God told John what to look for when he baptized the Messiah.

9) John was there when the heavens opened and the Spirit of God descended as a dove and came upon Jesus and the Father's voice declared, *"This is My beloved Son, in whom I am well-pleased"* (Matthew 3:16–17; Luke 3:21–22; John 1:32–34).

10) John hailed Jesus as *"the Son of God"* (John 1:34).

11) He saw himself as the *"friend of the bridegroom,"* and the fact that all were coming to Jesus was a fulfillment of John's purpose and ministry (John 3:22–30).

12) John consistently maintained an attitude of humility toward the Lord Jesus—*"He must increase, but I must decrease"* (John 3:30).

Did You Know?
ELIJAH AND JOHN THE BAPTIST

Jesus said John fulfilled the prophecies about the coming of Elijah, though John himself was not Elijah (Malachi 3:1; Matthew 11:10–14; Mark 9:11–13). Elijah did not die, but was carried into heaven in a whirlwind (2 Kings 2:11–12). John stated that he was not Elijah (John 1:21), and Gabriel said that John would come and minister *"in the spirit and power of Elijah,"* which John certainly did (Luke 1:17). Elijah appeared with Moses at the Mount of Transfiguration to meet Jesus (Matthew 17:1–4), and many think Elijah will be one of the two witnesses mentioned in Revelation 11:3–13.

"Are You the Expected One, or shall we look for someone else?" Matthew 11:3

Then, from prison John sent two of his disciples to ask, *"Are you 'the Expected One . . . the Coming One,' or shall we look for someone else?"* (Matthew 11:3). In the Greek New Testament the word for *"someone else"* literally means "a different one" (*heteros*—another of a **different** kind, not the same, or of a different quality). John asked if someone would come who would be different, act differently, do things differently—unlike the way Jesus conducted Himself at present.

 Think about your life. What has God done in your past? How are things right now? Do you doubt Him? If things are somehow mixed up, going the wrong way, not the way you expected, then are you looking for a "different" Messiah to match your expectations? Let's see how Jesus responded to John's questions.

📖 Read Luke 7:18–22. What did Jesus do and say to assure John that everything was as it was supposed to be—that He was in line with the prophecies given in the Scriptures?

_____

_____

_____

Jesus showed Himself to be the healer and deliverer and preacher of the good news of salvation. He then sent the disciples of John back with a report that included word of the fulfillment of prophecies made about the Messiah.

📖 Read Luke 7:23. What do you see in this verse? What does Jesus say to John? What is He saying to us?

_____

_____

_____

_____

Jesus made it very clear that it is not inevitable, but **possible** to stumble over the way He does things, over Who He is and how He acts. John was in the process of stumbling, perhaps over his being in prison, or over Jesus not fulfilling his expectations about His kingdom. Many expected the Messiah to establish His kingdom then and there, but Jesus was not ready to do that. There was still much to be done and much to be taught before all could be fulfilled. Jesus' invitation and call to John was a call to trust Him and His ways and His timing. Everything was on schedule, and He wanted John to trust Him. It would be a choice. To keep *"from stumbling"* would take a walk of faith in the Word of God and in the character and power of God that stood behind that Word.

Jesus said any man or woman who would trust Him and His ways and not stumble over Him would be *"blessed."* The Greek word for "blessed" is *makarios*, which means to be fully satisfied in the depths of one's heart and life. The possibility and the promise hold true for us as well. We can stumble or we can trust and be blessed. Trusting is believing what we **cannot see** based on what we **can see** through the reading of God's Word (Hebrews 11:1). We do not understand all His ways, but we can trust Him because of Who He is.

We know from Mark 6:27 that John was beheaded by order of Herod. Matthew 14:13 informs us that John's disciples reported this to Jesus at which time Jesus withdrew to a lonely place *"by Himself."* Even there the people followed Him, and He ministered to them out of His great compassion for them. Jesus never stopped caring for John or for the people who came to Him. But this is not the end of the story. . . .

📖 Read Acts 13:25, and note what the first part of the verse says about John. What insights do you receive from the statement, *"while John was completing his course"*?

_____

_____

_____

_____

_____

What does Paul say about his own course in Acts 20:24?

_____

_____

_____

_____

_____

The Lord had a "course" (Greek: *dromos*—a race course) set for John to run. This idea of "the course" is further explained in Acts 20:24, speaking of the course the Lord had designated for Paul to run, and in 2 Timothy 4:7, Paul speaks of completing this course. So, for John there was a course set, and he ran and completed it. John may not have known the end of the race would come for him so soon, but it did nevertheless. Just months before the end of John's course, Jesus had called on him to be careful not to be offended or frustrated over the way He did things. Though discouraged by the ways of Jesus toward the end of his race, John completed the work the Lord had given him to do, and he now is enjoying eternal rewards from his faithful and loving Lord.

FOR ME TO FOLLOW GOD

DAY FIVE

When we look back over the life and ministry of John the Baptist, it is evident that the ways of God were a surprise to many—to his parents, to the people around him, and to John himself. Perhaps you are facing some surprises about the ways of God in your life or in the life of someone close to you. What is the Lord saying to you about His ways in your life? Spend some time in prayer. Talk to Him about these things. And remember, *"Blessed is he who keeps from stumbling over Me"* (Luke 7:23).

We are all running in a race. The author of Hebrews picks up on this idea to encourage his readers in their race.

📖 Look at Hebrews 12:1-2a written below and circle every word that begins with the letter **"e."**

Therefore, since we have so great a cloud of witnesses surrounding us, let us also lay aside every encumbrance, and the sin which so easily entangles us, and let us run with endurance the race that is set before us, fixing our eyes on Jesus, the author and perfecter of faith. . . .

Now identify the four main ideas that come from these **"e"** words.

1. **e** _____

2. **e** _____

3. **e** _____

4. **e** _____

APPLY The first thing we must do in running the race is remove or "lay aside" any encumbrance. What are some **encumbrances**—some weights—that are slowing your pace in the race?

_____

_____

_____

Is there a sin that is **entangling** you, tripping up your steps?

_____

_____

📖 Looking at Hebrews 12:2–3, are you weary in your course, the path God has set for you? Are you in need of **endurance**? Are you growing weary and losing heart?

_____

_____

_____

_____

How well are you *"fixing"* your **eyes** on Jesus (12:2–3)? Are you focused on His love for you and on the strength that is available to you?

_____

_____

_____

_____

Consider these truths. The word translated *"lose heart"* (*ekluomai*) carries the idea of becoming weary, giving up and giving in. A synonym also translated *"lose heart"* is the word *egkakeo* or *ekkakeo*. It literally means giving in to evil—whether to our flesh, to the world's ways, or to enemy thought darts (Galatians 5:16–18; 1 John 2:15–17; Ephesians 6:16). In the context of Scripture, then, we can see the ideas of being weary and of giving in to evil. Many times it seems easier to give up instead of pressing forward.

Put Yourself In Their Shoes
FINISHING THE COURSE

Paul said, *"I do not consider my life of any account as dear to myself, in order that I may finish my course, and the ministry which I received from the Lord Jesus, to testify solemnly of the gospel of the grace of God"* (Acts 20:24). That was also John's heart cry as he completed his course and the ministry he received from the Lord. How are you running the course that God has given to you?

APPLY After reading the following passages of Scripture, think of some ways we can lose heart. Write any applications the Lord brings to mind.

📖 Read Galatians 6:7–10 (note verse 9).

_____

_____

_____

We must be aware that we are always sowing and preparing for reaping. Sowing to the flesh brings corruption, the natural product of our "flesh." It is always easier to give in to the "flesh" and opt for comfort and ease than it is to take up our cross and die to ourselves (Romans 6). However, if we will look to the Lord and heed His Word, we can walk in faith and do what is right, expecting a good harvest of righteousness in the future. Don't lose heart in doing good.

📖 Read Luke 18:1–8. Explain the significance of the phrase *"lose heart"* (note verse 1). What does this passage say about prayer?

_____

_____

_____

_____

The Lord wanted His disciples to know the reality of answered prayer—that their heavenly Father is a just and righteous God who hears the prayers of His children. He wants His children to trust Him and to do so even when our questions seem unanswered or the answers to our questions are long in coming. He also wants us to trust Him even when it seems like the unjust are winning the day. John certainly faced thoughts such as these, even to the point of questioning Jesus as to His Messiahship. Amazing! The Lord wants us to learn to endure the race, and part of that endurance comes through trusting Him in continual prayer.

📖 Read 2 Corinthians 4:16–18 (4:16—*"lose heart"*), and note what the Lord says through Paul. What personal applications do you see?

_____

_____

_____

_____

As we are housed in this earthly tent (2 Corinthians 5:1–10), we deal with a decaying outer covering (the outer, fleshly man) that is easily wearied, often tempted, and one that is unwilling to continue running the race. At the same time we are being renewed in the inner man by the power of the Holy Spirit. God is increasing our weight of glory, that which truly lasts and is truly beautiful. The key for us is to keep looking at the things that are not seen. A great example of this type of faith is evident in Moses, who turned away from Egypt and all its treasures because he saw *"Him who is unseen"* (Hebrews 11:24–27).

"For consider Him [Jesus] who has endured such hostility by sinners against Himself, so that you may not grow weary and lose heart."

Hebrews 12:3

Think of John the Baptist and some of the surprising ways of God in his life. Has the Lord surprised you with some of His ways? We can stumble over God's timing in our lives. Are you close to **stumbling** over Him? How do you feel about His **timing** right now in your life? Read the statement below, and check any box next to a topic that applies to you.

"I thought that by now God would have. . . .

- ☐ provided for a major material need I have.
- ☐ allowed me to be married.
- ☐ solved my problems at school.
- ☐ given me clear direction about my career.
- ☐ finally answered that prayer I've been praying for so long.
- ☐ helped me straighten out my financial problems.
- ☐ done something about that particularly difficult person in my life.
- ☐ _____.

_____

(Fill in your own unique problem and how you feel God should have responded to it.)

Are you coming close to stumbling over Him and His ways in the **place** He has you now? Consider the topics below, and check any that apply to you.

- ☐ My job or place of work
- ☐ The city where I live
- ☐ The state where I live
- ☐ Other _____

- ☐ My church
- ☐ My ministry area
- ☐ The country where I live

Talk to the Lord about these areas. Don't stumble over Him. Trust Him. Remember, right now you are a candidate for His blessing—inner satisfaction that only He can give. Keep running the race God has marked out for you and keep looking to Him, following God—God's way.

Lord, I know Your ways are higher than my ways and Your thoughts are higher than my thoughts (Isaiah 55:9). I know I can trust You and Your ways in my life because of the great love You have clearly shown (John 15:13). Forgive me for the times I have doubted You, the times I whine, complain, and grumble instead of trusting and resting in Your loving and sovereign hands. Help me remember that anything that passes through Your hands has first come through Your wise and loving heart. Thank You for Your care, Your concern, Your infinitely wise plans for me and for all Your children. Thank You that You are working all things together for good to those who love You and who are called according to Your purpose, that wonderful purpose of conforming us into Your image (Romans 8:28, 29). Thank You that, as we run the race, You are ever seeking to encourage and strengthen and to bring us to share more fully in Your holiness. Thank You that we will see You in Your glory at the finish line, and we will rejoice in You and Your ways for all eternity. In Jesus' Name. Amen.

In light of all you have seen of the ways of God in the life and ministry of John the Baptist, record your prayer in the space provided on the next page.

When the surprises of God come and you are tempted to stumble over the Lord, remember that you are a candidate for the blessing of God.

_____

_____

_____

_____

_____

_____

_____

_____

_____

_____

_____

Notes

TOO MUCH CONFIDENCE IN SELF

eter was a man of great heart and the recognized leader of the Lord's disciples. He was the "Rock" (Matthew 16:18), the man who could be counted on to lead the disciples and the early Church. A successful entrepreneur with a thriving fishing business, Peter was a natural leader who was willing to take risks. He was bold, impulsive, and willing to stick his neck out to keep walking with God. This zealous side of his character served him well but also frequently got him into trouble. At the core of many of his mistakes was that he placed too much confidence in self. He was "committed" to the Lord, but his actions were more often characterized by trying to "do something for God" instead of abiding and allowing God to do His works through Peter. It seems that before the resurrection Peter was committed to the Lord, but he did not yet fully understand what it meant to be surrendered. The word "commitment" doesn't appear much in Scripture, but when it does it is almost always negative. It means "to pledge or promise to do something." Surrender, on the other hand, means "to give over, or to yield." It puts the focus not on what we are able to do for God, but on our need for God to do what only He can do. This week we want to learn from Peter's life the dangers of placing too much confidence in self and of walking by commitment instead of walking by surrender.

THE NAMES OF PETER

Although most commonly referred to as "Peter," the character of this week's lesson was originally known as Simon Barjona. The name Simon was a common one in Palestine of Jesus' day. In fact, there are nine men in the New Testament who bear this name. At its root it means "listener." Barjona was derived from *"Bar"* (meaning "son") and *"Jona"* ("John" or "son of John"). The modern English equivalent would be "Simon Johnson." The name Peter was a nickname given to him by our Lord from the Greek word *"petros"* which means "rock."

A CHRONOLOGY OF PETER'S MINISTRY

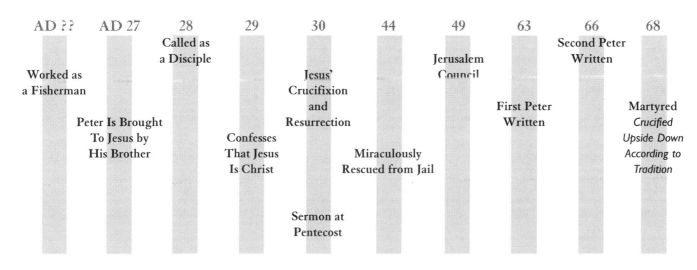

AD ??	AD 27	28	29	30	44	49	63	66	68
		Called as a Disciple						Second Peter Written	
Worked as a Fisherman				Jesus' Crucifixion and Resurrection		Jerusalem Council			
	Peter Is Brought To Jesus by His Brother		Confesses That Jesus Is Christ				First Peter Written		Martyred *Crucified Upside Down According to Tradition*
					Miraculously Rescued from Jail				
				Sermon at Pentecost					

"You Can Count on Me, Lord!"

Peter was a man capable of great things. When Jesus walked on water, it was Peter who stepped on the waves to join Him. When Jesus asked, "Who do you say that I am?" Peter gave his great confession, *"Thou art the Christ, the Son of the Living God."* Yet this same Peter was capable of great failures as well. Before God could do the work He desired **through** Peter, He first had to do a work **in** him. Peter had great zeal, but he placed too much trust in what **he** could do for God. He had to learn the hard way that God didn't need his help. God only desired his surrender so that He could do through Peter what Peter could never do on his own. "When the going gets tough, the tough get going!" seemed to be Peter's motto of life. But that "pull yourself up by your bootstraps" mentality doesn't work in the Christian life. Ours is not a life of independence and self-dependence, but of a growing dependence on our Lord. As John the Baptist put it, *"He must increase, and I must decrease."* Today we want to begin looking at Peter's greatest failure—his denial of our Lord—and how it happened. The first thing we want to see is that Peter thought he could handle persecution better than he did. Hopefully we can learn from his mistakes and avoid them for ourselves.

📖 Look at Luke 22:33. What exactly is Peter's boast?

_____

_____

_____

_____

Peter says he is willing both to go to prison and to lay down his life for Jesus. What Peter is saying is that no matter how hard the road gets, he will still follow Jesus. His heart is sincere, but he overestimates himself and what he will do when the pressure is on. How easily the words come, but the actions are harder in the face of reality!

📖 Now read Luke 22:7–32 to identify the context of Peter's boasting and what precipitated it.

When did this conversation between Jesus and Peter occur (vv. 7, 14)?

_____

_____

What did Jesus reveal about one of the disciples (vv. 21–22)?

_____

_____

_____

What discussion did this initiate (v. 23)?

_____

_____

Did You Know?
THE PASSOVER

The observance of the Passover was instituted just prior to God's deliverance of His people from Egypt in Moses' day. The first Passover was designated as an act of obedience to the command of God, and those who obeyed saw the angel of death "pass over" their house as it went through Egypt, killing each firstborn. After Israel was delivered from slavery, the observance of Passover was practiced annually. The first night of Passover week was marked with the Passover meal, which Peter and the disciples share with Jesus in the Upper Room. The meal consisted of an unblemished lamb, whose blood was applied to the doorposts (picturing the blood of Christ), unleavened bread (picturing sinlessness), and bitter herbs (to remind them of the bitterness of their enslavement). The Passover marked the beginning of the Hebrew calendar year. It is significant that Jesus was crucified during Passover week as God's Lamb. Jesus' observation of the Passover with the disciples instituted the sacrament of the Lord's Supper.

What seems to be the point of their discussion concerning who would betray Jesus (v. 24)?

_____

_____

What light does the context shed on Peter's boast?

_____

_____

_____

The setting of Peter's boasting is at the Last Supper. Notice that the discussion really began when Jesus revealed that one of the twelve would betray Him. Verse 23 by itself suggests that each asked himself, "Is it I who will betray the Lord?" Strangely, verse 24 suggests the opposite. It seems that they were arguing over who was the greatest and who would be the most faithful. They were essentially saying, "Maybe you will betray, but not me." It is in this context that Peter makes his boasts.

📖 Look at James 4:13–16, and identify what James has to say there about boasting.

_____

_____

_____

The hypothetical situation James offers is someone who boasts of their business plans assuming that they are able to fulfill them on their own. His admonition is that none of us knows for sure what tomorrow will hold, so we should recognize that all our plans are dependent on the will of the Lord. Anything else is merely presumption. James makes it clear that such boasting is both arrogant and evil.

What does Jesus have to say about the validity of Peter's boast (Luke 22:34)?

_____

_____

_____

Though Peter had confidence that he could be trusted to be faithful no matter the cost, Jesus knew better. In Luke 22:34, Jesus tells Peter that before the cock crows (i.e., before the sun rises that day), he will have denied three times that he even knows Christ. Jesus knows better than we do what our weaknesses and limitations are. Jesus had already warned Peter that Satan had requested permission to "sift" him like wheat (Luke 22:31). Notice Jesus did not pray that Peter would be able to avoid this sifting, but that his faith would not fail (22:32). When Peter stumbled, he was the only one who was surprised.

One of the things that gets in the way of our walk with God is our tendency to place too much confidence in ourselves. In Philippians 3:3 Paul says that the true believers are those who glory (boast) in Christ Jesus and *"put no confidence in the flesh."* One factor in Peter's failure was that while he may have been glorying in Christ, it would not be accurate to say that he *"put no confidence in the flesh."*

"Simon, Simon, behold Satan has demanded permission to sift you like wheat; but I have prayed for you, that your faith may not fail; and you, when once you have turned again, strengthen your brothers."

Luke 22:31–32

HOW MUCH DO YOU NEED TO PRAY?

A wise man once said, "You will only pray as much as you see your need to pray." If Peter's practice in Gethsemane is any indication, Peter didn't realize how much he needed to pray. Jesus knew what lay ahead for Him and for His followers. As a result, He prayed *"very fervently."* In fact, the intensity of His praying was such that *"His sweat became like drops of blood, falling down upon the ground"* (Luke 22:44). Jesus tried to impress upon His disciples the need for them to pray as well, but they did not share His passion. Today we want to continue looking at Peter's greatest failure and how it happened. Our focus is that, because Peter had too much confidence in himself and what he thought he could do for God, he prayed too little.

📖 Read Luke 22:39–46.

Where were Jesus and the disciples (v. 39)?

_____

_____

Why were they there (vv. 40–41)?

_____

_____

After taking the Passover meal with the disciples, Jesus led them to the garden of Gethsemane on the Mount of Olives. We know from verse 39 that this was where Jesus liked to go for prayer, for the text reads, *". . . as was His custom."* The example of the Lord Jesus was not one of prayer in crisis only, but of prayer as a way of life. Though the impending circumstances made the prayer more fervent, praying about everything was customary with Christ. Unfortunately, Peter had not yet discovered this dependence upon prayer.

From Luke 22:40, what exactly was Jesus' instruction to the disciples?

_____

_____

Jesus instructs the disciples to *"Pray that you may not enter into temptation."* The wording does not carry the idea of praying to avoid tempting circumstances, but of praying for the strength to avoid falling in the midst of temptation. It is not God's will that we never have to deal with temptation. In the parallel account of John 17, Jesus is seen praying in Gethsemane in verse 15: *"I do not ask Thee to take them out of the world, but to keep them from the evil one."*

Looking in Luke 22:45–46, make note of how well the disciples followed Jesus' instructions.

_____

_____

_____

Word Study
DROPS OF BLOOD

In reference to the fervency of Jesus' prayer in Gethsemane, Luke 22:44 says that His sweat *"became like drops of blood, falling down upon the ground."* The Greek word used here for blood is *"thrombos,"* a term used in medical language for a clot of coagulated blood. Some have suggested that Jesus prayed so hard that He actually began to bleed from His pores. It is more likely however that Jesus sweated so profusely that the perspiration was falling in huge drops like drops of blood from a wounded man. The text says His sweat was *"like"* drops of blood.

Verses 45–46 reveal that the disciples were sleeping when they should have been praying. It is unclear what the phrase *"sleeping from sorrow"* means. The New International Version translates Luke 22:45, *"When he rose from prayer and went back to the disciples, he found them asleep, exhausted from sorrow."* Whatever the reason it is clear from Jesus' words of rebuke that they should have been praying instead of sleeping.

📖 The Gospel of Mark also records this incident in the garden. Read Mark 14:32–42 and answer the questions that follow.

What did Jesus ask Peter, James and John to do (v. 34)?

_____

_____

_____

What were they doing when He came to check on them (v. 37)?

_____

_____

What warning did Jesus give to them (v. 38)?

_____

_____

_____

How many times did Jesus find them sleeping instead of praying (v. 41)?

_____

_____

In the parallel account of Mark's Gospel (Mark 14:32–42) we see that, when they got to the garden, Jesus took Peter, James, and John in with him to pray. He said, *"My soul is deeply grieved to the point of death; remain here and keep watch."* An hour later Jesus returned and found them asleep. Jesus roused them and said to Peter, *"Simon, are you asleep? Could you not keep watch for one hour?"* He warned Peter that *"the spirit is willing, but the flesh is weak."* Two more times Jesus would go back to pray, and each time He would return only to find His men sleeping again. Peter and the others were obviously tired; however, fatigue was no excuse for falling asleep at such a crucial time. If we only understood the importance of prayer, we would give up sleep before we would give up prayer. Jesus did.

What did Peter miss out on because he did not watch in prayer? What difference would it have made? We move to conjecture at this point, but, clearly, Peter would have been better prepared to face the temptation to deny Jesus had he spent more time praying and less time sleeping. Martin Luther is quoted as saying, "Busy, busy, busy . . . Work, work, work . . . I have so much to do today, I must spend the first three hours in prayer." The more we have ahead of us, the more we desperately need to pray. How else can we know God's perspective? How else can we make the wisest use of our time and resources?

PETER, JAMES, AND JOHN

During His earthly ministry, Jesus spent more time with the Twelve than He did with the multitudes. The twelve disciples were a key component to His strategy. But even among the Twelve there was a prioritizing of His relationship with His three key disciples: Peter, James, and John. Often these three were included in events when the rest of the Twelve were not included. The three alone were with Jesus on the Mount of Transfiguration (Luke 9:28–36) as well as at other times, like here in the Garden of Gethsemane.

Put Yourself In Their Shoes
SURRENDER TO GOD'S WILL

Of all the examples we can draw from Jesus' humanity, perhaps none is more compelling and more practical than the example He set for us with His prayer in Gethsemane. When He asks, *"Father, if Thou art willing, remove this cup,"* He shows us that we can ask the Father for the desire of our hearts. When Jesus concludes with *"...yet not My will, but Thine be done,"* He teaches us the importance of surrender to the will of the Father. When that is our heart, we can bring any honest entreaty to our Lord.

REACTING TO THE SITUATION INSTEAD OF RESPONDING TO JESUS

Because trials catch us by surprise, they reveal not so much the kind of people we want to be, but the kind of people we really are.

Don't you wish you could plan your trials? Wouldn't it be great if you could get out your calendar and say, "Lord, I'm going to be real busy on Wednesday, so why don't we have my next trial on Thursday afternoon?" Then you could make sure to have your quiet time, and you could pray and prepare so that when the trial arrived you would be ready to meet it. But unfortunately life doesn't work that way. Trials are the "pop quizzes" of life—we don't know in advance when they will come. Because they catch us by surprise, they reveal not so much the kind of person we want to be, but the kind of person we really are. Peter had an advantage most of us don't have. Jesus told him the trial was coming. He warned that Satan was about to sift him like wheat. He instructed Peter to pray so that he would not succumb to temptation, yet when the trial arrived, Peter failed miserably. He reacted out of his flesh to the situation instead of responding to the invitation of Jesus. As we will see in today's study, when the men came to arrest Jesus, Peter thought he knew what needed to be done. But he was dead wrong! Because he placed too much confidence in himself, he didn't take time to listen to Jesus, and with right motives he did the wrong thing. We need to be students of Peter's mistakes, or else we will make the same mistakes ourselves.

📖 Read through Luke 22:47–53 and write down the main details of Jesus' arrest.

_____

_____

_____

_____

📖 Look closely at Luke 22:49–51.

What is the question the disciples ask (v. 49)?

_____

_____

What is Jesus' answer?

_____

_____

What happens between their question and Jesus' answer (v. 50)?

_____

_____

While Jesus rebuked His men for sleeping, an approaching crowd appeared—led by Judas, who intended to betray Him with a kiss. One of those with Jesus asked, "Lord, shall we strike with the sword?" It was the right question to ask, but unfortunately one person did not wait for Jesus to answer. Before Jesus could respond, one of them struck the slave of the high priest and cut off his ear. We know from John's Gospel that it was Peter who did this (John 18:10). Jesus rebuked Peter by saying, *"Stop! No more of this."* It is obvious that the Lord did not want His men trying to defend Him.

📖 Read the parallel account of this incident found in Matthew 26:51–53.

What reminders does Jesus give to Peter (v. 53)?

_____

_____

_____

What do these reminders reveal about Peter's focus?

_____

_____

_____

Jesus reminds Peter that at any time He can appeal to His heavenly Father and have at His disposal *". . . more than twelve legions of angels."* Jesus' point seems to be, "Peter, stop trying to help God." If we focus on our circumstances instead of God, we will lose sight of His greatness.

Someone asked the right question. As mentioned earlier, one of the disciples responded to the crisis by looking to God for instructions instead of to himself for ideas. Unfortunately, that was not Peter's response. Not only did he fail to look to Jesus by asking what he should do, but he also failed to wait for the Lord's response when someone else asked. Instead, he cut off the ear of the slave of the high priest. Now, think about that for a moment. What benefit could be accomplished from hacking off a slave's ear? Absolutely none! All Peter did was make a mess that the Lord had to clean up. Jesus had to turn around and heal the slave's ear. Peter's problem lay in the fact that he acted way too fast. He reacted to the situation instead of responding to Jesus.

📖 Look at James 1:20, and record what you learn there about the outcome of reacting in anger.

_____

_____

_____

_____

James 1:20 warns us, *". . . the anger of man does not achieve the righteousness of God."* If we act on human impulse instead of hearing from God, we will end up doing the wrong thing. Our greatest need in crisis is to hear from God and then to do what He instructs. Anything else will not only fail to help, but will make a mess for the Lord to clean up. Failure results when we act before taking time to hear from God.

Did You Know?
TWELVE LEGIONS OF ANGELS

The "Legion" was the principal unit of the Roman army, containing about 6,000 men. Jesus reminded Peter that all He had to do was simply say the word and at the snap of a finger ("at once") His Heavenly Father would place at His disposal more than 72,000 angels. Since one angel slew 70,000 men after King David's ill-advised census (2 Samuel 24:15–16), it is obvious that twelve legions of angels would be a humanly unconquerable force.

HE FOLLOWED AT A DISTANCE

"The fear of man brings a snare," we are told in Proverbs 29:25. Peter boasted of great courage, but in truth, he was afraid of what men could do to him. He told Jesus that he was ready to go to prison or to die, but he was far from ready. Once Jesus was arrested, we find that Peter wanted to go with Him, but out of fear he followed at a safe distance. Isn't that the same struggle we have in our faith? We want to follow Jesus, but it isn't comfortable to stand out from the crowd and follow Him closely, so we follow at a distance. Jesus' words to Peter still had not "sunk in"—that (if necessary) He could ask and the Father would send at once twelve legions of angels. The only person the Scriptures ever tell us to fear is God. Peter needed to learn that the safest place he would ever find was with Jesus in the center of God's will.

📖 Read through Luke 22:54–62.

Where was Jesus going?

_____

_____

How did Peter follow the Lord?

_____

_____

_____

Jesus was now under arrest, and was in the process of being taken away to the house of the high priest for questioning. We know from other Gospel accounts that Caiaphas was the high priest. This hearing was to determine His religious guilt, and would be followed by the "official" trial before Pilate. Peter followed along, but at a "safe" distance. The implication is that Peter took great pains so as not to be noticed.

Why do you think Peter followed at a distance?

_____

_____

What does this suggest about his view of God?

_____

_____

_____

It would seem that Peter followed at this distance out of fear. He wanted to be with Jesus, but he had lost confidence in Jesus' ability to handle the situation. Peter had lost sight of the power of God as he had witnessed this demonstration of the power of man. The irony is that the men who arrested Jesus understood Christ's power. When they said they were seeking Jesus, He said *"I Am He,"* and they fell to the ground (John 18:6). Yet Peter feared these men, not realizing that his life was in the hands of God.

"And do not fear those who kill the body, but are unable to kill the soul; but rather fear Him who is able to destroy both soul and body in hell."

Matthew 10:28

What was the nature of Peter's failure?

_____

_____

_____

_____

How does Peter's failure compare with Jesus' prophecy of 22:31–34?

_____

_____

_____

_____

Did You Know?

"BEFORE A COCK CROWS"

Jesus told Peter in advance, after Peter boasted that he was willing to go to prison or to die, that before a cock crowed he would deny three times that he knew Christ. "Before a cock crows" was a Roman figure of speech that marked the end of the third Roman watch, which lasted from midnight to 3 AM. Jesus' words were also prophetic, for while Peter was still speaking his third denial, the first rooster crowed (Luke 22:60).

We read that Peter denied Christ three times before the cock crowed, just as Jesus said he would. He denied Jesus to two men and a servant girl. For all of his boasting, in the end his actions did not match his expectations. The contrast here is striking, for John also followed Christ after His arrest. It is worth noting that though Peter followed Jesus at a distance, John apparently did not keep such a distance. Yet John was kept safe. The bitter words of denial did not have to be uttered by Peter. John 18:15–16 indicates that John entered with Jesus into the court of the high priest and then later asked the doorkeeper to allow Peter to enter the court.

The further we go away from Jesus, the easier it is to get into trouble. As John beautifully illustrates, it is safer on the frontlines of the battle with Jesus than cowering on the fringe, separated from Him. We must follow closely if we are to experience God's power and provision.

FOR ME TO FOLLOW GOD

Peter   **DAY FIVE**

We have seen some of the reasons why Peter, the faithful disciple of our Lord and leader of the other disciples, failed in the hour of crisis. Peter thought that if the day ever came, he would be able to handle it. However, when push came to shove, he denied our Lord. With curses and swearing he vowed, *"I do not know the man!"* (Matthew 26:74). He had placed too much confidence in self. To trust in self is the opposite of faith, the opposite of confidence in God. Because he thought too highly of his own faith, Peter made great boasts, but could not follow through on them. Because of his confidence in self, he didn't realize how much he needed to pray and was found sleeping when he should have been watching. Because he trusted himself, he didn't wait to hear from Jesus at the crisis of arrest, but took matters into his own hands. He reacted to the situation instead of responding to Jesus. Finally, not only did Peter boast too much, pray too little, and act too fast, but lastly, he followed too far away. He feared what man could do to him more than he feared God. In fairness to Peter, at least he was there. He and John were the only disciples with the Lord during His night of mock trials. Yet looking closely at the mistakes Peter made, we can better understand his failure in denying our Lord.

APPLY One of the things that set Peter up for failure was that he had too much confidence in himself. Because of this, he boasted of things on which he could not follow through. Can you think of a time in your life when you boasted of what you would or wouldn't do, only to fail later on?

_____

_____

_____

What did you learn from this experience?

_____

_____

_____

APPLY We can see in Peter that one of the ways he exhibited too much confidence in self was that he failed to recognize how much he needed to pray. Looking at your own prayer life, what does it say to you about how aware you are of your need for God day by day?

_____

_____

Is there something you need to bring to God in prayer that you haven't yet addressed with God?

_____

_____

_____

What are some areas where you struggle with running ahead of God?

_____

_____

_____

First Peter 3:15 instructs the believer to always be *"ready to make a defense to everyone who asks you to give an account for the hope that is in you."* Yet sometimes we struggle with taking a stand for the Lord. Look at the list below, and identify the areas where you find it hard to take a stand.

___ Work	___ School	___ Social Gatherings
___ Neighborhood	___ Friends	___ Relatives
___ Strangers	___ Civic Clubs	___ Sport Activities
___ Other_____		

The solution is not simply to pull yourself up by your bootstraps and vow that next time you will take a stand. That would be just like Peter's futile boasts. Instead, we should pray honestly about our fears and focus on developing a growing relationship of trust in the Lord. The more secure we are in Him, the less we will fear what others may think about us or do to us.

In this week's lesson we begin to see why Peter failed as he did. He boasted too much, he prayed too little, he acted too fast, and he followed too far away. The good news, though, is that he learned from his mistakes. In the next lesson, we

> "But sanctify Christ as Lord in your hearts, always being ready to make a defense to everyone who asks you to give an account for the hope that is in you, yet with gentleness and reverence."
>
> I Peter 3:15

will look more closely at how the Lord brought Peter back to walk with Him, but we want to close this lesson with the encouragement that Peter didn't continue to make the same mistakes. In Acts 1:4, the Lord Jesus instructs Peter and the rest of the disciples to "wait" for what the Father had promised. This time Peter did not act too fast. In fact, he didn't pray too little either, for he spent the next ten days in prayer (Acts 1:12–14). The church was born on the tenth day. As God began to move through the apostles in a powerful way, Peter no longer followed at a distance. Acts 4:13–21 shows no evidence that Peter was still afraid of men, as he was during the time of Jesus' arrest. Instead he confidently challenged the elders and chief priests and refused to stop speaking in the name of Jesus. As he returned to the disciples after his arrest, Peter exhibited growth in the fact that he no longer boasted too much, but instead, walked in dependence on the Lord (Acts 4:23–31). In Acts 4:29, we read the prayer of Peter and the other early Church leaders, asking God to grant them boldness—evidence of yielded hearts.

We shouldn't be too judgmental towards Peter for all his early mistakes, for we make so many of the same mistakes ourselves. James wrote, *"for we all stumble in many ways"* (James 3:2). None of us has arrived. What a blessing it is to think that while I am down here making mistakes, Jesus is in heaven, praying for me that my faith will not fail. Out of my failure, perhaps Jesus will say as well, *"once you have turned again, strengthen your brothers"* (Luke 22:32). God **knew** Peter's mistakes before he made them, and God **grew** him through those mistakes and made a different man out of him. Isn't it wonderful to know that He can do the same work in us as well? To God be the glory!

Let's close out this week's lesson in prayer.

 Lord, I see so much of Peter in me. I know You must laugh when You hear me boast of what I will do for You. You know me better than I know myself. And yet You are infinitely patient with me. Help me to see how much I need to depend on You. Help me to recognize the bankruptcy of self, and the riches of Your power made available to me when I surrender control. Guard me from running ahead of You or following at a distance. Work **in** me so that You can do what You desire **through** me. Amen.

Prayer of Application . . .

Take a few moments to write down a prayer of application from the things that you have learned this week.

_____

_____

_____

_____

_____

_____

_____

_____

_____

Notes

COMING BACK TO
WALKING WITH GOD

One thing that makes the Bible so practical to our lives is its realistic picture of imperfect people walking with God. As we saw last week, Peter was a man of great ambition and the recognized leader of the Lord's disciples—yet, he was also a man who failed. Though he had boasted of great courage, he revealed a coward's heart when the pressure was on. Three times he denied that he knew the Lord, just as the Lord said he would. When that fateful cock crowed, the Lord turned and looked at Peter, and realizing what he had done, Peter went out and wept bitterly. Yet as we will see this week, his failure wasn't final. As the book of Acts records, Peter went on to be used greatly in the early days of the Church. This coward who feared the report of a servant girl would go on to boldly defy the entire religious establishment of Jerusalem. But to get to that point, Jesus had to do a work in Peter. Perhaps the most important thing to learn from Peter's life is how the Lord restores us to a right relationship with Him. In this lesson we want to learn from Peter's life how to come back to a close walk with God.

PETER'S SIGNIFICANCE

In each of the lists of the twelve disciples, Peter is mentioned first. It was he who preached the sermon on the day of Pentecost, when 3,000 were saved and the church was born. It is clear from the Gospels as well as the record in Acts that he was the most prominent leader of the early Church. He authored two books of the New Testament (First and Second Peter) and like most of the Lord's disciples, sealed his testimony of faith by dying a martyr's death. Tradition holds that he was crucified upside-down because he did not feel worthy to die in the same manner as Jesus.

A CHRONOLOGY OF PETER'S MINISTRY

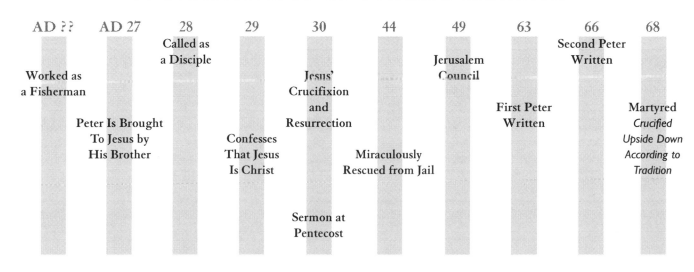

AD ??	AD 27	28	29	30	44	49	63	66	68
		Called as a Disciple		Jesus' Crucifixion and Resurrection		Jerusalem Council		Second Peter Written	
Worked as a Fisherman							First Peter Written		Martyred *Crucified Upside Down According to Tradition*
	Peter Is Brought To Jesus by His Brother		Confesses That Jesus Is Christ		Miraculously Rescued from Jail				
				Sermon at Pentecost					

A RETURN TO FISHING

Before Jesus called Peter as a disciple, his occupation was fishing. In fact, there is every indication that he was quite successful at it—prosperous enough to employ others in his business. During Jesus' earthly ministry it is obvious that Peter had no intention of going back to his former occupation. He planned on serving in the new kingdom that Jesus was to set up. Yet after his denials on the night of the crucifixion, we see a different Peter. Even though he was an eyewitness of the resurrected Lord, Peter no longer saw a place for himself in the Master's work. In John 21:3 Peter says, *"I am going fishing."* This statement is in the present tense in the Greek, which refers to continuous or repeated action. This means he wasn't simply going to catch one fish for a meal. It appears that he has decided to go back to his old job.

📖 Take some time to reflect on Peter's return to fishing, and then read John 21 and answer the questions below.

Why do you think Peter would go back to his old occupation of fishing, knowing that Christ was risen from the dead?

_____

_____

_____

Scripture does not give us a definitive right or wrong answer to this question. It does, however, imply certain things. It is not that Peter didn't believe in Christ—he had just seen that Jesus was alive. It seems that Peter no longer believed in himself. Even though Jesus had risen, from his vantage point he had failed the Lord, and things would never be the same. If in fact Peter had not yet repented of his failure, it would appear that he had returned to his old identity, what he did before he met Christ. Perhaps he felt that since he had failed so miserably and denied Christ, that he was no longer of any use to Jesus. Or perhaps, even if Jesus would take him back, he felt he had nothing to offer.

📖 Look at John 21:3.

What success did Peter and the other disciples find when they returned to fishing?

_____

_____

APPLY What application is there in this for us?

_____

_____

The text tells us, *"…that night they caught nothing."* The Greek word used here means "absolutely nothing." From dusk until dawn they worked with no success whatsoever. When we have not repented, we fail miserably at

> "Lord, with You I am ready to go both to prison and to death!"
>
> Luke 22:33

things in which we were once successful. If we want to return to our old way of living, God will not allow us to prosper. The old life has absolutely nothing to offer us.

Why do you think the disciples didn't recognize Jesus (v. 4)?

_____

_____

_____

There are differing opinions on this question. Some have suggested that the early morning light coupled with the morning mist on the sea made it difficult to see clearly. Verse 8 indicates that they were about a hundred yards from shore. Others suggest that the reason the disciples didn't recognize Jesus is because they weren't looking for Him. Sometimes we do not recognize the Lord when He shows up in our lives at an unexpected time.

When Jesus suggested that they cast their nets on the other side of the boat, remember that the disciples still didn't recognize Him. Their willingness to follow His suggestion, even though they didn't recognize who He was, is a reflection of how desperate they were. The result was a catch so great they could not haul it into the boat. When we turn from our own way to do things God's way, He graciously affirms that choice with blessing.

Compare this miraculous catch of fish with Luke 5:1–11, and write what stands out to you.

_____

_____

_____

_____

In this comparison we see that Jesus performed in John 21 the same miracle He used when He first called Peter into ministry. Peter was willing to follow Jesus when Christ first called him (v. 5). When he saw that Jesus was Lord, he saw himself differently, and it was at this point that he abandoned his old identity as a fisherman and followed Jesus. It would seem that by repeating the miracle He performed when He called Peter, Jesus is essentially "recalling" him to ministry.

📖 Look at John 21:7.

How did Peter respond when John recognized that the man on shore was Jesus?

_____

_____

Why do you think he responded this way?

_____

_____

_____

Did You Know?
FISHERMEN AND THEIR TRADE

The Sea of Galilee boasted a thriving fishing industry, since it was the only source of fresh fish for many in the area. Fishermen formed a distinct class of society and lived together as a community. The "Fish Gate" at Jerusalem probably had an adjacent prosperous fish market with both fresh fish from Galilee and salted and dried fish imported from Tyrian traders. Fishermen were strong and tough because of the work they did in all kinds of weather. They were also crude in manner, and rough in speech and in their treatment of others. Most fishing on Galilee was done with dragnets from a boat about fifteen feet long. Unending hours of sometimes fruitless toil built patience and character. With many of our Lord's disciples, their former occupation became a parable of their future ministry as "fishers of men."

When John said, *"It is the Lord,"* Peter *"threw himself into the sea."* Most interpret this to mean that Peter so longed to be back with the Lord that he could not wait for the boat to make it back to shore. Perhaps he had already made the connection between this miraculous catch and the way Jesus called him to ministry. His actions also suggest abandonment of his return to fishing.

THE CHARCOAL FIRE

After Peter failed our Lord and denied three times that he even knew Him, he was awash in self-doubt. His return to fishing reflects an assumption that he no longer had anything to offer in the Lord's service. Yet God had a purpose for Peter and a calling on his life. As a result, God would not allow him to go back to his old way of living. Perhaps the most miserable person on the planet is the Christian who is not walking in fellowship with God and in obedience to His will. A Christian in fellowship with God can enjoy his relationship with the Lord, and a non-Christian can at least enjoy his sin, fleeting though the pleasure may be. But the fleshly believer receives no enjoyment, for his sin keeps him from enjoying God, and the Spirit living in him keeps him from enjoying his sin. Peter could not rescue himself from this dilemma, but the Lord graciously intervened. When Peter arrived on shore, he found Jesus beside a charcoal fire. There are two main Greek words translated "fire" in the New Testament. One refers to a charcoal fire used for cooking, and the other refers to a simple wood fire normally used for light and heating or for burning rubbish. Keep these two meanings in mind as you work through today's questions.

📖 Look back at John 18. By what type of fire did Peter's denials occur? What is the significance of this?

_____

_____

_____

_____

_____

> ### "Now the slaves and the officers were standing there, having made a charcoal fire, for it was cold and they were warming themselves; and Peter also was with them, standing and warming himself."
> ### John 18:18

We see in John 18:18 that Peter's denials occurred beside a charcoal fire. Perhaps John included this minor detail because he connected the charcoal fire of Peter's denials with the same kind of fire beside Jesus on the shore. John 18:18 and John 21:9 are the only two places in the Bible where this particular Greek word for charcoal is used. It appears that Jesus was recreating the scene of Peter's failure in an intentional way so that He could deal with that issue of failure.

📖 As you look at verses 9–10, did Jesus need all the fish they had just caught in order to feed them? Why do you think He included some of their fish?

_____

_____

_____

> ### "And so when they got out upon the land, they saw a charcoal fire already laid, and fish placed on it, and bread."
> ### John 21:9

It is significant that when the disciples got to shore, Jesus already had fish on the fire. It appears that these fish were another of our Lord's miracles, perhaps reminding the disciples of the loaves and fish that He had multiplied. It would seem that the Lord was pointing out that He didn't need their help, and yet He included some of their fish in the meal. Because God loves us, He invites us to join in His work. He does not require our help, but He does desire our participation.

Three times Peter denied that he knew the Lord; the last time he even **cursed.** The bitterness of realizing what he had done and how he had failed still clung to him. In this passage, the Lord restores Peter with three directives to care for His sheep, one for each of Peter's denials. What a beautiful portrait of God's grace we see in the tender way He dealt with Peter's failure, and what a gift of hope to all who have ever failed the Lord.

In verse 15 Jesus asks Peter, *". . . do you love Me more than these?"* What do you think the word *these* refers to?

_____

_____

_____

_____

Some suggest that Jesus asked if Peter loved Him more than the other disciples did. This does not fit the context however, and would place the emphasis on Peter's effort. It makes more sense that Jesus simply asked Peter if he loved Him more than fish. Jesus was bringing Peter to a crisis point of deciding between going back to fishing or going on with the Lord.

What is the significance of the fact that Jesus never asked if Peter loved sheep. Whose sheep is Christ referring to?

_____

_____

_____

_____

Jesus asks Peter repeatedly, *"Do you love Me?"* Jesus never asked Peter if he loved sheep. In fact, Jesus' statements make it clear that these sheep were not Peter's sheep anyway—the sheep belong to Jesus. It is not our love for ministry that should propel us, for sometimes ministry is difficult and unpleasant. That which keeps us going is always and only the love of Jesus.

The first two times that Jesus asked Peter this question He used the Greek verb *"agapao"* for love. This refers to unconditional, committed love and is the highest form of love. Each time Peter answered with a different Greek verb, *"phileo." Phileo* refers to emotional, friendship love, a lessor form of love. The first two times, Jesus literally asked, "Peter, are you committed to Me?" and Peter answered, "Yes Lord, I'm your friend." The third time, Jesus used the word *"phileo."* He literally asked, "Peter, do you even love Me as a friend?" Peter was grieved and recognized that Jesus knew his heart. He replies in verse 17, *"Lord, You know all things; You know that I love (phileo) You."* Jesus reinstated Peter to ministry through this conversation, and through Peter, Christ gave hope to all who fail.

STRIPPED FOR WORK

Fishing was wet and dirty work. Normally a fisherman would take off his outer garments while working and wear merely a loincloth. When Peter recognized our Lord, he put on his outer garment for the sake of modesty and reverence. Instead of waiting for the boat to get to shore, he swam the hundred yards while the others brought the boat in, dragging the nets full of fish. The miraculous catch was not a result of luck, but the blessing of obedience to Christ. It was supernatural that 153 large fish could be brought in without tearing the nets.

 **DAY THREE**

"You Follow Me!"

P eter was at a crucial juncture of his life and ministry. Think how different things would have been if our Lord had just let him return to fishing. Think how miserable and unfulfilled the rest of his life would have been. It might have been easier. Given time, perhaps he would have once again prospered in fishing, but he would have never been satisfied. Burning in his chest would always be the painful memories of what was and what might have been. But Jesus did not leave Peter to himself. It is important that we recognize, however, that Peter had to be broken and repentant. He had to respond rightly to the Lord's convicting and prompting. Once Jesus had reinstated Peter to ministry, He began to reveal what the rest of Peter's life would look like. Twice in the last few verses of John 21, Jesus tells Peter, *"Follow Me!"* This is the same phrase Jesus used to call Peter into ministry in the very beginning. It is this same phrase Jesus spoke to the Twelve when He began teaching of the Cross, and many followed Him no longer. In characteristic gentleness, Jesus brought Peter back to the very beginning and reaffirmed his call to ministry.

📖 Look at John 21:18–19.

What exactly does Jesus say to Peter?

_____

_____

What does the text tell us He meant?

_____

_____

_____

In 21:18, Jesus indicates that when Peter is old, others would gird him and take him where he did not wish to go. Verse 19 clarifies that Jesus is telling Peter that he would die a martyr's death. When Jesus said, *"follow me,"* He wanted to make certain Peter understood what that meant. You see Peter wasn't wrong in saying that he would lay down his life for Jesus; it simply wasn't something he could do in his own strength. After the coming of the Holy Spirit, Peter emerged with boldness that only God could give.

📖 Read John 21:20–21.

What is Peter's question to Jesus?

_____

_____

Why do you think he asked it?

_____

_____

_____

PORTRAIT OF GOD'S GRACE

Three times Peter denied that he knew the Lord. Three times Jesus gave him the opportunity to affirm his love for Him, and three times Jesus reaffirmed his call to "shepherd my sheep." What a beautiful portrait of God's grace we see in the tender way He deals with Peter's failure, and what a gift of hope to all who have ever failed the Lord.

Remember that Jesus had just told Peter that he would die a martyr's death. Peter looked at John, the disciple whom Jesus loved and the author of this Gospel and asked, *"Lord, what about this man?"* In other words, Peter asked, "Lord, is he going to have to die for the faith, too?" Peter struggled with what Jesus had revealed. One should not look too harshly at Peter's statement without realizing the full weight of Jesus' revelation. How would we respond if the Lord revealed to us that we were going to die for the faith?

📖 Look at John 21:22.

How did Jesus deal with Peter's concerns about his death and how John would die?

_____

_____

_____

How does this apply to us?

_____

_____

_____

This passage of Scripture is one of the great illustrations of focusing on the call that God has given us. Jesus quickly brought Peter back into focus by basically saying, "Peter, what I do with John has nothing to do with your call—you just need to focus on your own call." Christians often struggle with the temptation to compare their calling with someone else's. In a very real sense, that is the sin of covetousness—wanting what someone else has. God wants us to be content in His calling for us and to trust Him with His calling for others.

📖 Look at John 21:22–23.

What did Jesus reveal about John's death?

_____

_____

What did believers understand this to mean?

_____

_____

How did John interpret Jesus' words?

_____

_____

_____

> *"For the love of Christ controls us, having concluded this, that one died for all, therefore all died; and He died for all, that they who live should no longer live for themselves, but for Him who died and rose again on their behalf."*
> 2 Corinthians 5:14–15

Jesus says, *"If I want him to remain until I come, what is that to you?"* He did not say that John would not die, even though this rumor spread among the brethren. By focusing on what Jesus did not say, John refutes this rumor. It is significant however that John outlived all the rest of the apostles and didn't die until nearly seventy years later. We know that near the end of his life, John was in exile on the isle of Patmos where the book of Revelation was written. According to traditon, John was boiled in oil but did not die from this persecution. He appears to be the only one of the Twelve who died of natural causes.

In this chapter which is devoted to Jesus' restoration of Peter (John 21), John presents clear truths on what it means to be restored. Believing in these truths will help us as we seek restoration and renewal from Jesus Christ. John closes his gospel by reminding us, *". . . there are also many other things which Jesus did, which if they were written down in detail, I suppose that even the world itself would not contain the books."* In reality, the things John could have written were limitless, but in John 20:31 he tells us that *". . . these have been written that you may believe that Jesus is the Christ, the Son of God; and that believing you may have life in His name."* We usually apply this verse to evangelism, but it applies equally well to our own sanctification.

Peter **DAY FOUR**

A Different Man

In the last lesson we saw why Peter failed. He boasted too much, he prayed too little, he acted too fast, and he followed too far away. The good news, though, is that he learned from his mistakes. In this lesson we have looked at how the Lord brought Peter back to walk with Him, and we have examined the process of Peter's restoration. But we want to close this lesson with the encouragement that Peter didn't continue to make the same mistakes. He became a different man altogether after Jesus restored him—different than he was immediately before his restoration, and even different than he was before his failure. In Acts we see Peter as one who walked in the Lord's strength, not his own. As his God-given name indicates, he became the "rock" of support for the early Church that Jesus had called him to be. He became the rock when he learned to lean on the Rock of Ages.

📖 Look at Acts 1:1–14.

How long did Jesus' post-resurrection appearances to Peter and the apostles last (1:3)?

_____

_____

What did Jesus tell Peter and the rest of the disciples to do after He left (1:4a)?

_____

_____

How did the disciples spend the days between the ascension and Pentecost (1:14)?

_____

_____

_____

_____

> **"And there are also many other things which Jesus did, which if they were written in detail, I suppose that even the world itself would not contain the books which were written."**
>
> **John 21:25**

For forty days after the resurrection Jesus presented Himself alive, proving His resurrection in many different ways. During this time, He taught them concerning the kingdom of God. In 1:4, we see the Lord Jesus instruct Peter and the rest of the disciples to *"wait"* for what the Father had promised—that they would be *"baptized with the Holy Spirit."* The old Peter was never very good at waiting. This time was different, however, for he spent the next ten days continually devoted to prayer (Acts 1:12–14). The Church was born on that tenth day.

📖 Read Acts 4:1–21, and answer the questions that follow.

Why were Peter and John arrested (v. 2)?

_____

_____

How would you characterize Peter's response to his interrogators (vv. 8–12)?

_____

_____

What command did the rulers and elders give to Peter and John (v. 18)?

_____

_____

_____

What was Peter's response (vv. 19–20)?

_____

_____

_____

On the night of Jesus' arrest, we saw that Peter *"followed at a distance."* In fact, his denials were evidence of his fear of men. But here we see a very different Peter. He boldly preached the resurrected Christ to the crowds at the temple and was arrested for it (v. 2). He was then called to stand before the rulers and elders and scribes, yet he exhibited no fear or timidity. Because he was filled with the Holy Spirit (v. 8), he spoke with divine boldness. When the rulers observed the confidence with which he spoke, knowing that he was uneducated, they gave Peter the highest compliment a believer could receive by recognizing him *"as having been with Jesus."* Even when the rulers commanded Peter and John to no longer speak or teach in the name of Jesus, the two men respectfully remained defiant—ready to pay any price to speak of their beloved Savior.

📖 Look at Acts 4:29–31.

What was Peter's request of the Lord after he had been released (v. 29)?

_____

_____

_____

How did the Lord answer that prayer (v. 31)?

_____

_____

_____

Did You Know?
PENTECOST

The name for the holiday of Pentecost was adopted from the Greek term for "fiftieth" because it was observed on the fiftieth day after the offering of the barley-sheaf during the festival of unleavened bread (Passover). Since Jesus' post-resurrection appearances covered a period of forty days, that tells us that the upper room prayer meetings of the disciples (Acts 1:14) lasted for a period of ten days, culminating in the outpouring of the Holy Spirit on the day of Pentecost.

"...but these things have been written that you may believe that Jesus is the Christ, the Son of God; and that believing you may have life in His name."
John 20:31

As he returned to the body of believers after his arrest, further evidence of Peter's growth is reflected in that he no longer boasted too much but instead walked in dependence on the Lord (Acts 4:23–31). In Acts 4:29 we read the prayer of Peter and the body of believers **asking God** to grant them boldness—evidence of yielded hearts. God answered that prayer by a fresh filling of the Holy Spirit, and we see the people speaking the word of God *"with boldness"*! Now Peter's confidence is in Christ instead of in himself.

Because of the immense persecution on the Church and possibly an unwillingness to put other believers in danger, Peter left Jerusalem for a time. Acts 12:19 tells us that he spent some time in Caesarea, and we know from Galatians 2 that he also spent some time in Antioch. The last information we have of Peter in Acts is at the Jerusalem Council.

📖 Read Acts 15:1–11.

What was the question of the Jerusalem Council (v. 1)?

_____

_____

What does Peter contribute to the debate (vv. 7–11)?

_____

_____

_____

The "Jerusalem Council" was formed to debate whether or not Gentile converts needed to be circumcised in order to be saved. Many prominent leaders were there, including James, Paul, Barnabas, and Peter. After much discussion it was Peter and James who brought the discussion to a conclusion. Peter reminded the group that **1)** God initiated the gospel going to the Gentiles, **2)** that He confirmed their conversion by giving them the Holy Spirit in the same manner as the Jews, **3)** that their hearts were cleansed by faith, **4)** that even the Jews were not able to carry the yoke of the law, and **5)** that all are saved by grace. After his own failure, Peter could understand that grace in a way had not understood before.

Peter went on to many more years of fruitful ministry. He eventually wrote two epistles to the persecuted believers. In the end, he died a martyr's death, just as the Lord had foretold. Tradition holds that when the time came for him to be crucified, he requested to be put to death upside down, not considering himself worthy to die in the same manner as our Lord. Through Peter's life we recognize that we can still be of useful service to the Master— **even after we have failed!**

Put Yourself In Their Shoes
HOW DID THE DISCIPLES DIE?

Here is what we have from the historical record and tradition:

Peter—crucified upside-down

Andrew—crucified

James, son of Zebedee—killed by sword

John, brother of James—died of old age

Philip—crucified

Bartholomew—crucified

Thomas—killed by spear thrust

Matthew—killed by sword

James, son of Alphaeus—crucified

Thaddaeus—killed by arrows

Simon the Zealot—crucified

Judas Iscariot—suicide (hanging)

In addition . . .

Stephen—stoned

James, brother of Jesus—stoned

Paul—beheaded

 **DAY FIVE**

FOR ME TO FOLLOW GOD

"**M**ankind is feeble and frail and prone to falling." These words, spoken by the "prince of preachers," Charles H. Spurgeon, adequately capture the reality of Peter (and of each of us). Like Peter, none of us are "fail-safe." Sooner or later every Christian will experience failure. If we didn't, then we wouldn't need a Savior. The most important question is not whether or not we will fail, but **when** we fail, will we fail to get up? In Peter we see a beautiful portrait of how the Lord comes alongside us to restore us when we fail. God will allow (and sometimes even engineer) our failure when we place too much confidence in ourselves. But we must recognize that failure doesn't have to be final. We cannot allow our failings to drive us back to our old way of living; it no longer has anything to offer us. When we fail, we must come back to the place of our failure (the charcoal fire) and do business with God. We must reestablish our relationship with God, and we must surrender afresh to His will and way in our lives. Peter did this, and as a result, he went on to be used mightily by the Lord in the founding of the Church. Clearly we see in Peter that failure doesn't have to be final.

 As you reflect on your own relationship with Christ, is there some failure in your past that still haunts you and makes it difficult for you to serve Him?

_____

_____

_____

Have you dealt with that failure in a biblical way?

_____

_____

Past failures can negatively affect the present in three ways. **First,** the failures of the past can stain the present when those failures are left unresolved with the Lord and with others. **Secondly,** we need to recognize that forgiveness does not always result in a removal of all of the consequences of our actions. Sometimes the Lord chooses to leave in place the consequences of our sins even when we are broken and repentant because He knows we need them for our own growth and protection. We must learn to hate sin as He does. **Thirdly,** even if we have made things right with God and man, the failures from our past may still haunt us if we listen to the condemning voice of the enemy.

How do you know if the guilt you feel is the convicting work of God or the condemning work of Satan? First, remind yourself of the objects each has. God has as His goal that we would repent and walk with Him. Therefore, when He is convicting us, everything points toward repentance, reconciliation, and restoration. Satan has as his goal, not that we would turn from our sin to God, but that we would continue to wallow in our sin. God's convicting words are always specific: "This is what you did wrong," and "This is what you need to do differently." The condemning words of Satan are always general: "You are a terrible person," and "You are worthless." Ultimately, we separate the convicting words from the condemning words by how they line up with the truth of God's Word.

 As you consider past failures, what have you listened and responded to more? (Mark where you are on the scale below.)

Condemnation ⟵————————————⟶ Conviction
from Satan   from the Spirit

"Search me, O God, and know my heart; Try me and know my anxious thoughts; and see if there be any hurtful way in me, And lead me in the everlasting way." Psalm 139:23–24

CONDEMNATION AND CONVICTION

Condemnation is not the work of God, but of the devil. Conviction is the ministry of God in our lives. Condemnation is usually general, focusing not on what we did wrong or on how to make it right, but on how worthless we are. Conviction, however, is always specific, pointing to the change that God desires.

What should we do about conviction by God's Spirit?

1) Confess (agree with God) about the specific wrong actions or attitudes.
2) Repent of running your own life; do so area by area.
3) Yield each area of your life to Christ.
4) Trust Him moment by moment with the details of your life.
5) If God has convicted you of trying to take back control over any area of your life, then you need to deal with this conviction promptly.

What do we do about condemnation from Satan?

We must respond as Jesus did in the wilderness; we must answer him with the Word of God. To do this we must continually study the Word, and we may need to seek wise counsel from others who can lead us to the truths of God that will help us combat the lies of the enemy.

APPLY Is there any area of your life that you are not yielding to God?

_____

_____

One of the things with which Peter struggled when Jesus renewed his call was how that call compared to John's. Do you need to take your eyes off of a "John" in your life?

_____

_____

_____

Look at God's will for your life, His "calling" for you. Check the areas you have struggled with accepting.

___ Where I work   ___ What I do   ___ Who I work for
___ Mate (or lack of one)   ___ Where I live   ___ Trials I have
___ Lack of opportunity   ___ Possessions others have
___ Other _____

In each of these, Jesus does not say, "Do you love My calling for you?" He simply asks, "Do you love Me?" How will you answer Him?

_____

_____

_____

_____

Jesus' directive to Peter is also His directive to us: "... *what is that to you*" (stop worrying about My calling for others), "... *You follow Me!*" (if you love Me, be faithful to what I have called you to do).

Let's take what we have studied to the Lord right now in prayer.

 Lord, I see so much of Peter in me. I boast too much, I pray too lit-tle, I act too fast, and I follow too far away. And I fall—oh I fall so short—not only of Your standards, but of what I expect of myself.

Jesus is not saying, "Do you love My calling for you?" He is asking, "Do you love Me?" How will you answer Him?

Thank You, Lord, that You are mindful that I am but dust. I praise You that my failures don't have to be final. Lord, You know all things, and You know that I love You (John 21:17). I want to surrender afresh to Your will, Your unique calling for me. Help me to keep my eyes off of others and keep them focused on You and Your call for me. Help me trust You with the hard parts of Your will. Most of all, when I fall, please help me back up. Don't let me continue to wallow in my sins. Amen.

Prayer of Application . . .

Take a few moments to write down a prayer of application from the things that you have learned this week.

_____

_____

_____

_____

_____

_____

_____

_____

_____

_____

_____

_____

_____

Notes

WALKING IN THE LOVE OF GOD

Deuteronomy 7:7 tells us the Lord *"set His love"* on Israel. Through Moses He promised them, *"And He will love you and bless you and multiply you"* (Deuteronomy 7:13). In Jeremiah 31:3, the Lord declared to His people, *"I have loved you with an everlasting love; therefore I have drawn you with lovingkindness."* We see that same love magnified when we open the pages of the New Testament. First John 4:8 declares, *"God is love."* The man who penned those words is the apostle John, sometimes known as "the Apostle of Love." John was greatly affected by this love of God. For him it was at the very heart of life. John went on to write,

"By this the love of God was manifested in us, that God has sent His only begotten Son into the world so that we might live through Him. In this is love, not that we loved God, but that He loved us and sent His Son to be the propitiation for our sins. Beloved, if God so loved us, we also ought to love one another." (1 John 4:9–11)

Following God for over seventy years, John wrote five books of the New Testament: The Gospel of John, 1 John, 2 John, 3 John, and Revelation.

THE LIFE OF JOHN THE APOSTLE

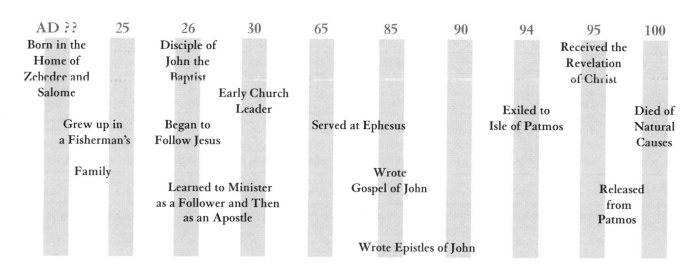

AD ??	25	26	30	65	85	90	94	95	100
Born in the Home of Zebedee and Salome		Disciple of John the Baptist						Received the Revelation of Christ	
			Early Church Leader				Exiled to Isle of Patmos		Died of Natural Causes
	Grew up in a Fisherman's	Began to Follow Jesus		Served at Ephesus					
	Family				Wrote Gospel of John				Released from Patmos
		Learned to Minister as a Follower and Then as an Apostle							
					Wrote Epistles of John				

If you want to know more about the love of God, one of the best teachers is a man who has experienced that love firsthand, a man who called himself *"the disciple whom Jesus loved"* (John 21:20). The Apostle John, the brother of James and one of the sons of Zebedee, followed God and experienced His love for over 75 years. But John did not always love God. We will see that as we study him and as he shows us what it means to follow the Lord, who loves us so much and who teaches us what it means to love others.

Did You Know?

JEWISH TIMEKEEPING

In the first century, some people used the Jewish method to measure time. They measured from sunset to sunset, evening and morning being a full day. When they counted their hours, they usually counted from 6:00 AM or 6:00 PM so that the third hour of the day was 9:00 AM, the sixth hour was noon, etc. Others used the Roman system, which counted from midnight or noon so that the sixth hour would be 6:00 AM, the tenth hour would be 10:00 AM, the ninth hour of the night would be 9:00 PM, etc.

CALLED TO COME AND FOLLOW JESUS

When we turn to the Gospels we find many lives intertwined with the life of the Lord Jesus. James and his brother John are two interesting examples of this special connection with Jesus. John 1:35–51 records Jesus' initial encounter with His first disciples. The first two disciples we meet are two disciples of John the Baptist (1:35), **Andrew** and **another** disciple with him. We know this other disciple as **the apostle John**, the author of the Gospel of John. He does not identify himself by name, but the evidence points to his eyewitness account of these events, including the exact hour he met Jesus. John 1:39 says they met Him at the tenth hour (most likely 10:00 AM) and *"stayed with Him that day."* Immediately, we see a hunger to know Christ and a desire to be with Him. The other disciples in John chapter one are Andrew's brother **Simon Peter**, **Philip** (from Bethsaida near the Sea of Galilee, the city of Andrew and Peter), and **Nathaniel**. It is also likely that **John** told his brother **James** about Jesus the Messiah just as **Andrew** had told his brother Simon. That brought the number to **six** initial followers of Christ. In these first days (around December, AD 26) they walked in the light of Jesus' invitation to *"Come, and . . . see"* (1:39).

During those first months (from December, AD 26 through September, AD 27) these disciples saw the miracle at Cana (John 2:1–11), the first trip to Capernaum (2:12), the first cleansing of the Temple in Jerusalem during the Passover (2:13–25), and the early ministry of Jesus in Judea (3:22–30). There they baptized many, even more than John the Baptist and his disciples baptized. Realizing that the Pharisees had become aware of this new ministry (4:1–3), they left Judea and went through Samaria to Galilee (John 4:4–42). It appears that when they arrived back in Galilee the disciples went home for a few months. Jesus travelled to Nazareth where He was rejected by the "home folk" (Luke 4:16–30). Jesus then returned to Capernaum, His new home (Matthew 4:13–16; Luke 4:31–37) and began teaching there. He even healed Peter's mother-in-law at her home (Luke 4:38–39), and He healed many others in the vicinity as well (Luke 4:40–42). From there He began to minister throughout the region of Galilee (Matthew 4:17; Luke 4:42–44).

As Jesus began this new part of His ministry in Galilee, He came to those who had walked with Him in ministry, who had gone through the "Come and see" first months. Luke 5:10 informs us that James and John were partners with Simon in their fishing business, and they had at least two boats (5:7), one belonging to Simon (5:3) and the other belonging to James and John (5:7).

📖 Read Matthew 4:18–22. What do you discover about John and his fellow fishermen?

_____

_____

_____

A short while later, still in the region around Capernaum, they had opportunity to work with their father Zebedee. Jesus met them once again while they were helping their father. When Jesus called them, they left their nets and followed Jesus (Matthew 4). What do you find in Luke 5:11?

_____

_____

_____

James and John were brothers, the sons of Zebedee, and were fishermen by trade. Matthew 4 informs us of their activities a few months after their first meeting with Jesus that is mentioned in the first chapter of John. After these first months of following and observing Jesus, they were now ready to leave the nets to follow Him more fully. In Luke 5 we find them even more surrendered to following Jesus. _"They left everything and followed Him"_ (Luke 5:11).

In the first 14 months of Jesus' public ministry, John and the others had gone from being full-time fishermen to those who soon left everything (family, careers, possessions, etc.) to follow Christ. John and his business partner, Andrew, had been disciples of John the Baptist for a time (perhaps a year). Now they were following Jesus. Their understanding of discipleship and "followship" was growing.

When we look at these disciples, we see a process of "followship." They didn't leave everything the first day they met Jesus. He taught them and brought them to greater and greater levels of surrender.

 What applications do you see for your life? Are you making progress in your following and walking with God? Is there a new level of surrender to which He is calling you?

_____

_____

_____

About a year and a half after first meeting John, Jesus went aside for a night of prayer after which He chose His Twelve Apostles (Luke 6:12–16, the summer of AD 28). John was one of the Twelve. What do we learn from the Scriptures about him and the others at this point in their walk with Jesus?

📖 Read Mark 3:17. What do you learn about James and John?

_____

_____

_____

✏️ **_Did You Know?_**
❓ **JESUS AND JOHN**

Some believe that Mary's sister who stood by her at the cross was Mary the wife of Clopas. Those of this interpretation form their belief by referencing the expression "his mother's sister" (John 19:25) with the words immediately following, "Mary the wife of Clopas." But by comparing Matthew 27:56 and Mark 15:40; 16:1 with John 19:25, we can deduce that Mary's sister was not Mary the wife of Clopas, but Salome, the wife of Zebedee and the mother of James and John. If Salome is indeed the sister of Jesus' mother, then James and John would be first cousins of Jesus, and the references to "his mother's sister" and "Mary the wife of Clopas" in John 19:25 are referring to two different people.

James and John had made an impression on Jesus, and He gave them a name as He had done with Simon (3:16). He called them *"Boanerges,"* which is translated *"Sons of Thunder,"* for they were men who spoke and acted in thunderous fashion. Apparently they were forceful, expressive men whose presence was easily recognized. They must have been men of deep conviction and intense zeal, perhaps even hot-tempered. Keep these things in mind as we look at the walk of the apostle John.

According to Mark 3:14, why did Jesus appoint these twelve men?

_____

_____

Mark 3:14 gives two reasons: **First,** *"that they might be with Him."* Jesus wanted them to spend time with Him so that they would know Him personally, listen and talk to Him, and learn from Him. He wanted them to see His relationship to the Father in prayer and in the Word, to see how He related to people and their sins, sicknesses, and other problems. They needed to see how He dealt with opposition and how He carried out the Father's will. **Second,** He wanted to *"send them out to preach."* He had a message on His heart that He wanted them to hear from Him and from the Father, and He wanted that message to be spread throughout the world through them. How well did they listen and heed what He said? We will see more in Day Two.

 *John* — DAY TWO

Did You Know?

PETER, JAMES, AND JOHN

In the Gospel records we see that Jesus ministered to both large crowds and small groups. Among the smaller groups were the Seventy (Luke 10:1, 17) and the Twelve (Matthew 10:1–5). Within the Twelve there was an inner circle with which Jesus often met, namely, Peter, James, and John (Matthew 17:1–9; Mark 5:35–43; 14:32–42). The three of them proved to be able leaders of the early Church both in Jerusalem and throughout the Roman Empire.

STILL FOLLOWING—STILL LEARNING

While John and the others walked with Jesus, they saw, heard, and learned priceless lessons. They ministered alongside Him, and He sent them out to minister in the cities and towns. They witnessed miracles and awesome evidences of the power and glory of Jesus Christ. One such incident was the Transfiguration. Three men, Peter, James, and John, saw that miraculous event. In Luke 9:27–36, Jesus stated that some of those hearing Him would see the kingdom of God before they died. In the context, Luke transitions immediately to eight days later, when Jesus took those three men up on the mountain to pray. There Jesus was transfigured before them, and Moses and Elijah appeared (9:29–31). The three disciples (who had fallen asleep) awoke to see this. Then they were overshadowed in a cloud and heard the Father say, *"This is My Son, My Chosen One; listen to Him!"*

How did this phenomenal event affect these men? Did this experience give them a full understanding of the kingdom of God? Did they comprehend what God was doing and how He was working?

📖 Soon after the Transfiguration, Jesus spoke of His coming crucifixion, but they did not understand (Luke 9:43–45). Read Luke 9:46–56. What do you discover about John (9:46–50)?

_____

_____

_____

What does the Samaritan situation reveal about John (Luke 9:51–54)?

_____

_____

_____

What was Jesus' response in each situation?

_____

_____

_____

When Jesus spoke of being *"delivered into the hands of men"* (9:44), it was as if the disciples didn't hear a word. They were arguing over which of them was the greatest, prompting Jesus to rebuke them. Jesus not only reprimanded them, but He also encouraged them to focus on being the least or the lowliest in order to exhibit the true sign of greatness. John then complained because someone who wasn't with their group was ministering in Jesus' name. At that point, Jesus made it clear that others could minister without being in their particular group. *"He who is not against you is for you"* (9:50). When the Samaritans proved unreceptive to Jesus and His disciples, John, along with his brother James, wanted *"to command fire to come down from heaven and consume"* the unreceptive village. Jesus rebuked them for their hot-tempered, vengeful spirit. He came to save lives, not to destroy them. James and John had some things to learn about ministry, about the ways of God, and about the love of God.

These things in Luke 9 took place after James and John had been with Jesus for almost three years. About five months later (February, AD 30) Jesus spoke again about His coming death, which was only another two months away.

📖 Look at Mark 10:32–45. Note what you find about James and John.

_____

_____

_____

What does Matthew 20:20–21 add?

_____

_____

_____

James and John, along with their mother, asked Jesus if they could have the two most prominent places in the kingdom. It appears that they were focused on their own personal greatness. The other disciples became indignant because they too wanted positions of greatness. Jesus focused their attention again on the fact that true greatness in the kingdom is based on being a servant or a slave to others. John and the other disciples were looking for greatness in the kingdom. They certainly did not understand the cross or what the cross would mean in their own lives. Nor did they understand how that cross would soon define the love of God so fully and so deeply for them and for those to whom they would one day minister.

> *"... whoever wishes to become great among you shall be your servant."*
> Mark 10:43

It is evident that Jesus does not choose to use only perfect people. He takes us as we are, but He does not leave us as we were.

JOHN, THE TEACHER

John was a discipler, teacher, and writer who often taught others about the love of God. One of the noted disciples of John in the second century was Polycarp, the Pastor of Smyrna, who lived from around AD 70 to 160. He testified that John penned the Gospel of John while in Ephesus. (Irenaeus, a disciple of Polycarp, wrote these facts in his *Against Heresies*.) Polycarp learned well from John. When about to give his life as a martyr Polycarp said, "Eighty–six years I have served Christ, and he has done me no wrong; how then can I blaspheme my King who has saved me?"

John along with his brother James had some things to learn about the kingdom of God. It is evident in the lives of James and John that Jesus does not choose perfect people. The Lord took John as he was and worked from there. He takes us as we are, but He does not leave us in that condition. He keeps working on us to bring us to maturity in Christlikeness.

APPLY What applications do you see for where you are right now? Is He showing you some new things about His love? His holiness? His kingdom ways?

_____

_____

_____

_____

_____

In the final week of Jesus' ministry, He spoke of the destruction of the Temple and of the buildings around it. On the Mount of Olives, Peter, James, John, and Andrew questioned Him privately about when these things would take place and what would be the sign of their fulfillment (Mark 13:3–4). They had a hunger to know the things of the kingdom and what was coming. Jesus explained to them many of the things pertaining to the "the end times." Later that week Jesus sent Peter and John to prepare for the Passover (Luke 22:8). At that passover meal on the night before His crucifixion, Jesus washed the disciples' feet. John is the only writer to include this in his Gospel. What can we learn from John about this?

📖 Read Luke 22:24–27. As you read, note that this event occurred sometime during the preparations, possibly as they determined who would sit where at the supper. Were the disciples focused upon serving Jesus, or upon serving themselves?

_____

_____

_____

📖 Read John 13:1–17. Note the careful detail of John's account. The one who wanted a prominent position in the kingdom (John [see Mark 10:32–45]) made careful note of the testimony of Jesus. What is the significance of John's detail?

_____

_____

_____

Luke 22 shows where the disciples (including John) were in their thinking. They wanted greatness, not servanthood. In John's account we see Jesus emphasizing the importance of being a loving servant as He washed the disciples' feet. Jesus said they would be *"blessed"* if they did as He taught and exemplified. To be *"blessed"* means to be fully satisfied. They tried to gain satisfaction by achieving greatness while Jesus taught them to live as servants. The fact that John gave this detailed account of Jesus' example reveals the significance of this event in his life.

📖 By example and by His words Jesus revealed what it means to be a follower of God and a disciple. Looking at John 13:34–35, what did Jesus say about a disciple's love?

_____

_____

_____

Jesus said the distinguishing mark of a disciple would be love—the kind of love He showed them. This servant-hearted love for others was the one thing He required of His followers, the supreme evidence of His relationship with them, and the sure promise of what the future held for them. John certainly saw the greatest example of this love in Jesus. He saw how Jesus loved them as He washed their feet, even the feet of Judas the traitor. John heard of this love in the words of Jesus, *"Greater love has no one than this, that one lay down his life for his friends"* (15:13). Then he was an eyewitness to that love at the cross, perhaps the only one of the Twelve who was actually at the cross (John 19:26–27, 31–37). The love of God in Jesus Christ made an eternal impact on the life of the apostle John.

What do you learn about John in John 20:1–10 (note carefully verse 8)?

_____

_____

_____

Mary Magdalene reported to Peter and John that Jesus' body had been taken out of the tomb, and they quickly ran to the tomb. Although he ran faster and arrived at the tomb before Peter, John did not enter the tomb until Peter had done so. He simply looked in and saw the linen wrappings neatly in place. In these verses, John testifies to us his belief that the body was not stolen. The linen wrappings would not have been laid out in such an orderly manner if the body had been stolen. Having seen this evidence, John believed Jesus had risen from the dead; however, he did not yet understand the necessity and promise of the Messiah's resurrection as taught in the Old Testament Scriptures. Soon, he and the others would have the mystery explained to them by the risen Christ (Luke 24:25–27), deepening their understanding of God's great love.

What do you discover about John in John 21?

_____

_____

_____

Some days after the resurrection, John was one of seven disciples who went night fishing on the Sea of Galilee (Tiberias). He recognized that the Lord Jesus was the one who told them to cast the net on the right side of the boat. Later, on shore, John followed close behind Jesus and Peter as they talked (21:20). In his writing he testified that his witness was true and he knew much more than he had written. If all the things Jesus did were written, John declared, *"I suppose that even the world itself would not contain the books which were written"* (21:25). These events identify John as a faithful witness who loved the Lord Jesus and knew he was loved by Him.

Word Study
THE WORD "LOVE"

In the Gospel of John, John uses the word "love" six times in chapters 1—12. Only John records the words of Jesus in chapters 14 through 16 and the Lord's intercessory prayer in chapter 17. In those chapters (13—17) he uses the word "love" 31 times. The time in the Upper Room, the walk through the city toward Gethsemane, and Jesus' prayer for His disciples revealed a depth of such love that John had not previously known. In the Gospel he penned, he never refers to himself by name, but he often speaks of the *"disciple whom Jesus loved,"* referring to himself (John 13:23; 19:26; 20:2; 21:7, 20).

Did You Know?
PETER AND JOHN TOGETHER

Peter and John were together when Peter denied the Lord near the charcoal fire (see John 18:15–16). John was most likely the disciple mentioned in John 18:16 that had access to the courtyard of the high priest. They were also together on the morning of Christ's resurrection [Sunday (John 20:2)], in the boat fishing when Jesus made the charcoal fire (John 21:1–7), and often in Jerusalem giving witness of Jesus and leading the church there (Acts 1–8).

During the final week of Jesus' ministry and for the period of forty days after His resurrection in which Jesus appeared to His apostles, John's life was radically changed. He began learning some truths about servanthood, about kingdom greatness, and about genuine love that forever impacted his life and the lives of those around him. But the journey was not over. There were yet many more miles to travel and many lives to touch. We will see that in Days Three and Four.

"YOU SHALL BE MY WITNESSES"

In Acts 1:4–12 we find the account of Jesus' final meeting with the apostles. It has now been forty days since His resurrection, and they still do not fully comprehend His kingdom plans, *"Lord, is it at this time You are restoring the kingdom to Israel?"* (1:6). They were looking forward to freedom from Roman domination and all the trappings of a hypocritical religious system. However, they did not fully understand what the Lord was about to do in sending the Holy Spirit and building the Church. That would take further revelation from the Holy Spirit. Jesus had promised them that when the Holy Spirit would come He would guide them into all truth. His coming was ten days away. They were instructed to wait in Jerusalem until He came, and then they would go to all the world empowered to witness of what they had seen and heard. The Lord had a significant role for John in these plans.

John was part of the prayer meetings in the upper room in Acts 1:13–14. He was there at Pentecost and the days following (Acts 2–5). What do you learn about John in Acts 3:1–11?

_____

_____

_____

Acts 3 records that Peter and John went to pray at the temple at 3:00 PM, the time of afternoon prayers. When a lame man asked for alms, both Peter and John fixed their gaze on him. Peter then offered him healing in Jesus' name. With this man's healing came rejoicing as he became overwhelmed with joy, *"walking and leaping and praising God"* (3:8). *"While he was clinging to Peter and John"* (3:11), the crowds gathered and Peter began preaching the gospel to them (3:12–26).

📖 Read Acts 4:1–14, and record your insights about the religious leaders and about John and Peter.

_____

_____

_____

📖 Looking at Acts 4:18–23, 33, what additional truths do you discover?

_____

_____

_____

"Many other signs therefore Jesus also performed in the presence of the disciples, which are not written in this book; but these have been written that you may believe that Jesus is the Christ, the Son of God; and that believing you may have life in His name."
John 20:30–31

In reaction to the disturbance caused by their preaching (4:1), the Sadducees (who did not believe in the resurrection) put Peter and John in jail overnight. The next day the authorities questioned them, noting the *"confidence of Peter and John"* (4:7, 13). The rulers saw them as *"uneducated and untrained men,"* but they recognized the evident influence that Jesus had over their lives (4:13). When they ordered them to speak no more in the name of Jesus, Peter and John boldly declared that they could not *"stop speaking what we have seen and heard"* (4:20). Acts 4:33 sums up the ministry that was occurring during this period of time, *"And with great power the apostles were giving witness to the resurrection of the Lord Jesus and abundant grace was upon them all."*

Acts 5:12–16 gives another summary of the ministry of the apostles in Jerusalem during these first years of the church. This led to yet more arrests by the high priest, but the Lord sent an angel to release the apostles. He instructed them, *"Go your way and speak to the people in the temple the whole message of this Life"* (5:20). When the authorities found them preaching again, they arrested them once again, flogged them, and released them (5:25–40), yet these faithful witnesses rejoiced that they were considered worthy to suffer shame for the name of Jesus. Acts 5:42 speaks of the kind of ministry they experienced, *"And every day, in the temple and from house to house, they kept right on teaching and preaching Jesus as the Christ."*

In these days John was recognized along with Peter as a leader among the apostles. In Acts 8 the apostles sent Peter and John to Samaria after great numbers came to Christ at the preaching of Philip. After that time (around AD 34) we do not read anything in Scripture about John until his writings appear.

John's first book was the Gospel of John (written around AD 85). Sometime after he finished writing his Gospel, he went on to write 1 John, 2 John, and 3 John (between AD 85 and 95). Sometime in the early nineties (around AD 94), John was exiled to a Roman penal colony on the island of Patmos. While there the Lord appeared to him and gave him the *"Revelation"* of *"what must soon take place"* (Revelation 1:1). That prophecy took John from his exile on Patmos to heaven and back, as well as to the end of world history and into eternity.

📖 Looking at the Gospel of John from John's vantage point in the year 85 AD, read John 1:1–18 and 20:30–31. What central thought does John convey in these passages?

_____

_____

_____

John had a clear perception of Jesus as the Lord God, the Creator, the Word made flesh, the Christ/Messiah, and the Son of God. He was confident that Jesus came to give eternal life and make all who believe in Him children of God (1:12, 20:31). He spoke as a firsthand eyewitness to all Jesus said and did in His ministry. What he wrote can be trusted as the truth. He wanted people to believe his witness and personally come to know Jesus Christ and the Life and love He offers.

📖 We have seen much about the life of John and his emphasis on the witness of who Christ is. We know John spoke of the necessity of believing

"...the name of Jesus Christ...And there is salvation in no one else; for there is no other name under heaven that has been given among men, by which we must be saved."
Acts 4:10, 12

John and other faithful witnesses rejoiced that they were considered worthy to suffer shame for the name of Jesus.

in Him and walking in truth and in love. In light of this, read 1 John 1:1–4, and record the focus of this passage.

_____

_____

_____

_____

Did You Know?

JOHN IN EPHESUS

On the cross, Jesus spoke to John about His mother Mary. He revealed His love and care for her in telling Mary to regard John as her son and John to accept and care for Mary as if she were his own mother (John 19:25-27). Church history records that John moved to Ephesus around AD 65, where he provided a home for Mary. He probably penned the Gospel of John and the letters of 1, 2, and 3 John while ministering there. John lived and ministered in Ephesus and in the churches of Asia Minor until his exile to the island of Patmos under the persecution of Emperor Domitian (around AD 94 to 97). Most likely he was personally acquainted with the seven churches of Revelation 2.

The focus of 1 John 1:1–4 is the manifestation of Christ as the God-Man. Christ was known by John and the apostles and can be known by any who believe. Here John again gives a very clear testimony of being an eyewitness of *"the Word of Life."* He knew Christ Jesus personally when He walked on earth. John uses the words *"see"* and *"hear"* in verses 1, 2, and 3 to refer to his personal knowledge of Jesus as the clear manifestation of the Father. He was confident that anyone who believes can enjoy the same kind of fellowship and love the apostles enjoyed—*"with the Father and with His Son Jesus Christ"* (1:3).

In 2 John and 3 John we see the same focus on knowing Jesus Christ. In these small letters, John shows his strong conviction, that "son-of-thunder" zeal, for the truth. He also emphasizes the necessity of love and obedience as the proof of love for God. In 2 John, he reveals his concern for believers walking in truth and love, and he focuses on the truth of Jesus Christ *"coming in the flesh"* (verse 7). In 3 John he continues his emphasis on love and truth and includes a strong rebuke for those who do not walk in that love and truth.

 Think back over what you have seen today. Are you walking in the truth? Are you walking in love? Are you giving a clear witness of who Jesus Christ is by your words and your deeds?

John **DAY FOUR**

THE REVELATION OF JESUS CHRIST TO JOHN

The apostle John was first a disciple of John the Baptist and would have heard all that he had to say about the coming Messiah. He then walked with Christ for over three years. He was there at the cross when the Lamb of God was crucified, and he witnessed His resurrection. Then, for over sixty years after Jesus' resurrection, John followed his risen Lord. He wrote the Gospel of John and 1, 2, and 3 John. What more could he learn? How much more could he write? What else could be revealed? We will see that in today's lesson. When John was past eighty years of age, perhaps past ninety (around AD 95), the Lord gave him what we know as the Book of Revelation—*"The Revelation of Jesus Christ"* (Revelation 1:1).

📖 Read Revelation 1:1–2, 9–19. How did John describe himself (1:1–2, 9)?

_____

_____

_____

What did Jesus reveal to him (1:9–19)?

_____

_____

_____

_____

John was a bondservant of God and a witness of the Word of God and of Jesus Christ. He saw himself as a *"brother and fellow partaker in the tribulation and kingdom and perseverance which are in Jesus."* He was on the island of Patmos because of his witness for the Word of God and his testimony of Jesus. There he saw the resurrected, glorified, enthroned Lord Jesus and fell at His feet as a dead man. The Lord laid His right hand on him and told him to not be afraid. After all that John had experienced and learned, the Lord had more to reveal. As well as John knew Jesus during those three years of His ministry, he had only begun to see Him as He was and is in His fullness.

John ministered in and around Ephesus for twenty or more years. The first of the seven churches to be dealt with in Revelation 2 is the church at Ephesus.

📖 Read Revelation 2:1–7, noting particularly verses 4 and 5. What is the main point upon which Jesus focused with this church that had heard so much about love?

_____

_____

_____

_____

_____

The church at Ephesus is a good example of the principle that every church must maintain a constant watchfulness—being ever watchful of sin, of the world's ways getting into the church, of **seemingly good** things getting in the way of the **right** things. This church that had heard so much about the love of God and love for God stumbled in its walk with Him. Its members had left their first love. Here again we see the Lord in His love, ever faithful to call His children back to first things, foundational things. It is a lesson for us all, and it is a warning about losing sight of the Lord in the midst of ministry. The Spirit is always speaking warnings such as this to the churches, and the churches must be alert to hear what He is saying.

In the early years, John and his brother James longed to be in a position of greatness in the kingdom. Luke 22:29–30 tells us Jesus promised the apostles that they would indeed reign with Him and judge the tribes of Israel. As John followed Jesus, he experienced His love and began to understand His reign as Lord. The Lord also revealed some things about how John would one day reign.

At the end of the Revelation, John witnessed a scene in the New Jerusalem. Think about John's desire to reign and what Jesus taught him.

Doctrine

THE LAMB—THEN AND NOW

In John 1:29, the apostle John records the testimony of John the Baptist. Jesus is the Lamb who takes away the sin of the world. In Revelation 5:6, 9, Christ is the Lamb slain who has purchased with His blood those from every tribe and tongue and people and nation. In that vision, John saw the throne of heaven and the Lamb there receiving the worship due Him. The redeemed, those bought out of slavery to sin, will reign on the earth with this Lamb who is worthy of all praise and worship by all of creation.

Did You Know?

THE ISLE OF PATMOS

The Isle of Patmos, a rocky island with little vegetation, is located just off the coast of Asia Minor (Turkey) in the Aegean Sea. Once used as a Roman penal colony, the small island is about ten miles long and about six miles wide on the northern end. John was placed there during the persecution of the Emperor Domitian and released around AD 97 during the reign of Emperor Nerva.

📖 Read Revelation 22:1–5. What is the mark of the citizens of this city (note particularly verses 3 and 4)?

_____

_____

_____

_____

What are they called (22:3)?

_____

_____

What characteristics of the love of God can you see in this scene?

_____

_____

_____

_____

The citizens of the New Jerusalem will walk in the light of the Lamb. They are known as bondservants, *"His bondservants,"* belonging to God. To be a bondservant in the kingdom of God is a great honor. Those bondservants are loved by their Lord, forever experiencing His personal provision and care for them. In the New Jerusalem their blessedness is found in seeing the face of Jesus, being owned by Him, and being identified with His mark, His name, on their foreheads. In this vision, John saw a glimpse of what it means to belong to God, to be loved by Him, and to reign with Him.

John walked in the love of God for over seventy years, and in that time he learned much about loving God and loving others. One of the lessons we learn from his life is that no one ever arrives at the final goal in this life. There is always more to learn, always more of the Lord to see and know and worship. There is always more growth and maturity needed in our walk with Him, and always a deeper love to experience and to show to others.

In Revelation it becomes clear that what John had seen and heard and handled in his years on earth will one day be revealed to all creation. The Lord Jesus will be distinctly seen as Lord of lords and King of kings, and He will reign over all. Not only will He reign supreme, but all who have believed in Him will reign by His side for all eternity.

Are you walking in the love of God, ready for His return?

APPLY How about you? Are you ready to reign with Him? Do you know and realize how much Jesus loves you? Are you loving others? Are you walking in the love of God, ready for His Return?

_____

_____

_____

_____

For Me to Follow God

John spoke much about love: God's love for us, our love for God, and our love for others. In speaking of love, the New Testament uses two Greek words, *agape* and *philos*, both translated *"love."* The word used most often is *agape* (or the verb *agapao*) which refers to the choice to act for the good and benefit of another whatever the cost. It is a selfless love. Jesus said people will know we are His disciples if we have that kind of love for one another (John 13:35). The command to *"love one another"* is found over a dozen times in the Scriptures, and that love is described in many ways through similar "one another" commands *("be kind to one another," "serve one another," "forgiving each other,"* etc.). How are you doing fulfilling these exhortations and commands?

 Read 1 Corinthians 13:4–8a. Fill in the blanks that describe love in the chart below. Then evaluate where you are. How are you doing? As you evaluate your life, check the box that best describes your love.

LOVE IS . . .		I AM . . .				
		Never	Seldom	Sometimes	Most of the time	Always
is		☐	☐	☐	☐	☐
is		☐	☐	☐	☐	☐
is not		☐	☐	☐	☐	☐
does not		☐	☐	☐	☐	☐
is not		☐	☐	☐	☐	☐
does not		☐	☐	☐	☐	☐
does not		☐	☐	☐	☐	☐
is not		☐	☐	☐	☐	☐
does not		☐	☐	☐	☐	☐
does not		☐	☐	☐	☐	☐
rejoices		☐	☐	☐	☐	☐
	all things	☐	☐	☐	☐	☐
	all things	☐	☐	☐	☐	☐
	all things	☐	☐	☐	☐	☐
	all things	☐	☐	☐	☐	☐
never		☐	☐	☐	☐	☐

How can these characteristics be part of our daily lives? What does it take to see them lived out even in the tough times? Galatians 5:22 says these things are *"the fruit of the Spirit."* In other words, the Spirit of God produces them. How do you and I experience that personally in our day to day lives?

📖 Read Galatians 5:16–17. What is essential to **not** seeing the works of the flesh in one's life?

_____

_____

_____

How can the fruit of the Spirit be seen in one's life according to Galatians 5:16?

_____

_____

Word Study
"LOVE NEVER FAILS"

In 1 Corinthians 13:8, the Greek word for "fail" is *"pipto,"* which means "to fall down, to perish." *"Pipto"* was used in Greek literature of a ship that failed to reach port, and was unable to complete its journey. This word for failure paints a beautiful picture of the love of God and also illustrates the meaning of genuine love for one another. Genuine love will not fail. It will reach its "destination." In His love God will guide us through our setbacks. He will complete the work He is doing in our lives (Philippians 1:6; 2:13). When we are showing genuine *agape* love to others, we too will faithfully give ourselves to meet the need or finish the task. *"Love never fails."*

If we are to **avoid** the works of the flesh, then we must say **"no"** to the desires of the flesh. This verse does **not** say that we won't have the desires of the flesh, nor does it say that we won't battle with these desires. It says we don't have to **carry out** the desires of the flesh. How do we keep from giving in to the flesh? By walking in the Spirit. That means obeying the Word of God, surrendering to the Spirit each day, actually each hour, really each minute! When we do so, the Spirit is free to produce His fruit in us and through us so that we might enjoy that fruit and that walk as He intended.

📖 What additional insights do you glean from reading Ephesians 5:15–21, especially verse 18?

_____

_____

We must *"be careful how* [we] *walk"* making sure we act as wise men who make the most of their time because the days are filled with opportunities for evil (see Ephesians 5:16). At the same time, opportunities abound for deeds and words marked by wisdom and goodness. The will of the Lord is not for us to be controlled by wine or any other intoxicating thing, alcoholic or non-alcoholic (like success, money, careers, leisure time, sports, etc.). His will is for us to be controlled by His Spirit, to *"be filled with the Spirit."* An understanding of the Greek language here can be helpful. The action verb *"be filled"* in the present tense means "keep on being filled," but in the passive voice means "let the Spirit fill you." In this verse the phrase is used in the imperative mood; i.e., it is a command to be obeyed, not an option to take or leave open for debate. We could translate the phrase, "keep on being filled with [controlled by] the Spirit." When we combine that thought with Galatians 5, we could add, "and you will walk by the Spirit with the fruit of the Spirit and not carry out the desires of the flesh." That kind of walk is described in Ephesians 5:19–21. If you practice this kind of walk, then you will walk with a song in your heart as you rejoice in your relationship to the Lord, full of thankfulness and marked by a servant's attitude toward the Lord and toward others.

📖 Read 1 Thessalonians 4:9–10. What assurance and exhortation do you receive from these verses?

_____

_____

_____

"Be filled with the Spirit"—It is a command to be obeyed, not an option to take or leave or an idea to be debated.

When we become children of God, He becomes our Father and begins training us as His children. Included in that training are several courses in *agape* love—selfless giving, serving others even when we don't feel like it, and giving up things [our time, our money, our energy] for the sake of helping someone else. The Lord is a patient Father, and He takes us through many courses on this kind of love so that we experience more and more of His love. He wants us to *"excel still more."* He is raising us up to walk in the image of Christ, who gave His life for us and to us. He's teaching us to live by His power and to purposefully give our lives away through love.

📖 Finally, what do you find in John's writings about this life of love? Read 1 John 4:7–11, and note what you find about the love which John experienced.

_____

_____

_____

John experienced the love about which he wrote. He saw the love of God face to face in Jesus Christ, *"the only begotten Son,"* whom God sent *"into the world so that we might live through Him"* (4:9). John knew this love was from God, and he had experienced this redeeming love. Those who are born of God know this love and by His power are able to show this love. He has loved us, forgiven us, and offered us His life. Therefore, we can love Him in return and show love to one another. John knew this was a growing love. Knowing God in Jesus Christ means growing in the understanding of how much we are really loved. Through this knowledge of God's love we also learn how to love God and others more fully. Such growth can only come through walking in the love of God.

Take some time to thank the Lord for His unconditional love for you.

🙏 *Lord,* thank You for the great love You have for me and for the patience You have shown me. Thank You for the gift of Your Son, for the forgiveness of my sin, and for eternal life. I know I have much to learn about Your love and about how to love You and others. May I share that love with many others that they too can come to know You and the love You have for them. Thank You for teaching and training me, for using those around me—at home, in my neighborhood, at work, at church—to teach me more about Your love and about how to love others in practical ways. I have so far to go to comprehend Your love for me. Help me by Your Spirit to see the breadth and length and height and depth of Your love. May my life reveal a heart overflowing with Your love. May I show You more and more the gratitude that equals the measure of Your love. I know it will take all eternity. I thank You for Your eternal love in giving me an eternal home with You as my eternal Father and Lord. In Jesus' Name, Amen.

In light of all you have seen in this lesson about walking in the love of God, write your own prayer to the Lord.

_____

_____

_____

_____

_____

_____

_____

_____

_____

_____

_____

> **We live through Christ, and we love through Christ.**

Notes

Thomas

A FAITH FOUNDED ON FACT

Perhaps none of Christ's twelve disciples has been more unjustly maligned than the one we call "Doubting Thomas." History unkindly remembers him only for his incident of doubting that Jesus had been resurrected. Yet in reality, this aspect of his character is deserving of applause, not shame, for though he was skeptical of Christ's resurrection, his doubt had a purpose. Thomas wanted to know the truth. His doubt gives evidence, not of a lack of faith, but of a desire to have a faith founded in fact, not fancy. Though Scripture is not long on information about his life and ministry, it is rich in encouragement from his example. Once he dealt with his doubt, he went on to serve the Lord faithfully for the remainder of his life. Like most of the Twelve, he likely sealed his testimony of belief with his own life. He is credited as the father of Christianity in India, where tradition holds he was martyred for the faith, pierced through with a spear as he knelt in prayer for his persecutors. The book of Revelation indicates that in the New Jerusalem there will be a foundation stone with Thomas' name on it (Revelation 21:14). Surely it is wrong to forever brand one as a doubter who is honest enough to ask for evidence upon which his faith can rest.

DID THOMAS GO TO INDIA?

Tradition holds that when different mission fields were assigned to the apostles, India was given to Thomas. The connection of his name with India was widely accepted after the fourth century by both East and West. The Malabar "Christians of St. Thomas" still count him as the first evangelist and martyr of India. Early church accounts hold that he was pierced through with a spear while praying for his enemies on the Indian coast, near Bombay.

THE LIFE OF THOMAS

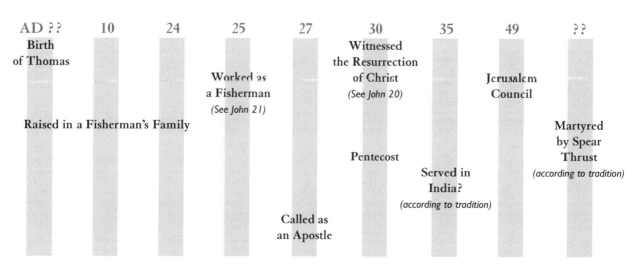

AD ??	10	24	25	27	30	35	49	??
Birth of Thomas			Worked as a Fisherman *(See John 21)*		Witnessed the Resurrection of Christ *(See John 20)*		Jerusalem Council	Martyred by Spear Thrust *(according to tradition)*

Raised in a Fisherman's Family

Pentecost

Served in India? *(according to tradition)*

Called as an Apostle

CALLED BY CHRIST

S cripture tells us nothing about Thomas' background. We have no idea where he was born or where he grew up. Concerning his occupation, we can only surmise that he was a fisherman, since we see him included with Peter and five other disciples who return to fishing in John 21. Tradition holds that he was born of poor parents who brought him up in this trade of fishing. Today we will begin looking at the three different gospel accounts of Jesus calling the Twelve. By examining these accounts you will get a feel for where Thomas fits in this group of disciples.

Take a few minutes to read each of the accounts (Matthew 10:1–4; Mark 3:13–19; and Luke 6:12–16). Write down the names of the Twelve in the order they appear in each list. List any similarities or differences that occur in each passage of Scripture.

Matthew 10:1–4	Mark 3:13–19	Luke 6:12–16
1. _____	1. _____	1. _____
2. _____	2. _____	2. _____
3. _____	3. _____	3. _____
4. _____	4. _____	4. _____
5. _____	5. _____	5. _____
6. _____	6. _____	6. _____
7. _____	7. _____	7. _____
8. _____	8. _____	8. _____
9. _____	9. _____	9. _____
10. _____	10. _____	10. _____
11. _____	11. _____	11. _____
12. _____	12. _____	12. _____

_____

_____

_____

_____

_____

In each of the lists, Peter is always mentioned first, and the first four disciples are always the same (Peter, Andrew, James and John), though not always in the same order. We know from other passages that these four, or at least three of them (Peter, James and John), were often with the Lord even when the others weren't. The next grouping of four is the same in each list (Philip, Bartholomew, Matthew and Thomas) with one exception—Mark and Luke put Matthew on the list before Thomas, and Matthew, with characteristic humility, places Thomas before himself. The third group of four (James the son of Alphaeus, Thaddaeus, Simon, and Judas Iscariot) is identical in each list with the exception that Luke calls Thaddaeus *"Judas, the son of James"* and places him with Judas Iscariot.

Did You Know?

❓ FISHING IN NEW TESTAMENT TIMES

Fishing was a major source of commerce around the Sea of Galilee during New Testament times. While some fishing was done with a rod and line (Matthew 17:24–27), most of the fishing in Jesus' day was done with nets. Although fishermen were not necessarily poor, their profession would be considered what we call today a "blue collar" type of work, not associated with the educated elite of Palestine. The fishing trade was known for its strong work ethic, and Jesus drew many of His disciples from this occupation. His call for them to become *"fishers of men"* was a challenge they could understand.

Mark 6:7 states: *"And He summoned the twelve and began to send them out in pairs; and He was giving them authority over the unclean spirits."* Luke, the most detailed of the gospel writers, seems to give his list in groupings of "twos." Compare all three lists, and identify who would normally be paired with each other.

_____

_____

_____

_____

_____

Peter it would seem was normally paired with Andrew, and James and John were usually together as well. Philip and Bartholomew (Nathaniel) are listed together, as are Matthew and Thomas. James and Thaddaeus usually appear together as do Simon the Zealot and Judas.

In comparing John 11:16, 20:24 and 21:2 what other identifying characteristic do you discover about Thomas?

_____

_____

_____

_____

In each of these lists he is called *"Didymus"* which is Greek for "the twin." Actually, Thomas was not his given name. Thomas (transliterated "Tomas" in Greek) is the Hebrew term meaning "twin." Eusebius, one of the earliest church historians, says that Thomas' real name was "Judah" in Hebrew and "Judas" in Greek. His nickname, "Twin," may well have been used by his companions to distinguish him from the other two Judahs—the brother of James who was also called Thaddaeus, and Judas Iscariot. We also know that Simon's name was changed to "Peter," possibly to distinguish him from Simon the Zealot. Obviously Thomas was a twin, though who his twin sibling was is anybody's guess.

📖 Read Acts 1:13, and notice the final list of the apostles. As you read the list, remind yourself that normally such lists would be given in order of prominence. Comparing the order here with the Gospel lists, what does this new list tell you about Thomas and the order of the disciples?

_____

_____

_____

_____

_____

Obviously, Peter was the most prominent of all the disciples. Here we see him grouped with John, who had apparently moved into the number two spot. These two are often found together in the narratives of Acts (Acts 3:1, 3, 11; 4:13, 19; 8:14). Andrew moves into a team with James. The interesting thing is that apparently Thomas moves up. Instead of being listed below Matthew, he now is listed above both Matthew and Bartholomew and is paired with Philip. The only other irregularity of this list is the omission of Judas Iscariot.

Thomas **DAY TWO**

A READINESS TO DIE

It is in John's gospel that we find the most comprehensive mention of Thomas in Scripture. Though history has branded him "Doubting Thomas," John paints a very different picture. Of course, John honestly portrays the incident of his doubting, but in two other scenes from Thomas' life we see another side revealed. We will see that Thomas was actually a courageous and faithful disciple who took a stand when others wouldn't. We will also see him willing to admit what he didn't understand. For the remainder of this lesson we will be looking at these three incidents from the life of Thomas, and we will attempt to learn from them what we can about his character. But more importantly, we will try to find the common ground of identity he shares with each of us and seek the lessons from his life that will move us ahead in our walk with God.

📖 Take some time to read John 10:31–39; 11:1–16. Why were the disciples afraid to go back to Judea?

_____

_____

_____

_____

_____

It is important to recognize that Jesus and the disciples had just come from Judea, and while they were there the Jews twice tried to seize Christ that they might kill Him (John 10:31–39). In John 11:8, responding to Jesus' statement, *"Let us go to Judea again,"* the disciples tried to dissuade Him by reminding Him of the threats on His life. Even though they knew Jesus loved Lazarus (John 11:3), they were fearful of this risk.

Look closely again at verse 16. What exactly does Thomas say here, and to whom does he say it?

_____

_____

_____

_____

_____

Thomas' statement was directed to the disciples, not to Jesus. In verse 16 he tells the whole group, *"Let us also go, that we may die with Him."* Notice that Thomas had already accepted that Jesus was going to Judea, though the others tried to talk Him out of it. Thomas recognized the full impact of what

THE HOSTILITY OF THE PHARISEES

As Jesus' popularity began to increase and news of His miracles began to spread, the Pharisees became increasingly hostile. They viewed Jesus as a threat to their positions of power. This is made evident in John 11:47–48, where there is no attempt to deny the validity of Jesus' miracles—only a fear that *"all men will believe in Him, and the Romans will come and take away both our place and our nation."* It is important to recognize that if a person is unwilling to submit to God in humility, they will eventually end up attacking Him. One cannot remain neutral about Christ.

going back to Judea might involve, but he was not willing to shrink back from the journey. It was a very brave and courageous statement Thomas made in this verse, for he believed the journey would cost them their lives.

Who asked Jesus to come back to Judea, and who invited the disciples to come with Him?

_____

_____

_____

_____

_____

It appears that Martha was the one who had invited Jesus to come (John 11:5). It was Jesus who invited the disciples to come with Him. This is significant, for it is one thing to turn down an invitation from a friend because of fear, but another thing altogether to turn down an invitation from the Master. Thomas seems to have recognized that even death in the will of God was better than shrinking back in fear and avoiding the will of God.

What do you see as the attitude behind Thomas' statement to his comrades?

_____

_____

_____

_____

_____

His statement is not one of pessimism, but of realism. He fully recognized what following the Lord might entail, but in spite of his fears he refused to desert Christ. Thomas' exhortation belies an attitude of courage, loyalty and devotion. It certainly stands in stark contrast to the portrait of a spineless skeptic that history has unkindly painted of him.

What, according to John 11:47–54, were the consequences of this visit back to Judea?

_____

_____

_____

_____

_____

As soon as Jesus performed the miracle of raising Lazarus from the dead, the news was brought to the Pharisees, who immediately began plotting His death. Because of this, John 11:54 indicates that Jesus no longer continued to walk publicly among the Jews. The disciples' fears of what could happen on this visit were not far removed from reality.

We read in Day One's discussion that Thomas was at the bottom of the second tier of disciples mentioned in almost exactly the same order in the Gospels of Matthew, Mark and Luke. Even though Thomas was not the

> *"If anyone wishes to come after Me, let him deny himself, and take up his cross, and follow Me."*
> **Mark 8:34**

recognized leader among the Twelve, it is he, not Peter or John, who exhorts his fellowmen to obedience. His words here resound with a deep and true love for the Lord, and an unwillingness to desert Him in treacherous times. How unlike the arrogant boasting of Peter, *"Lord, with You I am ready to go both to prison and to death!"* We know that Peter's boast was mere words. Thomas actually put feet to his declaration, for he goes with Jesus to Judea even though he expects that it will mean death. Jesus had taught His disciples that unless they were prepared to hate their own lives for His sake, they could not be His disciples. Thomas gives evidence of a life devoted to the will of God.

Thomas **DAY THREE**

HONEST QUESTIONS

The next vignette from the life of Thomas is found in John chapter 14. It makes up part of what is known as the "Upper Room" discourse, that conversation our Lord had with His disciples on the night before His crucifixion. This dialogue between Jesus and His men began in the upper room where they observed the Passover together and then He washed their feet. It was during this evening, of course, that Judas departed and made arrangements to betray the Lord. The discourse continued with the eleven faithful disciples as they walked to Gethsemane, and it culminated in Jesus' arrest.

📖 Read John 13:31—14:4. Identify the sorrowful news Christ gave to His men, and how He tried to comfort them.

_____

_____

_____

_____

> **"Let not your heart be troubled; believe in God, believe also in Me."**
>
> **John 14:1**

It was an extremely sorrowful occasion, for Jesus had just revealed that He would only be with them a little while longer. The thought of Jesus dying weighed heavily on the disciples' hearts. Jesus exhorts them in 14:1, *"Let not your heart be troubled,"* and He relates to them the hope of heaven and the promise that He was going to prepare a place for them. Although Jesus' words in John 14:1–4 were meant to encourage, they did not provide the comfort for which Thomas was looking.

What exactly does Thomas say in John 14:5, and what does this reveal about him?

_____

_____

_____

_____

_____

Thomas says, *"Lord, we do not know where You are going."* One can see that as soon as Thomas heard the Lord was to leave them, he could focus on nothing else. As we have already observed, Thomas cared more to be with Jesus than for his own life. Death was less to be feared than being separated from the Lord he so loved. Although it is easy to identify weaknesses in Thomas' statement, what shows through most prominently is his passionate love for Christ. The second half of his statement, *"how do we know the way?"* reveals that Thomas sought deeper truth or, in essence, "How do I get to where you are going to be?" To Thomas that was all that really mattered, and no price would be too great to pay as long as he could be with Jesus.

What is Jesus' answer to Thomas' question, and what does it mean?

_____

_____

_____

_____

In John 14:6 Jesus says to him, *"I am the way, and the truth, and the life; no one comes to the Father, but through Me."* In other words, Jesus says, "Thomas, you don't have to bear the responsibility of finding me. I am your way to the Father." Thomas' question resulted in one of the richest revelations of Christ in all the New Testament. Christ Himself is our way, our truth, and our life. He is the sum-total of all we need to know and believe. He is **how** we find the Father, He is **what** truth is, and He is **where** we find life.

What does the fact that Thomas asked this question say to you personally?

_____

_____

_____

_____

_____

As I grapple with Thomas' question, I find great encouragement in the knowledge that it is perfectly okay to ask questions of the Lord. James 1:5 states, *"But if any of you lacks wisdom, let him ask of God, who gives to all men generously and without reproach, and it will be given to him."* Often we are guilty of only expressing to the Lord what we think we "should" say instead of honestly exposing our hearts to him with all our questions and doubts. Thomas was probably not the only one who considered asking such a question, but he was the one bold enough to voice his confusion.

> **Christ Himself is our way, our truth, and our life. He is how we find the Father, He is what truth is, and He is where we find life.**

LOOKING FOR A FAITH FOUNDED ON FACT

Thomas DAY FOUR

The most extensive look into Thomas' character is found in John 20, after our Lord's resurrection. It is, of course, the incident for which he is forever remembered as "Doubting Thomas," though unfairly so, for he did not remain a doubter. History records that after Thomas saw the Lord and had his doubts erased, he went on to useful service for the Master. As we saw in our study in Day One, with the approach of Pentecost we find him in the "Upper Room" praying with the rest of our Lord's disciples (except for Judas). The outcome of Thomas confronting his doubts was a solid faith from which others could draw encouragement. What a blessing it is that Scripture portrays its heroes so honestly!

📖 Read John 20:19–26, and record the details of Thomas' doubting and his encounter with the risen Lord.

_____

_____

_____

_____

_____

We see from this passage that ten of the Twelve were gathered together on the evening of the resurrection when the Lord appeared to them. Unfortunately Thomas was not with them, and it would be ludicrous to attempt to state clearly why he was not there. We should go no further than Scripture goes and simply accept the fact that he was not there. Though he did not embrace the other disciples' accounts of seeing the Lord, it is significant that he was with them eight days later when the Lord reappeared. He had not abandoned them, nor had he abandoned the faith.

📖 When did the other disciples believe, and how was their doubt different than that of Thomas (see Luke 24:38–39; John 20:19)?

_____

_____

_____

_____

It must be recognized that the other disciples **did not believe** until they had seen the risen Lord themselves and touched His wounds (Luke 24:38–39). On the night of the resurrection, they hid themselves in a locked room out of fear of the Jews (John 20:19). Thomas asked for nothing more than what the other disciples had already experienced. In Luke 24:25–26, Jesus spoke a word of rebuke directed at all of His followers: *"O foolish men and slow of heart to believe in all that the prophets have spoken! Was it not necessary for the Christ to suffer these things and to enter into His glory?"* We must not single Thomas out as if his doubts were any more pronounced than the others. Instead, we should applaud the fact that, when given the evidence, he quickly believed.

How did Jesus deal with Thomas' doubts, and what does that say to us about our own doubts (John 20:27)?

_____

_____

_____

The Lord answered the doubts of Thomas by giving him evidence. The manner of Christ's answer reveals His omniscience, for He answered Thomas' question (which was asked in His absence) and even used the same words Thomas did. It should be of great encouragement to us when we doubt, first, that even the Lord's disciples experienced doubt. Second, we should be encouraged that the Lord is willing and able to answer the uncertainties of an

"Because you have seen Me, have you believed? Blessed are they who did not see, and yet believed."
John 20:29

honest seeker. And third, what a blessing it is to know that our faith is built not simply on our own willingness to believe, but on the fact of His resurrection.

Once Thomas had his questions answered, how did he respond?

_____

_____

_____

_____

_____

There is no record in the text that Thomas found it necessary to touch the wounds of Jesus. Seeing Jesus and His wounds was probably sufficient for him. His reply, *"My Lord and my God!"* is the grandest expression of faith in the New Testament. It is significant that Thomas is the **only person in the New Testament** to address Jesus as God. The outcome of Thomas' doubts was a stronger faith, a faith founded on fact.

FOR ME TO FOLLOW GOD

What are some lessons we have learned from the experience of Thomas? First, we learned from both John 14 and John 20 that Thomas was inquisitive, and that his questions were accepted and embraced by the Lord. We observed that Jesus does not reject doubts that are honest and accompanied by a willingness to believe once evidence is given. We also learned from Thomas that it is better to give voice to our doubts than to hide our disbelief, for the Lord is willing to provide answers. In Thomas we find a very human portrait of what it means to be a follower of Jesus. But let us never call him "Doubting Thomas" again, for clearly his doubts lasted but a fleeting moment while his faith made him strong for the rest of his life.

Which faith is greater: the one that never doubts or the faith that having doubted investigates and is satisfied? Many of us can relate with Thomas' doubts because we have had some doubts of our own. Often when we struggle with theological issues, unlike Thomas, we keep our doubts to ourselves. But doubts handled in such a fashion never have a chance to get resolved. God, who created us with a mind and intellect to ask questions, is not offended with honest doubt if it is coupled with a sincere desire for truth.

For non-Christians, however, doubts are often nothing more than smoke screens hiding an unwillingness to believe. I can remember discussions with many non-Christians who professed doubts, but I have learned a simple way to cut through the fog of disbelief. Before addressing someone's doubts, I ask, "If I answer your questions to your satisfaction, are you willing to accept Christ?" Their response tells me very quickly if they are honest seekers or if their doubts are merely an excuse for them to continue to live as they please.

Many great men of faith began as spiritual skeptics. The apostle Paul did not believe the testimony of Stephen (Acts 7:58), but when he encountered the risen Lord on the road to Damascus, his doubts were converted to a dynamic faith. Attorney Frank Morrison, a once-avowed skeptic of the resurrection, set out to disprove that Jesus rose from the dead. But upon investigating the facts with his legal mind and training, he had to change his opinion. He eventually wrote the best-seller, *Who Moved the Stone?*—with its first chapter titled, "The Book that Refused to Be Written." Another former skeptic, Lew Wallace, intended to write a book about Christ as a mere man, but in the process he became convinced of Jesus' divinity and went on to write the classic historical novel, *Ben Hur*. God is willing to meet us with our honest doubts.

Have you had doubts about the faith? The legendary reformer, John Calvin, wrote, "The heart is never so established and the mind so enlightened that there remain no vestiges of doubt." Three key lessons we should learn from Jesus' dealings with Thomas include: **1)** Jesus already knows our doubts, **2)** He does not reject us because of our doubts, and **3)** He is willing and able to deal with our doubts.

> "The heart is never so established and the mind so enlightened that there remain no vestiges of doubt."
> —John Calvin

APPLY Can you think of a time when you struggled with doubts about the faith?

_____

_____

Around what did your doubts revolve?

_____

_____

_____

How did you deal with those doubts?

_____

_____

_____

People try to deal with their doubts in different ways. Sometimes you can publish your doubts, but in doing so, you run the risk of leading others into doubt. Or you can simply ignore your doubts, but this will result in a faith divorced from your intellect. Renowned Christian apologist, Josh McDowell wrote, "My heart cannot rejoice in what my mind rejects." Still another way you can deal with doubt is to keep your doubts to yourself, but they will fester and spread like a poison in your system.

> "My heart cannot rejoice in what my mind rejects"
> —Josh McDowell

📖 Look at Psalm 73.

What was the source of Asaph's doubts (see 73:1–3)?

_____

_____

_____

What did he say would be the outcome if he "published" his doubts to others (v.15)?

_____

_____

_____

Asaph knew the correct spiritual answer: *"God is good to Israel, to those who are pure in heart."* But his experience didn't seem to be matching with that doctrine. From where he sat, it looked like the wicked were prospering. The whole psalm is an honest account of his struggle with this troublesome question. In verse 15 he honestly concedes, *"If I had said, 'I will speak thus,' behold I would have betrayed the generation of Thy people."* Clearly the solution to doubts is not to air them indiscriminately. Even pondering them over in his mind proved troublesome for Asaph, and a solution did not come until he took his doubts to the Lord. The turning point of the whole Psalm is found in verse 17: *"Until I came into the sanctuary of God; Then I perceived their end."* Like Thomas, once he met with God his doubts were put to rest.

APPLY Where have you struggled with doubts?

___ Mysteries of the Bible   ___ Jesus' miracles   ___ God's goodness
___ Your own salvation   ___ Heaven   ___ Science & the Bible
___ Judgment of sin   ___ God's love   ___ The resurrection
___ Other _____

Have you ever "published" your doubts to others?

_____

_____

What was the result?

_____

_____

_____

Do you know someone who simply tries to ignore their doubts?

_____

_____

_____

How strong is his/her faith?

_____

_____

_____

How is he/she perceived by others?

_____

_____

_____

Put Yourself In Their Shoes
WHEN YOU DOUBT

When you doubt, you can:

• Publish your doubts—leading others to doubt with you.

• Ignore your doubts—separating your faith from your mind.

• Hide your doubts—allowing them to fester and spread.

Or you can:

• Take your doubts honestly to the Lord.

Can you think of an example of hiding doubts from the Lord?

_____

_____

What was the outcome?

_____

_____

"I do believe; help my unbelief"

Mark 9:24

Thomas shows us that we can take our doubts honestly to the Lord. In Mark 9 we see an example of just that. A man brought his demon-possessed son to Jesus, hoping that Jesus could help where others had failed. Jesus encouraged his weak faith by saying, *"All things are possible to him who believes"* (Mark 9:23). In a prayer of total honesty the man replies in the very next verse, *"I do believe; help my unbelief."* Jesus did just that. Likewise, if we take our doubts to the Lord He is willing and able to help our unbelief.

Why not take your doubts to the Lord right now in prayer?

Lord, I am ashamed to admit that I have doubted You, Your power, Your truth, and Your goodness. Thank You for providing me with the assurance of knowing that I am not the only one who struggles with doubt. Thank You for the example of Thomas. I know that I believe in You, but I ask that You help me with my unbelief, just as You helped with Thomas. In my moments of weakness, meet with me and help my unbelief. Give me the assurance that I need. Amen.

Prayer of Application . . .

Take a few moments to write down a prayer of application from the things you have learned this week.

_____

_____

_____

_____

_____

_____

_____

_____

_____

_____

_____

_____

_____

Notes

Notes

James

GROWING IN GENUINE FAITH

Can you imagine what it was like to grow up as the little brother of Jesus? You follow Him through school, and He probably made perfect scores. Whenever you get into an argument with Him, you're always in the wrong. He never does anything bad, never gets into trouble. He never swears when He bangs His thumb with a hammer in the family carpentry shop. Whenever you do something wrong your mom probably says, "Why can't you be more like Jesus?" To make matters worse, He becomes a well-known speaker and begins to imply that He is God incarnate. Imagine trying to explain your brother to your friends. Finally, your family is disgraced when He is executed like a common criminal. This is how James grew up, and yet, this man James eventually became a devout follower of Christ as well as the chief leader of the mother church in Jerusalem. He is even author of one of the books of the Bible. And what is the theme of this book? Authentic faith—the real thing. We are ready to begin looking at James, the brother of Jesus. We will see what his life teaches about walking with God.

JAMES, THE BROTHER OF JESUS

James, the brother of Jesus, may have begun as a skeptic, but he ended his life as a devout follower of Jesus and a beloved and respected leader. After his miraculous release from prison, Peter asked that a report be given to James (Acts 12:17), and Paul sought out and acted on James' advice concerning his testimony before the Jews (Acts 21:15–26). He authored the tolerant statement of the Jerusalem Council (Acts 15), but his main focus was assimilating Jews into the Church.

THE LIFE OF JAMES

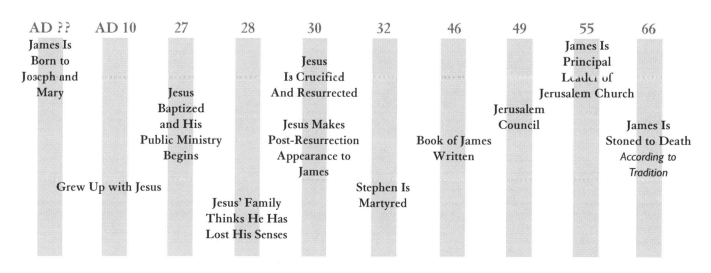

AD ??	AD 10	27	28	30	32	46	49	55	66
James Is Born to Joseph and Mary		Jesus Baptized and His Public Ministry Begins		Jesus Is Crucified And Resurrected				James Is Principal Leader of Jerusalem Church	
				Jesus Makes Post-Resurrection Appearance to James		Book of James Written	Jerusalem Council		James Is Stoned to Death *According to Tradition*
	Grew Up with Jesus		Jesus' Family Thinks He Has Lost His Senses		Stephen Is Martyred				

THE UNBELIEVING BROTHERS

The Bible reveals very little about the formative years of Christ. Other than that His infancy was spent in Egypt and that He made a trip to the Temple at age twelve, there is no written record of His life from the time He was a baby until He began His public ministry at age thirty. But there were many witnesses to these years, including family witnesses, for Jesus had four brothers, and He also had sisters, though we have no indication of how many.

📖 Look at the context of Matthew 13:55–57 and Mark 6:3, and write everything that stands out to you about Jesus' family.

_____

_____

_____

_____

_____

As mentioned above, Jesus had four brothers: James, Joseph, Simon, and Judas. We also see in these passages that Jesus had sisters. The text tells us that the family business is the carpentry trade. But one thing that stands out about His family from this context is that they must have been a very ordinary family, for all in Nazareth were amazed at the thought that Jesus would be a teacher. Jesus' statement in verse 57 is striking: *"A prophet is not without honor except in his home town,* **and in his own household"** (emphasis mine).

Christ's brothers are mentioned in Mark 3:20–35. The incident occurred in the town of Capernaum on what is known as the "busy day" of Jesus' ministry (in the fall of AD 28 after about two full years of ministry). Jesus' ministry had drawn great crowds and a measure of controversy.

What does Mark 3:21 reveal about James and the rest of the family's initial response to Jesus' public ministry?

_____

_____

_____

_____

The obvious thing revealed here is that all of Jesus' siblings, James included, thought He was crazy. Mark 3:19–21 says He went into a house (most likely His home in Capernaum), and while He was there great crowds again gathered. His family in Nazareth (*"His own people"),* hearing of all that was going on *"went out"* (from Nazareth to Capernaum) seeking *"to lay hold of Him, for they said, 'He is out of His mind'"* (NKJV). Verse 21 in the New American Standard Bible says, *"He has lost His senses."* The Greek word translated *"lost his senses"* means to lose one's mental stability. Something not quite as obvious here is that Jesus' siblings really did care for Him. Rather than abandoning Him or ignoring Him, the family went out to take custody (care) of Him.

✏ **Did You Know?**

② **CARPENTRY**

The family business in the home where James grew up was carpentry. In the days before power tools, the wood had to be cut, sawn and hewn by hand through hours of backbreaking labor. Carpenters were known to be quite strong. While most of the homes in Palestine were made of brick and mortar, carpenters were the ones sought for hewn support beams and rafters. Wood-working was applied in the building of carts (the word "carpenter" is actually a contraction of *"cartpenter"),* as well as making wooden tools, basic furniture, and various repair jobs.

📖 Matthew 12:46–50, Mark 3:31–35, and Luke 8:19–21 are most likely three different gospel accounts of the same incident. Comparing them, write any observations you have about Jesus' family's view of His ministry.

_____

_____

_____

Again, we see Jesus' family holding a posture of unbelief. Jesus' response here is significant. Essentially what He reveals in this account is that His family must grow accustomed to relating to Him as His followers did. Christ's response did not come out of an uncaring position but was intended to force them to move beyond the understanding they had of Him as He was growing up.

📖 In John 7:1–10 we get our last glimpse of James and the rest of the brothers' unbelief. Read the passage, and write what stands out to you.

_____

_____

_____

Two important things are revealed here about James and the other brothers. We learn in verses 3–4 that the brothers saw Jesus as one who *"seeks to be known publicly,"* and essentially what they were asking Him to do was to prove Himself to the world. We also read in verse 5 that *"not even His brothers were believing in Him."*

One important question—from what you know of Jesus' family, who is missing from all these verses that we have looked at today, and why do you suppose this is so?

_____

_____

_____

Glaringly absent from each of these passages is any reference to Joseph, the father of the family. Most scholars believe that he had already died. This would mean that with Jesus going into public ministry, James had more responsibility in the household for a time as the oldest male at home, and perhaps he resented this.

It is easy for us to condemn Jesus' family for their initial unbelief, but it takes very little reflection to begin identifying with it. Regardless of what a person goes on to accomplish in their lifetime, the family always tends to view them in the role they have in that relationship. Add to this the difficulty anyone would have accepting the idea that God would become a man, and it is easier to understand the struggle that faced James and his siblings. During the remainder of this lesson on James, we will focus on the transformation that James experienced in his faith as he moved from seeing Jesus as His brother to recognizing Him as his Savior and Lord.

> "For not even His brothers were believing in Him."
> John 7:5

A CHANGE OF THINKING ABOUT JESUS

Although most of Jesus' family did not believe in Him during His earthly ministry, it is significant that all of them end up becoming believers. James and the rest of Jesus' family had undoubtedly heard the testimony of their parents about the uniqueness of Jesus' birth. They would have witnessed and/or heard about many of His miracles. But the most convincing evidence of all was His resurrection from the dead. From that point forward there is no mention of any more doubts about His divinity. Let's look at the process of how James and the others came to believe in Christ as the Son of God.

📖 Read John 19:26–27. Identify the context of these verses, and write your thoughts on why James was not given the care of his mother.

_____

_____

_____

_____

This passage obviously reflects the special relationship that existed between Jesus and John, the disciple whom He loved. Mary's presence there and the connection with John suggest that she was now a believer. The fact that James was not given this responsibility implies that he was not yet a believer. Jesus undoubtedly had a reason for bypassing his brothers as caretakers of His mother.

📖 We next see James mentioned in Acts 1:14. Read this verse, along with the surrounding context, and write what you learn about James.

_____

_____

_____

_____

From this passage we can see that James is among those gathered in the Upper Room for prayer those ten days between Jesus' ascension and Pentecost. We are told that *"these all with one mind were continually devoting themselves to prayer."* To be of *"one mind"* with the disciples, obviously means that James and the other brothers were all believers now. In 1 Corinthians 9:5, Paul links the brothers of the Lord with the apostles.

📖 Now look at 1 Corinthians 15:7, and see what it suggests concerning what had brought about this change in belief for James.

_____

_____

_____

Though not the first person to whom Jesus appeared (Peter, then the whole group of disciples, and then some five hundred people all witness the risen Lord before James), he is specifically singled out for a post-resurrection

> *"These all with one mind were continually devoting themselves to prayer, along with the women, and Mary the mother of Jesus, and with His brothers."*
>
> **Acts 1:14**

appearance. Perhaps this is because James was so skeptical that only this would convince him. Maybe it was also because of the special role that James would play in the life of the early Church. In any case, the Lord came to him and removed all doubt.

A Leader in Jerusalem

Nothing is said in Acts concerning how James assumed the role he held in Jerusalem, but somewhere in the intervening years he rose to a position of prominence in the early Church. While the Lord's disciples focused on expansion of the faith, taking the gospel first to the Jews, then to the Samaritans, and ultimately to the Gentiles, James stayed in Jerusalem. He had moved from mere sibling to skeptic to prayer participant to the recognized leader of the church in Jerusalem. With 3,000 souls converted on the day of Pentecost (Acts 2:41) and some 5,000 men coming to faith in one day a short time later, most theologians estimate that the church in Jerusalem expanded very quickly to 20,000 or more people. James was at the helm of one of the largest congregations in history. This transformation of James from skeptic to leader had not happened overnight, but he certainly was a changed man by the time the Church was started. Today we want to study his leadership position and how James filled it as we look at the passages where he is mentioned.

📖 Look at Acts 12:17. Identify the context, and write what you see there about James.

_____

_____

_____

The context is the miraculous deliverance of Peter from prison. Once he had fellowshipped with believers upon his return, his instruction is for them to *"Report these things to James and the brethren."* It is significant that he didn't just say to report it to the brethren or to the leaders. Apparently James is already the recognized leader of the church in Jerusalem. Equally significant is the fact that although Peter was the recognized leader of the disciples, he is not the main leader of the Jerusalem church.

📖 Read Galatians 1:18–19, and make note of what you learn about James there.

_____

_____

_____

_____

We see here in Galatians that James spent some time with Paul three years after Paul's conversion. Probably they had already met, but the relationship was strengthened here. Paul identifies James in two significant ways: **1)** as "the Lord's brother," and **2)** as an apostle in Jerusalem.

Did You Know?
"CAMEL KNEES"

James was known as an unusually good man, and was called "James the Just" by his countrymen. Tradition holds that, like Samson and John the Baptist, he was a Nazarite from his mother's womb. In the early church he was also nicknamed "camel knees" because his long hours in prayer caused thick callouses on his knees, giving them an appearance like those of a camel. He was probably married (1 Corinthians 9:5), but nothing is ever mentioned of his wife and family.

Take a few minutes to read Acts 15:1–31. The new church is at a critical juncture. What was at first a body made up solely of Jews had begun to attract scores of Gentiles. The central question of the Jerusalem Council was "how does a Gentile come into the church?" Must he first become a Jew? Certainly there was nothing wrong with the Jews continuing to honor the Law, provided that they recognized that the Law could not save. For the Jewish Christians, neglect for the Law would offend the fellow Jews they were seeking to reach. But was it right to put the burden of the Law on the Gentiles, a burden which Peter says, *"neither our fathers nor we have been able to bear"*? Take a few minutes to answer the questions below, and learn what you can about this circumstance of the Jerusalem Council.

📖 Looking at Acts 15:2, 4, and 6, exactly to whom do Paul and Barnabas address this question, and what do we know about them?

_____

_____

_____

_____

Three times the passage identifies the audience as the *"apostles and elders"* in Jerusalem. Jerusalem was the hub of the Jewish faith since the time of King David. With the birth of the church in Jerusalem, the city became the "home office," so to speak, of the Christian faith as well. The apostles spoken of here were those eyewitnesses of the resurrection who were the core leadership of the universal Church. The elders were separate and distinct from this group, though some apostles may have also been elders. They were the leaders of the local church.

📖 Now look at Galatians 2:1–10, and identify who is reporting to whom. What else do you learn about the identity of these leaders.

_____

_____

_____

_____

_____

It is noteworthy that Paul and Barnabas reported to the church in Jerusalem to see if they had *"run in vain."* In other words, they trusted the leadership there to make sure they were on the right track. From the leadership at Jerusalem, Paul identifies James, Cephas (Peter), and John as the key leaders and calls them *"pillars."* Most likely, these three men are listed in order of authority, placing James over Peter.

📖 Look again at Acts 15.

Who had the final say in the debate (v. 13)?

_____

_____

Did You Know?

? THE JERUSALEM COUNCIL

In Galatians 2:1–10, Paul details the visit to Jerusalem that he and Barnabas made before a group of men commonly called "The Jerusalem Council." At question was whether Gentile Christians needed to follow the Old Testament rite of circumcision. The conclusion of the council was a definitive answer of "no." One added suggestion, probably from James, was given though—"to remember the poor" (Galatians 2:10). The poor were always important to James. In his epistle he mentions them repeatedly with concern (1:9, 27; 2:2, 5–6, 15), while warning and admonishing the wealthy (1:10; 2:6,15–16; 4:1–4,13–16; 5:1–6).

What was his message (vv. 14–21)?

_____

_____

What resulted from the message (vv. 25, 31, 33)?

_____

_____

_____

_____

Many spoke on both sides of the issue, but it was James who seemed to be the moderator and the one who brought the discussion to closure. Notice that he took into consideration all the information that had been shared, but his answer hinged on what God had already said. The result, according to the letter sent to Antioch, was that they had *"become of one mind"* (15:25). Notice that Acts 15:28 credits the Holy Spirit with the Council's conclusion, indicating that the group recognized that God had spoken through James. The outcome was renewed rejoicing from the letter's encouragement (15:31), peace (15:33), and an unhindered continuation of the ministry of the Word of the Lord.

What does Acts 21:18 reveal about the role of James in Jerusalem?

_____

_____

_____

_____

_____

Although there was a plurality of elders in Jerusalem, James is clearly the principal leader at this time (probably AD 55–56). There is no mention of John or Peter as both men had probably left Jerusalem for reasons of safety and/or ministry.

📖 Read Galatians 2:11–12, and make note of what you learn of James from this passage. Be careful not to jump to conclusions. Simply observe the text.

_____

_____

_____

_____

_____

We see here that certain men *"from James"* (who were obviously Jews) encouraged Peter to separate from the Gentiles. Although the men gave Peter bad advice, one important thing to learn about the incident is that the men were **from James**, implying that **he** was the leader of the church in Jerusalem.

Doctrine
"HAVING BECOME OF ONE MIND"

Two important principles on determining God's will are revealed in this verse. **First,** the leadership group knew they had heard from God, not when one of them had the right answer, but when all of them were in agreement. They operated on the principle of unanimity. **Second,** this statement discloses that they didn't start out being of one mind. The most important thing to learn from this statement is that discerning God's will is a process that takes time.

A BOND-SERVANT OF GOD AND OF THE LORD JESUS CHRIST

THE BOOK OF JAMES

The book of James has been likened to the Old Testament book of Proverbs because of its emphasis on practical wisdom. It was probably the first of the New Testament epistles to be written (about AD 46) and is Jewish in flavor. It also shares a great similarity to Jesus' "Sermon on the Mount" with at least ten direct parallels. Martin Luther thought little of the book at first, calling it "a right strawy epistle, having no true evangelical character." Being deeply affected by the message of Romans, he bristled at James' emphasis on works. Luther's view changed in time, and he came to see James as a practical complement to Romans.

James authored the book of the New Testament that bears his name. His audience was *"the twelve tribes who* [were] *dispersed abroad."* In other words, he wrote his epistle to members of the twelve tribes of Israel who had come to Christ and who were scattered outside of Jerusalem because of the persecution. It would seem, from all we have learned of James so far, that his primary ministry was not to the Gentiles (that was Paul's ministry) but to the Jews. In Jerusalem, where the church was made up mostly of Jews, it was necessary to have a man such as James as pastor. Another of Jesus' younger brothers, Jude, also wrote one of the books of the New Testament, and in Jude 1:1 he identifies himself as a *"brother of James."* While this may not seem significant, the only reason Jude would mention this is because of how well known James was in the body of Christ. Today we want to begin looking at the epistle that James wrote and see what we can learn about this younger brother of Jesus.

📖 Read James 1:1.

How does James identify himself?

_____

_____

What things are true about his relationship to Christ that he chose not to mention?

_____

_____

_____

James identified himself as a "bond-servant" of God and of the Lord Jesus Christ. Remember that James is the brother of Christ, and yet he did not see himself in those terms. He saw his relationship to Christ not as a younger brother but as a devoted follower. Even though he was senior pastor of the mega-church in Jerusalem, he saw his service as unto God and unto Christ. A man of God may minister his call in serving people, but ultimately he is called to serve God. Therefore, it is God, not the people, who defines one's service.

📖 Now, look at James 2:1, and make note of how he referred to his older brother.

_____

_____

_____

James never referred to Jesus as the one with whom he grew up. Here he calls Him *"our glorious Lord Jesus Christ."* What a title of reverence! As Paul wrote in 2 Corinthians 5:16, *"Therefore from now on we recognize no man according to the flesh; even though we have known Christ according to the flesh, yet now we know Him thus no longer."* James saw Jesus not through the eyes of the flesh, but through the eyes of the Spirit and of faith.

📖 James called himself a "bond-servant." To us this may not mean much, but to a Jew it called to mind a very specific type of relationship. Look up these Old Testament passages, and write everything you can find out about "bond-slaves" or "bond-servants."

Exodus 21:5–6:

_____

_____

_____

Deuteronomy 15:12–18:

_____

_____

_____

The Law permitted a Jew to sell himself into slavery for seven years as a means of paying off debt. If, at the end of that time, he felt that it would be beneficial to continue working for his master, he could choose to be his servant for life. The servant would forever commit to do only the will of his master. His master would commit to provide for and to protect him as long as he lived. The covenant relationship was sealed by the master by piercing the ear of the "bond-servant" with an awl—providing visible evidence to all of the master-servant relationship.

So, when James calls himself a *"bond-servant of God and of the Lord Jesus Christ,"* what does he imply about himself (James 1:1)?

_____

_____

_____

James essentially said that he had become a "slave" of God and of the Lord Jesus Christ. Notice that he identified Jesus as both his Lord and the Messiah. James said that God had been such a good Master to him that he would be thrilled to spend the rest of his life serving his Master, Jesus. Serving Jesus was not a requirement for James' salvation, but a loving response of gratitude for all that God had done in saving him.

For Me to Follow God

James DAY FIVE

Jesus was a tough act for James and His other brothers to follow. Indeed, each of us would struggle with our own identity as the younger brother of Jesus. But clearly James was his own man. He came to realize that Jesus was not just his brother; He was the Messiah. Thoroughly Jewish, James had been well schooled in the Law, but he realized that simply keeping the Law

> "Paul and James do not conflict. They stand not face to face, beating each other, but back to back beating off common foes."
>
> A. T. Pierson

Did You Know?
HOW DID JAMES DIE?

According to Josephus, and Hegesippus (a second century church historian):

Shortly before Jerusalem was destroyed by the Roman army in 70 AD, during a time that many were coming to faith in Christ, Ananus, the High Priest, assembled the Sanhedrin and commanded James, "the brother of Jesus who was called Christ," to proclaim from one of the galleries of the Temple that Jesus **was not** the Messiah. But instead, James cried out that Jesus **was** the Son of God and Judge of the world. His enraged enemies hurled him to the ground and stoned him, till a worker ended his sufferings with a club, while he was on his knees praying, "Father, forgive them, they know not what they do."

"But the fruit of the Spirit is love, joy, peace, patience, kindness, goodness, faithfulness, gentleness, self-control; against such things there is no law."
Galatians 5:22-23

was not what a genuine faith was all about. Real faith—not just being religious—was about trusting Christ and cultivating a growing relationship with God through Him. In the book of James, he laid out his formula for godliness by warning us not to be carried away and enticed by our own fleshly desires, but to let the trials of our lives drive us to God, seeking His wisdom. Having found God's wisdom, we must act on it and apply it to our own lives. We must prove ourselves "doers" of God's Word and not just "hearers" (James 1:22) who deceive themselves into thinking they are spiritual because of how much they know instead of concentrating on how they live. *"The root of the righteous yields fruit,"* we are told in Proverbs 12:12. James rather bluntly tells us that a genuine faith will reveal itself by good works. *"Show me your faith without the works, and I will show you my faith by my works"* (James 2:18). As a bond-servant of Christ, his life was more than words. It was a day-by-day manifestation of a real faith that was seen in his good works.

Since the "root" of the righteous yields "fruit," we can draw some conclusions about the health of our root by the fruit it is bearing in our lives. In Galatians we are given two lists of "fruit" that can be helpful in evaluating the health of our spiritual roots. The first list is called *"the deeds of the flesh"* (Galatians 5:19–21). The second list is called *"the fruit of the Spirit"* (Galatians 5:22–23).

 Take a look at each of these lists and place a number from 1–5 (1=seldom and 5=always) beside each item that shows up on a regular basis in your life.

The Deeds of the Flesh (Bad Fruits)

___ immorality	___ impurity	___ sensuality
___ idolatry	___ sorcery	___ enmities
___ strife	___ jealousy	___ outbursts of anger
___ disputes	___ dissensions	___ factions
___ envying	___ drunkenness	___ carousing

The Fruit of the Spirit (Good Fruits)

___ love	___ patience	___ faithfulness
___ joy	___ kindness	___ gentleness
___ peace	___ goodness	___ self-control

As you look at the fruit that normally shows up in your life, what does that tell you about where your roots are?

_____

_____

_____

_____

We won't change our shortcomings by gritting our teeth and trying harder. These fruits are merely the evidences that show where our roots are growing. Tying apples on a pine tree won't fool anyone about what kind of tree it is. In the same way, trying to "act" loving with an unloving heart won't change who we are. We can't fake patience or gentleness. Joy will not come because we try hard to be joyful. Real faith, the kind James lived and wrote about, only comes from yielding our lives to Christ's control. James expressed his relationship with Christ this way: *"James, a **bond-servant** of*

God and of the Lord Jesus Christ." In other words, he so loved the Lord that he was a servant by choice. A bondservant was one who chose to surrender his freedom so that he could forever serve his kind and loving master. If we want our lives to reflect the fruit of the Spirit instead of the deeds of the flesh, we must walk in surrender as James did.

APPLY Have you ever come to a place where you surrendered control of every area of your life to Christ?

_____

_____

If not, why not?

_____

_____

_____

If so, are there areas you have taken back from His control that need to be surrendered afresh?

_____

_____

_____

James earned the respect of all in Jerusalem for his godly manner of living, and his epistle focuses on what it means to be a righteous man, a man with an authentic faith. When he says, *"the effective prayer of a **righteous** man can accomplish much"* (James 5:16), James puts the focus not on having effective prayer but on being a righteous man. His point seems to be, "if you become righteous, your prayers **will** be effective." Often we try to become godly by praying more, rather than realizing that doing things in this fashion is like "putting the cart before the horse." Our prayer life will never go any further than our walk with God. The more godly we become the more effective our prayers will be.

What does your prayer life say about the progress of your spiritual maturity?

_____

_____

_____

_____

_____

If your prayer life isn't what it ought to be, you won't change it by determining to pray harder. You will only change it as you grow in a real faith relationship with Christ, and that begins with surrender—becoming a **"bond-servant"** as James did.

Why not spend some time right now in prayer?

 Lord, I thank You for all You are teaching me through these New Testament saints who walked with You. Thank You for the testimony of James and the reality of his faith. I want that kind of relationship

> **Our prayer life will never go any further than our walk with God. The godlier we become the more effective our praying will be.**

with You. I want my roots to be so deeply grounded in You, that Your fruit is born in my life. You have been such a good and faithful Master to me, I want to be Your bondservant. For the rest of my life, I want to do always and only Your will, knowing that You will care for me and meet my needs. Give me a real faith. Amen.

Prayer of Application . . .

Take a few moments to write down a prayer of application from the things that you have learned this week.

_____

_____

_____

_____

_____

_____

_____

_____

_____

_____

_____

_____

Notes

Notes

Barnabas

THE ENCOURAGING POWER OF A HUMBLE HEART

One of the most important realities is that we minister out of what God has done in us. We can take others no further than we ourselves have been. What God desires to do in our lives is to work **in** us, so that He is then able to work **through** us. He desires complete integrity in our actions as well as our words. Barnabas was a man whose deeds matched his words. He was highly esteemed by all the apostles and new converts for his bold witness, clean testimony, and encouraging words. Because of his humility and surrender, God used him mightily as he mentored men like the apostle Paul and John Mark, who wrote the Gospel of Mark. Barnabas complemented Paul, for where Paul's strengths were in the assets he brought to the ministry, Barnabas' strengths were shown in the ability he had to comfort and encourage other ministers through God's Word. Whenever we follow God, we become useable by Him and an agent of His blessing to others. As you read examples in this lesson of how Barnabas became an encourager to many fellow believers, may the lesson encourage you to do likewise.

"THE SON OF ENCOURAGEMENT"

Barnabas' character is so associated with his ministry that he is known not by his real name (Joseph), but by his nickname, Barnabas, which means "son of encouragement."

CHRONOLOGY OF BARNABAS' MINISTRY

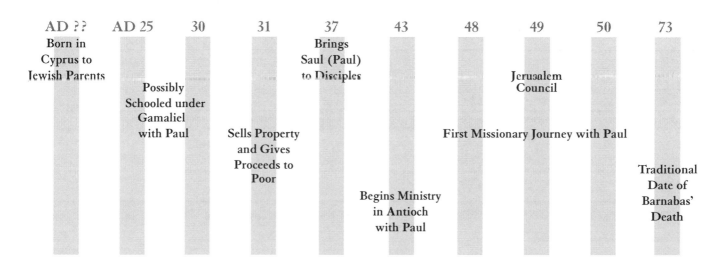

AD ??	AD 25	30	31	37	43	48	49	50	73
Born in Cyprus to Jewish Parents				Brings Saul (Paul) to Disciples			Jerusalem Council		
	Possibly Schooled under Gamaliel with Paul					First Missionary Journey with Paul			
			Sells Property and Gives Proceeds to Poor						Traditional Date of Barnabas' Death
					Begins Ministry in Antioch with Paul				

A MODEL OF HUMILITY AND ENCOURAGEMENT

It may surprise you that many theologians consider Joseph the Cyprian to have had the most significant ministry of the fledgling Church, greater even than the apostle Paul. Perhaps this is a surprising statement, for you may be saying, "I have never even heard of Joseph the Cyprian." Scripture doesn't spend a lot of time talking about him, but every mention of him is significant. One of the reasons his name doesn't ring a bell, however, is because most of us know him by his nickname, Barnabas. Through his mentoring of men such as the apostles Paul and Mark, he left a spiritual legacy that continues to have an impact today. Although he was probably a participant in the earthly ministry of Jesus, he is not mentioned directly by name until Acts 4:32–37. It is there that we find him singled out as a significant example of the early church practice of sharing common property.

📖 Read Acts 4:32–35 carefully, and answer the questions that follow.

What was the attitude of the early church toward possessions (4:32)?

_____

_____

What was the result of this attitude (4:34a)?

_____

_____

_____

How were the needs of the needy being met (4:34b–35)?

_____

_____

_____

Did You Know?

COMMUNITY PROPERTY

The early church had many diverse needs. Because many of those saved at Pentecost and thereafter were Jews from outside of Jerusalem who decided to stay to be taught by the apostles, a temporary welfare system had to be established to care for the physical needs of those unemployed. This was compounded by the fact that many who converted to Christianity would have lost their employment because of persecution and unbelieving employers.

The attitude of believers at this time was that all they possessed belonged to God instead of themselves. People would take their surplus (unneeded houses or land) and sell it, giving the proceeds to the church to distribute. The result was that *"there was not a needy person among them."* O, that the same could be said of the modern Church!

📖 Look at 4:36–37. What do you learn about Barnabas, who is given as a positive example of this practice of selling possessions and giving the proceeds to the needy?

_____

_____

_____

_____

_____

First, we learn that he was of the tribe of Levi. This tells us that he was an educated man. As a Levite, he would have been responsible for Temple duties. He was also from the Isle of Cyprus. We know from the Scriptures and historical writings that he was a bachelor and a man of integrity. Perhaps more telling about him than anything else in this passage is that his life was so characterized by encouragement that the apostles began calling him "Barnabas" which means "Son of Encouragement." This nickname stuck, and from this point on, he was never called "Joseph" again, but always "Barnabas."

Looking at the actions of this passage, why do you suppose the apostles gave this man Joseph the nickname, "Barnabas"? What was it about him that so associated him with encouraging others?

_____

_____

_____

_____

We need to appreciate the fact that Galilee was not highly regarded by the people of Jerusalem. In fact, it was said of Nazareth, a town in Galilee, *"Can any good thing come out of Nazareth?"* (John 1:46). And yet, the apostles were mostly from Galilee. Barnabas, the sophisticated Levite, who owned a tract of land, sold it and brought the money and laid it at the feet of these Galilean peasants, an act of deference and honor. That must have been a great *encouragement* to them. In fact, one must logically ask, "Why is Barnabas applauded for his actions when many people were selling property and donating the money to the Church?" We move into conjecture at this point, but it may very well be that Barnabas was the first believer to do so. The sale of homes and property was not a mandated practice, and we see no place in Scripture where it was commanded. It may be that the example of Barnabas was the impetus for the whole practice. In any case, of all that participated in this practice, Scripture singles out Barnabas as the best positive example. Barnabas had a stewardship view of life. He saw all that he had as belonging to God and viewed himself as merely the steward of it.

Did You Know?
CHRISTIAN PRIESTS

When God brought His people up out of Egypt, He set aside the tribe of Levi for His service. The Levites were to devote themselves as students of the Law and servants of the people. The people were to support them by their offerings. The tribe included the priests, the scribes, and all the other supporting roles in public worship. Acts 6:7 tells us that many of the priests became obedient to the Christian faith. Barnabas was among them.

BARNABAS AND SAUL

Barnabas DAY TWO

We don't hear from Barnabas again until Acts chapter nine when he appears in the middle of the conversion of Saul of Tarsus. Let's talk about Saul for a moment. We are introduced to Saul in Acts 7 where he is mentioned as the coat keeper at the stoning of Stephen (Acts 7:58). Saul was a zealous Pharisee and, like most devout Jews of the day, believed that if Israel wasn't pure, the Messiah wouldn't come. He probably saw the elimination of this group who believed in Jesus (called *"the Way"* [Acts 9:2]) as necessary. In Acts 8 we are told that Saul was in *"hearty agreement"* with the killing of Stephen. Very quickly he had stepped to the forefront of the great persecution against the church in Jerusalem. But Saul was not satisfied with persecuting only believers in Jerusalem. Acts 9 opens with Saul on his way to Damascus, *"breathing threats and murder against the disciples of the Lord."* Saul intended to take Damascus by storm, but ended up having to be led into town by the hand, for he was intercepted by Christ on the Damascus road. Saul was converted through this confrontation with Jesus. For more detail concerning this miraculous conversion of Saul, read Acts 9:1–22.

After news about Saul's conversion to Christianity spread, the Jews plotted to kill Saul (Acts 9:23), and his new Christian friends had to sneak him out of the city by helping him through an opening in the wall, lowering him down in a large basket. After his escape from Damascus, Saul went back to Jerusalem and tried repeatedly to associate with the disciples there, but everything that Saul tried to do to form a relationship with them failed. The text says, *". . . they were all afraid of him, not believing that he was a disciple."* Who could blame the disciples for reacting this way to Saul? After all, we must realize that Saul had killed some of their friends and relatives, so naturally they would have been hostile and bitter towards him. Many probably thought he was faking his conversion to trap more believers. Imagine how Paul must have felt. He no longer had the security of being a Pharisee, for his former associates were now trying to kill him (9:29), and the believers in Christ with whom he now identified himself were continually rebuffing him. Surely he felt dejected and in need of a friend who could encourage him. Barnabas, the "son of encouragement," was God's perfect choice to bring Saul much needed words of support and affirmation.

📖 Look at verses 27 and 28 of Acts 9. What is Barnabas' role, and what are the results of it?

_____

_____

_____

_____

THE IMPORTANT ROLE OF BARNABAS

When Paul left Damascus and came to Jerusalem, he kept trying to associate with the disciples, but they feared that his conversion was just another trap. Luke tells us that Barnabas *"took hold of"* him and brought him to the apostles (Acts 9:27). The word indicates that he physically held on to him. Luke uses this same word in Luke 23:26 when he says that they *"layed hold of"* Simon of Cyrene and made him carry Jesus' cross. He also uses it in Acts 16:19, saying that they "seized" Paul and Silas to arrest them, and again in Acts 18:17 when the crowd *"took hold of"* Sosthenes to beat him. It may have been that by this time Paul had given up, and Barnabas was making him go meet with the disciples. In any case, Barnabas took a very active role.

We must realize that it was not Peter, the "Rock," nor James, the leader of the Jerusalem church, but Barnabas who went to meet with Saul to see if he was genuine. Barnabas may have felt that he was risking his own life by meeting with Saul, for considering all he knew about Saul, he could have been walking directly into a trap. Notice that the apostles had such confidence in Barnabas and his spiritual discernment, that upon Barnabas' recommendation Saul was completely accepted into the fellowship of believers. Barnabas believed in Saul when no one else would, and surely Saul never forgot this.

The next mention of Barnabas is found in Acts 11. About six years had passed since Saul's conversion, and God had begun to move and work in a mighty way among the Gentiles in Antioch. In fact, the gospel had come to Antioch as a direct result of the persecution that Saul had orchestrated.

📖 Look at Acts 11:19–26, and answer the questions below.

What happened when the gospel of Jesus Christ began to be preached to the Greeks (Gentiles) in Antioch (v. 21)?

_____

_____

_____

_____

What was the response of the Church in Jerusalem (v. 22)?

_____

_____

_____

What did Barnabas do when he arrived (v. 23)?

_____

_____

_____

How does Luke describe Barnabas here (v. 24a)?

_____

_____

_____

What was the result of Barnabas' ministry in Antioch (v. 24b)?

_____

_____

_____

 **Word Study**
"SENT"

The Greek word for "sent" that is used of Barnabas being commissioned by the church in Jerusalem has as its root the word *"apostle."* The word portrays the idea of someone being sent out as an authoritative representative. Barnabas was the official representative of the mother church, investigating this new phenomenon of Gentiles coming to faith in Christ.

Although the persecution of the church would naturally seem to be of human origin, through the reading of Scriptures we can clearly see the hand of God behind it. Through this persecution the gospel came to Antioch with tremendous results among the Greeks. News of Christ's message spreading to Gentile regions would soon reach the church in Jerusalem. Wanting assurance that this was of God's doing, the Jerusalem believers selected a man of proven discernment—Barnabas—to investigate. What did Barnabas do when he arrived? He was convinced that God was at work among the Gentiles, and he *encouraged* the new converts in this region. Look at the words Luke used to describe Barnabas in verse 24: *"a good man . . . full of the Holy Spirit and of faith."* Verse 21 tells us that a large number had believed before Barnabas arrived. The statement *"considerable numbers"* indicates that even more people were converted **after** Barnabas came on the scene. We tend to underestimate the significance of encouragement because it is an indirect ministry, but the reality is that encouragement makes everyone more effective and motivated to use his or her gifts for the Lord.

Look at Acts 11:25–26.

Once Barnabas got a handle on this new work of God and was accepted as the key leader, what did he do?

_____

_____

What does this say about his character?

_____

_____

Rather than setting up shop and glorying in all that God was doing through him, he went to get someone else involved. Instead of hoarding the work

BARNABAS' IMPACT

Because Barnabas was more concerned with the work than with his own part in it, he was able to build a team by balancing many different gifts to maximum effectiveness. Not only were considerable numbers "brought" to the Lord (Acts 11:24), but we also see that considerable numbers were "taught" as well (Acts 11:26) over the course of the next year. The ministry not only grew in numbers but also in depth.

and credit to himself, he remembered Saul and decided he would fit in well. This was admirable of Barnabas to want to include Saul in the ministry, for throughout the ages many Christians have been too insecure to share their work with anyone. But if we are concerned with God's glory and not our own, it shouldn't matter who does the work. All that should matter is that the work gets done and that God gets the glory. Although we recognize God's sovereignty, humanly speaking, if it weren't for Barnabas, Saul (eventually identified as Paul) wouldn't have gone into the ministry. What impact for Christ the world would have been robbed of, if not for the encouraging ministry of Barnabas! Because he was willing to share the work, we see that his heart was more concerned with God's glory than with who got the credit. It is worth noting that this work of God at Antioch became so significant that the believers were first called "Christians" there.

> "...and the disciples were first called Christians in Antioch."
>
> Acts 11:26

Barnabas **DAY THREE**

THE FIRST MISSIONARY JOURNEY

God's hand was on the ministry of Barnabas and Saul in a mighty way. Not only did the work in Antioch prosper, but as we will see today, God had even larger plans for them was well. Before we move into today's study, we need to remind ourselves of a few things. Remember that when the church at Jerusalem first heard of the response to the gospel among the Gentiles, they commissioned Barnabas presumably to make certain this work was of God. Once he was convinced that this was a work of the grace of God, he stepped into a teaching/administrative role. Seeing the needs and opportunities, it was Barnabas who went to get Saul.

📖 Look at Acts 11:30 and 12:25.

Who is the leader in this relationship?

_____

_____

_____

_____

Who else is part of it?

_____

_____

_____

_____

In these two passages of Scripture, Barnabas is always mentioned first, and Saul plays a supporting role. John Mark is also mentioned as some sort of an apprentice. This pattern of taking along quality young men, presumably for the purpose of training, was a practice Saul would emulate with such notables as Timothy, Silas, Titus, and others. Colossians 4:10 identifies John Mark as Barnabas' cousin. As we move into chapter 13 we see the establishment of the first missionary journey in which Barnabas also involved John Mark (13:5).

Who is mentioned first in the list of church leaders in verse 1, and who is mentioned last?

_____

_____

_____

The list is probably given in order of priority, and Barnabas is mentioned first, with Saul falling last. This means that Barnabas was the key leader, the "senior pastor" if you will, and that Saul was the leader with the least seniority and significance. It is important to recognize that, although there would seem to be a healthy relationship between Barnabas and Saul, they weren't exactly peers.

📖 Look at verses 2–8. As the missionary journey was initiated by God and then begun, what was the apparent leadership structure of the team?

_____

_____

_____

We see this relationship played out as the Holy Spirit sets the two of them apart to the missionary work. In verse 2 we see that the Holy Spirit mentions Barnabas first. That same order is reiterated in verse 7 by the proconsul Sergius Paulus. Clearly Barnabas was viewed as the leader of this team. John (Mark) is listed in verse 5 as *their helper.*

When the team was confronted by the magician, Elymas, however, it was Saul who spoke, and at this point it appears that the leadership structure began to change as Saul (identified for the first time as Paul in v. 9) came to the forefront as the spokesman of the missionary journey.

📖 Read the rest of chapters 13 and 14 and make note of how the team is identified from this point forward and what this identification implies.

13:13—

_____

_____

13:42—

_____

_____

13:43—

_____

_____

13:46—

_____

_____

Did You Know?

? HERMES AND ZEUS

When the people of Lystra witnessed the miracle of Paul raising a lame man, they thought the gods had become like men and had come down to them (Acts 14:11). Although Paul is the one who performed the miracle, they had some recognition of the relationship between Barnabas and Paul. They called Barnabas "Zeus," and they called Paul "Hermes." In Greek mythology Zeus was the chief god and Hermes was the messenger of the gods. Clearly the people recognized Barnabas as the main leader of the group even though Paul was now the spokesman.

13:50—

_____

_____

14:12—

_____

_____

14:14—

_____

_____

Instead of *"Barnabas and Saul"* (13:2), it now became *"**Paul** and his companions"* (13:13) or *"**Paul** and Barnabas"* throughout most of the rest of the missionary journey (13:42, 43, 46, 50) until they got back to Jerusalem. Back in Jerusalem, they are identified as "Barnabas and Paul" again (15:25), for there Barnabas had the greater respect and credibility. In 14:14, we see that Barnabas is mentioned first again in reference to tearing their robes (a sign of humility before God) at the thought of being worshiped by the people. Verse 14 may suggest that Barnabas took the lead in rebuking the people's errant worship. It is worth noting, however, that it was Paul, not Barnabas, who was stoned in Lystra.

Think about what had happened here: Barnabas was in charge, and then Paul took over. How would you have handled that? Is there any evidence at all of Barnabas struggling with this? Most people would be hurt and offended; many would rebel, but not the "Son of Encouragement." It would seem that Barnabas matured to the point that his ministry was to Paul and to encourage others through Paul. Barnabas was secure enough in himself to allow Paul to blossom into perhaps the world's greatest missionary.

Barnabas DAY FOUR

THE HUMAN SIDE OF MINISTRY

By the time Paul and Barnabas' first missionary journey was completed many new churches were born. God enacted a mighty work among the Gentiles. With this first journey finished, Paul and Barnabas returned to Antioch to give a report. They proclaimed all that God had done and rejoiced at *"how He had opened a door of faith to the Gentiles"* (14:27). Then Barnabas and Paul settled down and spent a lengthy amount of time in Antioch. While there, a debate arose about whether a Gentile convert should be circumcised. As a result of the conflict, the two of them took the issue to the church in Jerusalem. Incidentally, in Jerusalem we find Barnabas mentioned first again (15:12), indicating that there he still had the greater credibility. When the apostles concluded in Paul and Barnabas' favor, the two returned to Antioch to give a report and to continue their teaching and preaching ministry (15:35). It is at this point that we see a conflict arise between Paul and Barnabas. What can we learn from this seemingly negative situation about Barnabas and encouragement? Plenty! Let's look closer. Who is right and who is wrong?

📖 Look at Acts 15:36–41 and answer the questions that follow.

For what is Paul burdened (15:36)?

_____

_____

What is Barnabas' burden (15:37)?

_____

_____

What does that suggest about the core of the conflict?

_____

_____

_____

CONFLICT OF BURDENS

In Acts 15, what at first glance appears to be a conflict of personalities is in reality a conflict of burdens. You see, it is not that Paul was right and Barnabas was wrong or vice versa. Both were correct, it would seem, and were being faithful to God's call on their lives. Paul was concerned about the "ministry," while Barnabas was concerned about the "minister."

The idea of a second trip is Paul's burden. Barnabas on the other hand, has a burden for John Mark. What at first glance appears to be a conflict of personalities is in reality a conflict of burdens. You see, it is not that one is right and the other is wrong. Both are correct, it would seem, and are being faithful to God's call on their lives. Paul is concerned about the "ministry" while Barnabas is concerned about the "minister." It would seem that being an encourager to other ministers might have been Barnabas' primary contribution on the first journey as well. His ministry was probably more to Paul than to the mission field. Again, this is indirect ministry, for Paul would not have been who he was without the discipling and *encouraging* work of Barnabas. When the two of them separated they divided between them the itinerary of the first missionary journey. Barnabas took John Mark and followed the first leg of their journey to Cyprus, while Paul took Silas and followed the latter part of their trip.

Although the partnership between Paul and Barnabas ended here, the friendship didn't. We see in the epistles that Paul speaks fondly of Barnabas. Perhaps this was God's way of kicking Paul out of Barnabas' nest, and enabling Barnabas to concentrate on John Mark. Although Mark had shown signs of immaturity, Barnabas obviously saw beyond Mark's weaknesses to his potential. Remember that John Mark was the author of one of the Gospels. As with Paul, one could logically argue that, humanly speaking, John Mark would not have had his significant ministry were it not for the discipling and *encouraging* work of Barnabas, the minister to ministers. Never underestimate the significance of this ministry of *encouragement*, for it is a catalyst to the saints.

Barnabas and Peter

Our last look at Barnabas shows some very human failure, and yet it still has much to say about the man, Barnabas. Paul, in his letter to the Galatian church, relates an incident involving Barnabas and Peter.

📖 Read Galatians 2:11–13 and answer the questions that follow.

What is the mistake being made (2:12)?

_____

_____

At whom is Paul most surprised (2:13)?

_____

_____

"... even Barnabas was carried away by their hypocrisy."

Galatians 2:13

This is a very different vantage point from which to view Barnabas, but in some respects, it is almost the exception that **proves** the rule. In this passage Paul explains this negative situation at Antioch involving Peter, Barnabas, and others. These men had been drifting back into Jewish legalism as they began treating the Gentiles as second-class saints. Look at what Paul says, though, in Galatians 2:13: "... _with the result that_ **even Barnabas** _was carried away by their hypocrisy._" Paul was more surprised at Barnabas than he was at Peter. Apparently, Paul had greater respect for Barnabas than he did for Peter. This respect is a reflection of their relationship and the _encouragement_ Barnabas had been to Paul. Because of who Barnabas was, Paul was surprised when he stumbled. The phrase in verse 13, "_even Barnabas,_" was an indirect compliment of sorts, for Barnabas' life and character were such that Paul expected that he would always do the right thing.

Barnabas DAY FIVE

FOR ME TO FOLLOW GOD

As we have focused in this lesson on the man the disciples nicknamed the "Son of Encouragement," we have begun to learn what a ministry of encouragement is all about, and how significant such a ministry can be. We should never think that because its operation is indirect, it is any less important to the work of God. A saint who has been encouraged will be able to fulfill his own ministry. A discouraged believer cannot consistently minister as God desires. In order for Barnabas to be an encourager, his life had to be washed in humility. As we look back over what Scripture reveals of this man, think of how beautifully God blended together humility and encouragement in Barnabas.

A humble heart encourages ...

1) by forgetting whose position is higher (Acts 4:32–35)
2) by believing in people when no one else does (Acts 9:26–31)
3) by sharing the work and the credit (Acts 11:19–26)
4) by letting others bloom (Acts 13–14)
5) by being faithful to God's call (Acts 15:36–41)
6) by surprising others when he stumbles (Galatians 2:11–13)

Truly Barnabas had earned his nickname. Encouragement is a form of ministry that all of us are called to as well.

📖 Look at Hebrews 3:13. What is our motivation to encourage each other?

_____

_____

_____

_____

"... encourage one another day after day, as long as it is still called 'Today,' lest any one of you be hardened by the deceitfulness of sin."

Hebrews 3:13

We are called to "*. . . encourage one another day after day, as long as it is still called 'Today,' lest any one of you be hardened by the deceitfulness of sin.*" Not only is this a ministry that each of us is required to fulfill, it is also a ministry each of us needs. Without encouragement, each of us is in danger of suffering from "hardening of the attitudes."

📖 Look at Hebrews 10:24–25 and answer the questions that follow.

How long do we need to continue this ministry of encouragement?

_____

_____

_____

How far do we go with it?

_____

_____

As Hebrews 10:24–25 instructs, we need to think of ways we can encourage and stimulate each other toward love and good deeds. To do this we must be together with other Christians. We must not forsake "*our own assembling together, as is the habit of some,*" but encourage one another. The ministry of encouragement is no less needed today than it was in the first century. In fact, this ministry is needed more and more the closer we get to our Lord's return.

APPLY Can you think of a situation where worrying about whose position was higher got in the way of your encouraging a brother?

_____

_____

_____

_____

Is there someone you know who needs words of encouragement right now?

_____

_____

_____

_____

It is often our own self-protection that keeps us from being willing to risk and to trust people. It may be our pride as well. We worry that someone will let us down and that we will be chided for having believed in them (or perhaps we will chide ourselves). We don't want to appear to be gullible or to make it obvious to everyone that someone has taken advantage of us. Yet these selfish attitudes may get in the way of us ever experiencing the joy of being surprised by those who truly have been touched by God. Wouldn't it be better to err on the side of believing in a person even when no one else believes in that person?

> "*. . . and let us consider how to stimulate one another to love and good deeds, not forsaking our own assembling together, as is the habit of some, but encouraging one another; and all the more, as you see the day drawing near.*"
> Hebrews 10:24–25

Think of the opportunities to serve that the Lord has given you. Are there any places where you could encourage someone by letting them join you in the work?

_____

_____

_____

It should never matter to us who gets the credit for the work of God as long as He gets the glory. If this truly is our heart, it should free us up to involve others who would benefit from being involved. We need to allow others to bloom into what God wants them to be, even if it means taking ourselves out of the limelight.

Sometimes we misinterpret encouragement to mean that there will be no conflicts or disagreements. Even Paul and Barnabas, godly though they were, experienced conflict. Sometimes the most encouraging thing we can do is to be faithful to our call even if it means parting company with those we love. It is our surrender to God and His will that encourages others, not our surrender to them and their will.

One of the ways we can encourage others is to live our lives in such a way that those in our inner circle show surprise when we stumble. Along with that principle is the realization that it is not our stumbling itself that causes people to lose confidence in us, but how we deal with our stumbling. Do we try to prove ourselves right because the other person was **more** wrong? Do we worry more about our reputation than our relationships, or do we humble ourselves and do all we can to make things right? Spiritual health is seen not in the absence of problems, but in the willingness to deal with problems the right way.

 If the Lord has directed an admonishing finger on anything in your life that needs to be corrected, make note below of what applications are needful for you.

Confession:

_____

_____

_____

Repentance:

_____

_____

_____

Restitution:

_____

_____

_____

Put Yourself In Their Shoes
A HUMBLE HEART

A humble heart encourages. . . .

• by forgetting whose position is higher.

• by believing in people when no one else does.

• by sharing the work and the credit.

• by letting others bloom.

• by being faithful to God's call.

• by surprising others when you stumble.

Humility:

_____

_____

_____

Surrender:

_____

_____

_____

Why not spend some time in prayer right now?

Lord, I want to be an encourager. I want to be someone through whom You can touch others for Your glory. Help me to see those around me who are discouraged—who need someone to believe in them. Make me sensitive to Your Spirit as You move me from selfish to selfless. Guard me from worrying about who will get the credit or what people will think of me. Use me to make those around me more effective. And Lord, when I do stumble, let my character be such that it is the exception rather than the rule. Finally, Lord, make me quick to make things right. Amen.

Prayer of Application . . .

Take a few moments to write down a prayer of application from the things you have learned this week.

_____

_____

_____

_____

_____

_____

_____

_____

_____

_____

Notes

LEARNING TO DRAW
FROM THE RIGHT SOURCE

*I*n the book of Acts, the apostle Paul is given two different identities. He is introduced to us at the stoning of Stephen as a young man named Saul. Yet throughout most of the book he is called Paul. The difference is more than just a name change. Saul the persecutor of the church before meeting Christ was the opposite of Paul the missionary. Both thought they were following God, yet how differently that following found its expression. **Saul** was in *"hearty agreement"* with putting Stephen to death (Acts 8:1). He invested his energies in *"ravaging"* the church, putting both men and women into prison (Acts 8:3). **Paul,** however, defended the church and ended his life in prison (2 Timothy 4:6). **Saul** had a zeal for God, but it was not in accordance with knowledge (Romans 10:2). He wanted to do the right thing, yet he allowed culture and tradition to define righteousness instead of the Word of God. On the other hand, **Paul** ignored tradition and followed the risen Christ. His life was no longer directed by ambition or zeal, but by surrender. What has that to do with us? Everything! You see, Saul, before the Damascus road, was not an unbeliever in the strictest sense of the term. He believed everything he knew about God, but he had not yet learned the difference between doing things **for** God and allowing God to do mighty things **through** him. He had to learn how to draw from the right source.

PAUL'S MINISTRY

Through his missionary journeys, Paul preached the gospel from Jerusalem all the way through Asia Minor, Greece, and to Italy. We know from Romans 15:24 that he had plans to go to Spain, though there is no record of whether or not he ever made it there. Paul started many of the early churches. Yet his greatest ministry (one that continues today) was through his writings. He wrote nearly half of the New Testament (13 books), and many believe him to be the author of Hebrews as well.

THE LIFE OF PAUL

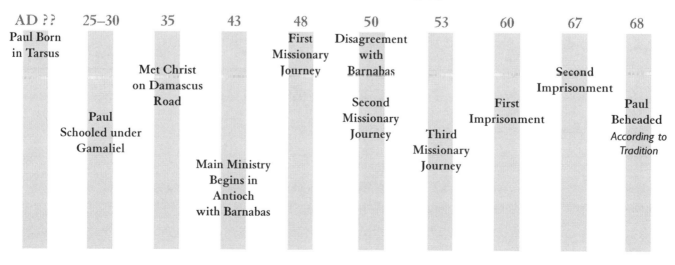

AD ??	25–30	35	43	48	50	53	60	67	68
Paul Born in Tarsus		Met Christ on Damascus Road		First Missionary Journey	Disagreement with Barnabas			Second Imprisonment	
	Paul Schooled under Gamaliel		Main Ministry Begins in Antioch with Barnabas		Second Missionary Journey	Third Missionary Journey	First Imprisonment		Paul Beheaded *According to Tradition*

FINDING HIS IDENTITY IN CHRIST

For the apostle Paul, becoming a Christian meant a complete change of identity. He ceased to be a self-made man. And he began the adventure of learning to find his identity in Christ, learning to draw from the right source. No doubt Paul grew up studying the Old Testament Scriptures. He studied under Gamaliel, one of the most conservative rabbis of his day. He became a Pharisee, and the indication was that he was outstanding among that group. When the church became a target of persecution, he surpassed his contemporaries at purging Israel of this new sect. In fact, it was that pursuit that placed him on the Damascus road. But when he met the risen Christ, his whole identity changed. No longer did he find his significance in what he did for God. This type of significance actually became something he viewed as worthless. Instead, his identity was found in what God had done for him. This week we will study what changed Paul from simply being religious to walking with God. Today, let's look a little while at what changed him.

📖 Read Acts 7:58–8:3.

What was Saul's (Paul's) role in the stoning of Stephen (7:58)?

_____

_____

What did Saul think about Stephen (8:1a)?

_____

_____

What happened after Stephen was put to death (8:1b)?

_____

_____

What was Saul's role in the persecution of that day (8:3)?

_____

_____

Word Study
SAUL'S HATRED OF THE CHURCH

Luke describes Saul's (Paul's) persecution as *"ravaging"* the church. This is a gruesome Greek word *(lumainomai)* used only here in the New Testament. In common Greek it referred to causing physical injury, particularly of mangling by wild beasts. The verb is in the imperfect tense, which pictures continual action. The fact that Acts mentions several times that Saul's persecution was aimed at both men and women is significant, indicating he went to extremes in his pursuit of believers, as normally women would be left alone. We know from Paul's own testimony that he did *"many hostile things"* to Christians (Acts 26:9) and even had some put to death (Acts 22:4; 26:10).

The stoning of Stephen was a pivotal point in the early church. It marked the beginning of a persecution that would scatter believers from Jerusalem into the rest of the world. We see in Acts 7:58 that Saul was present at the stoning of Stephen and that he even held the coats of those who put Stephen to death. Not only was Saul in *"hearty agreement"* with putting Stephen to death, but he also became the prime instrument in the persecution of the church. He entered house after house, arresting Christians. We learn from other verses that Saul actually tortured some to death.

📖 Look at Acts 9:1–9.

Who initiated the persecution of believers in Damascus and why (vv. 1–2)?

_____

_____

What did Jesus say to Saul (v. 4)?

_____

_____

What is Saul's question, and how does Jesus answer it (v. 5)?

_____

_____

What instruction did Jesus give to Saul (v. 6)?

_____

_____

What did Saul do (vv. 8–9)?

_____

_____

It is obvious from the text that Saul was the main initiator of expanding the persecution to other cities. When Jesus confronted Saul, He asked, "...why are you persecuting Me?" At first this may seem a strange question, but clearly Jesus saw all that Saul was doing as aimed at Him, not simply the Church. Since He is the head of the Church, what hurts the Church hurts Him. Saul's immediate question is "Who are You, Lord?" Jesus identified Himself and instructed Saul to go to Damascus to wait for further instructions. Saul obeyed Jesus, and spent three days there fasting (and we can assume praying).

Three days pass and then God spoke to Ananias, a Christian in Damascus. God sent Ananias to Saul and revealed to Ananias that He had chosen Saul as a witness to Gentiles, to kings, and to the Jews (Acts 9:15). God had also chosen Saul to suffer the same persecution he had been giving to others (Acts 9:16). Saul's conversion was immediate and dramatic. Though years would pass before his main ministry would begin, from the very first Paul (Saul) proclaimed Christ. It was while Paul was in prison, suffering persecution as the Lord promised, that he wrote his letter to the Philippian church. Beginning with Philippians 1, let's see how Paul learned to draw from the right source.

📖 Read Philippians 1:7–20, 30. What do you learn about the circumstances in which Paul found himself when he wrote this letter to Philippi?

_____

_____

_____

_____

Four times Paul mentions that he is in prison (vv. 7, 13, 14, 17). The Greek word here translated prison literally means "bonds," indicating that he was chained. Verses 20–21 show that it was highly possible that Paul would not come out of these circumstances alive. Verse 29 implies that his imprisonment also involved physical suffering.

Did You Know?
SAUL'S CONVERSION

Saul's conversion was an answer to prayer. When God spoke to Ananias about going to Saul, Ananias responded by saying, "Lord, I have heard from many about this man, how much harm he did to Thy saints at Jerusalem; and here he has authority from the chief priests to bind all who call upon Thy name" (Acts 9:13–14). Notice what good information the Damascus believers had. They knew who was coming, why he was coming, and with what authority he came. We can be sure they were praying, and praying hard. Imagine their surprise when Ananias came in and declared that Saul had become a Christian. It might not have been exactly what they were praying for, but God knew their hearts. Often we pray for God to remove someone who is unkind or harsh, when we should be praying for God to change them.

Paul mentions positive results that came out of his negative circumstances. What were they?

_____

_____

_____

Did You Know?

? THE PRAETORIAN GUARD

The Praetorian Guard was a group of Imperial soldiers in Rome, separate from the police or the army, who were charged with guarding the emperor. This elite unit was about 9,000 strong in Rome, so Paul's imprisonment was beneficial in that he was able to penetrate this group of men that would have been difficult to reach in any other way.

We learn several things about this imprisonment. First, we learn that his negative circumstances brought the positive result of further advancement of the gospel (v. 12). Secondly, we are told that those circumstances opened the whole Praetorian Guard to the gospel (v. 13). Third, we discover that the brethren trusted the Lord because of Paul's imprisonment and that the brethren had more courage to speak the word without fear. Finally, we learn that through Paul's imprisonment Christ was exalted (v. 20).

📖 Look at verse 27. What does Paul indicate will give evidence that we are conducting ourselves in a manner worthy of the gospel of Christ?

_____

_____

_____

In verse 27, Paul mentions two specific things that identify one who would conduct themselves in a manner worthy of the gospel of Christ: **1)** standing firm in one Spirit (this focuses on our unity with Christ), and **2)** with one mind striving together (this focuses on our unity with one another which flows out of unity with Christ).

Also in verse 21 Paul says, *"For to me, to live is Christ, and to die is gain."* There are two Greek words for "life." One is *"bios,"* from which our English word "biology" is derived, and the other is *"zoe,"* from which we get our term "zoology." Just as biology is the study of all life forms and zoology is limited to the higher life forms, *"zoe"* is a higher life than *"bios."* You might distinguish the two by defining *bios* as "mere existence," or "just getting by" and *zoe* as "the essence of life" or "a higher life." The word Paul used in verse 21 for life is *zoe.* He is saying that the essence of his life is Christ. Jesus Christ is where Paul found his identity and his purpose in life. Because the essence of Paul's life was Christ, prisons didn't bother him anymore, for prisons could not separate him from Christ. Prisons could not even hinder Paul's ministry, for though he was often bound in chains, the gospel was unfettered and unhindered (see vv. 12–13). In fact, his prison became his pulpit or his place of ministry once it was surrendered to the Lord.

APPLY Philippians 1:6 tells us that it is God's job, not yours, to complete His work in you. Chapter one makes it clear that imprisonment may be part of His agenda for you. Are there any "prisons" in your life right now? If so, what does your attitude need to be about them?

_____

_____

_____

_____

Christ is our life and the source we are to draw our strength and joy from, and yet it is often that in difficult circumstances we discover that we have been drawing our joy from the wrong well. What do your responses to your present circumstances reveal about the degree to which you are finding your life in Christ?

_____

_____

_____

_____

IF CHRIST IS THE ESSENCE OF MY LIFE, HIS ATTITUDE BECOMES MY ATTITUDE

Paul DAY TWO

Paul said, *"For to me, to live is Christ, and to die is gain"* (Philippians 1:21). These were not idle words. Death was a real possibility for Paul as he wrote these words from prison. But through having Christ as the essence of his life, Paul had learned something important about prisons—God makes our prisons into our pulpits. If God has placed us in a prison, then that is where He wants to use us. Paul had already seen that at work. He was so focused on God that instead of moaning about his lost freedom, or complaining of his dire circumstances, he rejoiced that his going to prison had turned out, *". . . for the greater progress of the gospel."* His focus was not on his suffering, but on how many people his sufferings had brought into his life for the sole purpose of ministry. Because the essence of his life was Christ, Paul could have the same attitude of humility that Christ had. We can also have that same attitude today, for if to us *". . . to live is Christ,"* then we are drawing from the right source, and we will begin finding our identity, our security, our significance, our sufficiency, and our joy in Him. And when Christ is the essence of our lives, His attitude becomes our attitude. Today we will focus on the second chapter of Philippians, looking at the attitude of Christ.

📖 Look at verse Philippians 2:5 What is the command Paul gives to us there?

_____

_____

_____

_____

Word Study
THE ATTITUDE OF CHRIST

In Philippians 2:6, Paul states that although Christ existed in the form of God, He did not regard equality with God a thing to be *"grasped."* The Greek word translated *"grasped"* here does not mean that Christ was not God, nor does it mean that He was not equal to the Father. The word actually means "to seize, to cling to." In other words, even though Christ was God, He didn't demand His rights as God or exploit His divinity to His own advantage. He didn't cling to His divinity, but chose to humble Himself as a servant.

Paul encourages us to have the same attitude that Christ had. The Greek verb used in verse 5 is known as a "present imperative." The present tense means continual action—we are always to have this attitude of Christ. The "imperative" mood means that this is a command, not a suggestion. Since we are commanded to have this attitude of Christ, then it is something we are enabled to do by grace or else God would not expect it of us.

📖 Read through verses 1–8, and identify everything you see there about this "attitude of Christ."

Verse 1—

_____

_____

_____

Verse 2—

_____

_____

_____

Verse 3—

_____

_____

_____

Verse 4—

_____

_____

_____

Verse 7—

_____

_____

_____

Verse 8—

_____

_____

_____

> *"Have this attitude in yourselves which was also in Christ Jesus, who ... emptied Himself, taking the form of a bond-servant...."*
>
> *Philippians 2:5,7*

When Christ is the essence of our lives, His attitude becomes our attitude. Practically speaking, this means that we will do the following things:

1) show encouragement, consolation, fellowship, affection and compassion (v. 1),
2) walk in unity and love (v. 2),
3) do nothing from selfishness or empty conceit (v. 3a),
4) have humility of mind (v. 3b),
5) regard others to be more important than myself (v. 3c),
6) not merely look out for my own interests (v. 4),
7) empty myself (v. 7a),
8) become a servant (v. 7b), and
9) express humility through obedience at all costs (v. 8).

How different this is than what Christians often live out!

Agree/Disagree

_____ **1)** If Christ is the essence of my life, I won't have any problems.

_____ **2)** The difficulties in my life are always opportunities to minister.

_____ **3)** I can imitate the attitude of Christ if I try hard enough.

_____ **4)** If the essence of my life is Christ, then His attitude will become my attitude.

We can see clearly that when we find meaning and purpose in our relationship with Christ, it changes our attitudes about everything. Our sufferings begin to be viewed as opportunities. Our attitudes toward people move from selfish to selfless. Why? If Christ is in control of our lives, then He begins to express Himself through us. The result is a life very different than when we were apart from Him. We see this astonishing difference in the apostle Paul. He was devoutly religious, but it wasn't until he began walking in a relationship with Christ, allowing Him to control his life that he became the person God wanted him to be. Having a right relationship with Christ is what it means to draw from the right source.

IF CHRIST IS THE ESSENCE OF MY LIFE, HE BECOMES MY GOAL

Paul   DAY THREE

W hen Paul was a Pharisee, he put his confidence in what he could do for God. And he probably felt that he did a lot for God, for He was so zealous for religion that he considered killing Christians to be a righteous act of valor. But it is obvious that God was not in him because there was none of the softness of God's love in him. When he met Christ, all that had to change. One of the ways we can see that he was drawing his significance from Christ instead of his own accomplishments was that none of his accomplishments mattered to him anymore. All that mattered was for him to know Christ. Today, as we move into chapter three of Philippians, we will learn from Paul what it means for Christ to be our goal.

📖 Look at Philippians 3:1–3.

What two groups of people does Paul contrast?

_____

_____

What is each like?

_____

_____

Word Study
TRUE CIRCUMCISION

Paul uses a play on words here, when he refers to the "true circumcision" and the "false circumcision." The term "false circumcision" is the Greek word *katatome* (to mutilate), and the term "true circumcision" is *peritome*. The idea is that some have perverted the meaning of circumcision to the point that it is only mutilation.

Paul contrasts the "false circumcision" crowd (make-believers—those who are religious but don't really have a relationship with God) with the "true circumcision" crowd (true believers). He tells us that true believers are characterized by three things: **1)** they worship in the Spirit (inwardly not merely outwardly),

2) they glory in Christ Jesus (not self), and **3)** they put no confidence in the flesh (human efforts). By contrast we can conclude that the believers of false circumcision have the opposite characteristics—they worship only outwardly, they glory in themselves, and they trust only in themselves.

📖 Paul states that the true circumcision belief puts *"no confidence in the flesh"* or in the efforts of self. As you read through verses 4–6, make a list of all the things in which Paul had the potential of placing his confidence.

_____

_____

_____

_____

_____

_____

Paul was circumcised the eighth day (exact observance of the Law), of the nation of Israel and the tribe of Benjamin (the right family lines), a Hebrew of Hebrews (outstanding when compared to others), a Pharisee (extreme devotion to the Law), a persecutor of the church (very zealous), and blameless according to the Law.

What was Paul's attitude toward his former accomplishments?

_____

_____

Why?

_____

_____

_____

Paul counted all those accomplishments as loss (not gain) or as rubbish (literally, "manure") when compared with the value of knowing Christ, of gaining Him, and being found in Him with the right kind of righteousness (that which comes from faith in Him, rather than from self).

📖 Read Philippians 3:12–14.

What does Paul identify as his goals?

_____

_____

How much progress did he have in reaching them?

_____

_____

_____

In this sequence of verses, Paul essentially says that he wants to lay hold of that for which he *"also . . . was laid hold of by Christ Jesus,"* namely, the upward call of God in Christ Jesus. In other words, Paul found his identity, his security, his significance, his sufficiency, and his joy in Christ. The great encouragement to us is that Paul makes it abundantly clear that this attitude was not something he had already attained, but rather something he continued to pursue. Philippians 1:6 reveals that God will not be finished working on us until the day we meet Christ.

If Christ Is the Essence of My Life, He Is My Strength and Supply

Paul DAY FOUR

What a glorious truth it is that I can do all things through Christ who gives me strength (see Philippians 4:13). Coupled with this, Paul also adds the promise that God will supply all our needs according to His riches in Christ Jesus (Philippians 4:19). What a fruitful well to draw from! And yet sometimes we are as guilty as Israel was in Jeremiah 2:13—*"For My people have committed two evils: They have forsaken Me, The fountain of living waters, To hew for themselves cisterns, Broken cisterns, That can hold no water."* The message from Paul's life is that we must learn to draw from the right source. We need Christ, not self, to be our life. We need to draw on His strength and His supply, not on our own. Paul had learned how to draw from the right source. He had come from boasting in his abilities to boasting in his weaknesses (2 Corinthians 12:9) and Christ's power. He had come from boasting in what he did for God, to only boasting in *"what Christ has accomplished through me"* (Romans 15:17–18). And He had learned to draw from the right source. Take a moment to read through chapter four of Philippians as we look at Christ being our strength and supply.

📖 Look at verses 10–13, and write down everything Paul indicates that he has *"learned."*

_____

_____

_____

_____

_____

_____

Paul says that he has learned, first of all, to be content in whatever circumstance he finds himself (v. 11). No wonder his prison was able to become his pulpit. Second, in verse 12 he indicates that he has learned how to deal with *"humble means"* or tight, difficult times. Also in verse 12 he states that he has learned how to *"live in prosperity."* Living in prosperous times is probably more difficult than living humbly, for when we are in tight spots, we sometimes have no choice but to trust God. However, in times of abundance, trusting God is a choice made more difficult because we have other options available. Finally, he indicates that he has learned a *"secret"* which enables him to handle being filled or going hungry, having abundance or suffering need: *"I can do all things through Him who strengthens me"* (v. 13).

> **"Therefore in Christ Jesus I have found reason for boasting in things pertaining to God. For I will not presume to speak of anything except what Christ has accomplished through me, resulting in the obedience of the Gentiles by word and deed."**
> **Romans 15:17-18**

How do you think Paul "learned" the things mentioned in these verses?

_____

_____

_____

The things that Paul mentions in this passage seem to have been a part of his maturing process as he grew in his relationship with Christ. One worthwhile observation we can make as we look at Paul's life and ministry is that it is obvious the Lord had guided him through all the circumstances mentioned. He had found himself with *"humble means,"* and he had known prosperity. He had gone through times of *"going hungry"* and times of *"being filled"*— times of *"having abundance"* as well as times of *"suffering need."* It is important to realize that Paul probably made some of the same mistakes that we make, and he grew through them—he even *"learned"* from them.

📖 What is the promise of verse 19, and how does God indicate He will fulfill it?

_____

_____

_____

_____

Put Yourself In Their Shoes

IS CHRIST THE ESSENCE OF YOUR LIFE?

When Christ is the essence of your life …

• your prison becomes your pulpit

• Christ's attitude becomes your attitude

• Christ becomes your goal

• Christ becomes your sufficiency

The promise here is that God will supply all our needs. The indication of the text is that He does this *"according to His riches . . . in Christ Jesus."* Ephesians 1:3 teaches us that God *"has blessed us with every spiritual blessing in the heavenly places in Christ."* In other words, we have everything we need in Him.

Do you see any prerequisites in the text to Paul offering this promise to the Philippians?

_____

_____

It should be noted that the Philippians were not selfish or self-focused. They were giving to meet the needs of Paul. It could be argued that this is not a universal promise, but only applies to those who are manifesting a trust in God, which is expressed in their willingness to give.

Paul **DAY FIVE**

FOR ME TO FOLLOW GOD

"*For to me, to live is Christ,*" wrote Paul. He had come to the place in his life and walk where the essence of his life was Christ, not Paul. One can almost hear the words of John the Baptist ringing in the background: *"He must increase, but I must decrease"* (John 3:30). That had happened in Paul's life. He had learned to find his identity, his security, his significance, his sufficiency, and his joy all in Christ. Because Christ was the essence of Paul's life, prisons didn't bother him anymore. In fact, he had learned to let his prison become his pulpit. Because Christ was the essence of Paul's life, people didn't bother him anymore. He had learned to have the attitude of Christ—humility. Because Christ was the essence of Paul's life, ambition didn't trip him up anymore. Christ had become his goal. Finally, because Christ was the essence of Paul's life, need didn't cause him to stumble. He had learned a *"secret"*—*"I can do all things through Him who strengthens me"* (Philippians 4:13). Paul had learned to draw from the right source. We, too, need to draw from the right source. If to us *". . . to live is Christ,"* then we are drawing from the right source.

APPLY Is there a "prison" that God has allowed in your life—something unpleasant that you cannot change?

_____

_____

_____

_____

Prisons come in all shapes and sizes. They may be physical limitations or handicaps, or they may come in the form of lingering trials. Prisons may come in the form of relationships or the lack thereof. Your "prison" might be a job that you hate or a marriage that is unfulfilling, or it may be an actual prison! Whatever it is, from Paul we learn that a "prison" is something God can use. He can turn that prison into a pulpit—a place of ministry.

What are some ministries that God could be raising up through your "prison"?

_____

_____

_____

📖 Look at what Paul wrote in 2 Corinthians 1:3–4.

What does God want to do for us in all our afflictions?

_____

_____

_____

What does God want us to do with the comfort He gives us?

_____

_____

_____

> "Blessed be ... the Father of mercies and God of all comfort, who comforts us in all our affliction so that we may be able to comfort those who are in any affliction with the comfort with which we ourselves are comforted by God."
> 2 Corinthians 1:3–4

What a beautiful pair of titles for God! He is the *"Father of mercies"* and the *"God of all comfort."* The less comforting news of these verses is that the verses assume we will have afflictions, but the good news is that we have a source of comfort in these afflictions. God wants us to draw on Him. He wants us to experience His comfort. But after we have done so, He doesn't want the process to end there. God wants every affliction for which we receive comfort to become a platform from which we can minister. We can comfort others from the comfort we receive. When we draw on God's comfort in our affliction, then our prisons become our pulpits.

If we have begun drawing from the right source, then our identity is being found in Christ and He becomes our attitude. Look at the list below, and mark on a scale of 1–5 how you would rate your own attitude (1=never, 2=seldom, 3=sometimes, 4=often, 5=always).

___ do nothing from selfishness or empty conceit (2:3a)
___ have humility of mind (2:3b)
___ regard others to be more important than myself (2:3c)
___ do not merely look out for my own interests (2:4)
___ empty myself (2:7a)
___ become a servant (2:7b)
___ express humility through obedience at all costs (2:8)

Having the essence of Christ was Paul's goal. Personal ambition didn't rule him anymore, and he no longer put any confidence in his flesh (what he could do for God).

 What are some ways you are tempted to put confidence in your flesh?

_____
_____
_____
_____
_____

Have you counted those things as loss yet?

_____
_____
_____
_____

Paul had been a Christian 25–30 years when he wrote the book of Philippians. Yet he still didn't consider himself as having "arrived." He knew he had not become perfect. He still saw room for growth as he pressed on toward the goal of having a closer walk with Jesus.

Do your goals lean more towards knowing Christ, or serving God by doing great works for Him? Look at the scale below, and mark where you feel your Christian walk leans.

Knowing Christ ⟵————————————⟶ Serving God

Paul recognized that his ministry grew out of his relationship with Christ. Living for Christ meant nothing to him before he embarked on the Damascus road. He was so caught up in doing things **for** God, that he didn't know God when He walked in his midst.

When Christ became the essence of Paul's life, Christ became his sufficiency. When he had a need, he could be grateful when others met it. But Paul didn't look to others—he looked to Christ as his source, his sufficiency.

Paul had been a Christian 25–30 years when he wrote the book of Philippians. Yet he still didn't consider himself as having "arrived." He still saw room for growth as he pressed on toward the goal of having a closer walk with Jesus.

APPLY To whom do you tend to look to meet your needs?

_____

_____

What should you change?

_____

_____

Put Yourself In Their Shoes

"PARDON OUR PROGRESS"

We are a work in progress . . .

• We are not yet what we ought to be.

• But we are not what we used to be.

• And we are not what we are going to be.

Paul clearly explains in Philippians that the Christian life is not perfection but a pursuit. In 1:6 he promises that, _"He who began a good work in you will perfect it until the day of Christ Jesus."_ God is still perfecting in us the work He began when we met Him. Paul gives his own testimony of this truth: _"Not that I have already obtained it, or have already become perfect, but I press on in order that I may lay hold of that for which I also was laid hold of by Christ Jesus"_ (3:12). When we look at our own lives, we should not beat ourselves up for what we are not, but rather, we should press on toward the goal of Christ. I hope that you will surrender your life afresh to Christ!

Why not spend some time right now in prayer?

Lord, I want so much for You to be my life. I want to find my identity in You. I want Your joy and Your sufficiency so that You can change my prisons into pulpits. I want Your attitude of humility to be my attitude. I want You to be my goal, not selfish ambition. Help me to have confidence in You that You will supply all my needs. Lord, I am painfully aware of my imperfections. Thank You for the promise that You are going to complete the work You have started in me. Give me grace to press on toward You as my goal. Amen.

Prayer of Application . . .

Take a few moments to write down a prayer of application from the things that you have learned this week.

_____

_____

_____

_____

_____

_____

_____

_____

_____

_____

_____

_____

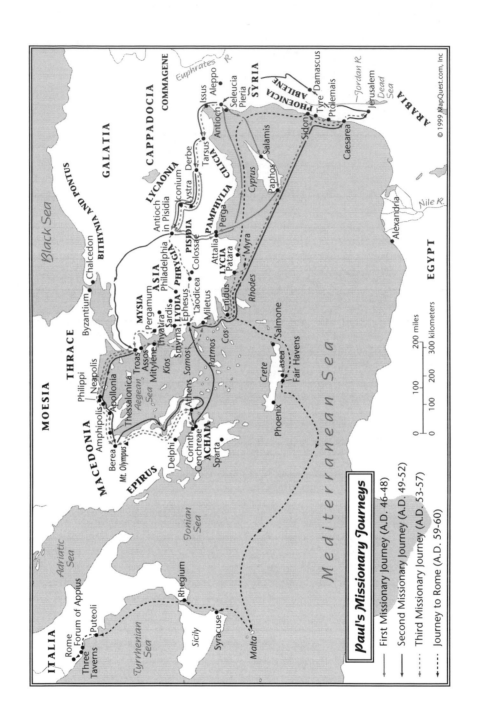

Paul's Missionary Journeys

First Missionary Journey (A.D. 46-48)
Second Missionary Journey (A.D. 49-52)
Third Missionary Journey (A.D. 53-57)
Journey to Rome (A.D. 59-60)

© 1999 MapQuest.com, Inc

Notes

Notes

WALKING IN THE WILL OF GOD

he Apostle Paul is probably one of the best known Christians of the first century. He was a man whose heart was captivated by his Lord and Savior, Jesus Christ. In fact, for Paul, Christ was his very life. *"For to me to live is Christ,"* he wrote to believers in Philippi (Philippians 1:21). To those in Rome he spoke of himself as a *"bondservant of Christ Jesus,"* whom he served with a willing spirit and to whom he was forever grateful for the grace shown him (Romans 1:1, 9; 2 Corinthians 9:15). Paul was marked as a man surrendered to the Lord and to His will (Ephesians 1:1). The phrase he often used to describe himself, *"Paul, an apostle of Christ Jesus by the will of God,"* became his signature throughout his years of ministry. This signature phrase reveals both the heart of Paul and the purpose of God. Paul wanted to walk and minister in the will of God, and God chose to use him in His will as the apostle to the Gentiles and a messenger to his fellow countrymen, the Jews. He desired to walk in the will of God all day, every day, knowing that God had a purpose for him.

How can we walk with God and see His will worked out in our lives? As we look at the life and journeys of Paul, we will discover many truths about how

PAUL'S MINISTRY

Paul was born around AD 2 and met Christ around AD 35. He ministered throughout much of the Roman Empire until his martyrdom in AD 68. He wrote thirteen letters of the New Testament through which he continues to minister to millions of believers in Jesus Christ.

THE EPISTLES OF PAUL THE APOSTLE

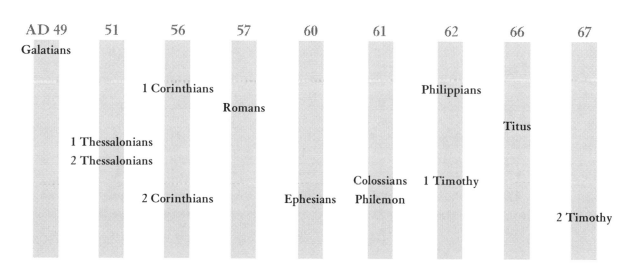

AD 49	51	56	57	60	61	62	66	67
Galatians		1 Corinthians	Romans		Philippians		Titus	
	1 Thessalonians							
	2 Thessalonians				Colossians	1 Timothy		
		2 Corinthians		Ephesians	Philemon			2 Timothy

Paul walked with God, and we will find some valuable lessons for knowing His will in our lives. We will also uncover some rich treasures about the ways of God in our lives and discover much about His will for us today.

SURRENDER TO GOD'S WILL

After his conversion on the road to Damascus, we see Paul with a heart submitted to doing the will of God. As he began his walk with the Lord Jesus Christ, he also began to discover that often with God's will comes opposition from others as well as many changes in plans. We find the first mention of the phrase *"if God wills"* while Paul was in Ephesus in the autumn of AD 52. This was at the close of his second missionary journey. (For an overview of the life of the apostle Paul, see the chart **An Outline of the Life and Ministry of the Apostle Paul** at the end of this lesson.) After a ministry of almost two years in Corinth, he came to Ephesus (Acts 18:19) and stayed a short while. The Jews asked him to stay, and he told them, *"I will return to you again if God wills."* He left and sailed back to Caesarea and then traveled on to Antioch. What can we learn from Paul about the will of God? What did he understand about God's will? What does Luke show us in his account of Paul's life in Acts?

From the Scriptures it is evident that it was God's will for Paul to return to Ephesus on his third missionary journey. He arrived there in AD 53 and stayed three years (Acts 20:31).

📖 Read Acts 19:8–10. What was Paul's main focus (19:8)?

_____

_____

_____

What kind of opposition did Paul face, and what did he do about it (19:9–10)?

_____

_____

_____

_____

✏️ *Did You Know?*

❓ EPHESUS

Ephesus, with a population of 250,000, was the fourth largest city in the world in the first century. It was located on the coast of southwest Asia Minor (modern Turkey), where the Cayster River empties into the Aegean Sea, with the Maeander River Valley to the south of the city and the Hermus River Valley to the north. Ephesus prospered as a major crossroads for shipping and trade. The theater stadium could seat 24,000 and the Temple of Artemis (Diana) was one of the Seven Wonders of the Ancient World. The cities of Smyrna, Sardis, Colossae, Hierapolis, and Laodicea were all within one hundred miles of Ephesus.

✏️ *Did You Know?*

❓ THE SCHOOL OF TYRANNUS

The School of Tyrannus was a lecture hall either owned by Tyrannus or used by Tyrannus to teach his students. Some ancient manuscripts note that Paul used this hall each day from 11:00 AM to 4:00 PM, a time when it normally would have been vacant.

Paul had an open door of ministry in the synagogue for three months and used the opportunity to reason and persuade many about the kingdom of God. While there, he faced opposition from some whose hearts became hardened as they heard the message, but Paul continued speaking to the spiritually hungry, the learners (*"disciples"*). After leaving the synagogue, Paul taught at the school of Tyrannus for two years *"so that all who lived in Asia heard the word of the Lord, both Jews and Greeks"* (19:10).

Ephesus was a major crossroads and port city for travel and trade. Many people would have traveled through there in a two-year span of time, and God placed Paul at this strategic place to get His message out. Paul's stay in Ephesus was all part of God's plan.

📖 Read Acts 19:11–20. What was God doing through Paul (19:11–12)?

_____

_____

_____

What happened as a result of the activity of the seven sons of Sceva (19:13–17, note especially verse 17)?

_____

_____

_____

What other results occurred (19:18–19)?

_____

_____

What result was foremost (19:20)?

_____

_____

"God was performing extraordinary miracles by the hands of Paul" (19:11). God was at work. As a result the name of the Lord Jesus was magnified. People confessed their sins and repented of their evil deeds. Their actions corresponded with their words. Verse 20 points out that the emphasis was not on miracles. It was on the word of the Lord growing and prevailing. The message of God's heart was getting out, according to His will.

 What is God doing in your life right now? Are you walking in His will? Is His message getting out through your life, your words, your deeds, and the people with whom you come in contact on a day-to-day basis? Ask the Lord to speak to you concerning these questions.

What do we find occurring after these days in which the Lord worked in such an awesome way? Acts 19:21 reports that *"after these things were finished, Paul purposed in the spirit"* to go to four areas—first, to Macedonia (northern Greece), then Achaia (southern Greece), then Jerusalem, and finally Rome. Was this Paul's will or God's will or both? [NOTE: Some translations say, *"purposed in the Spirit,"* referring to the Holy Spirit and His guidance.]

Here it is wise to compare Scripture with Scripture and get the full picture of what transpired during this time. We know that Paul *"purposed"* this itinerary toward the end of his time in Ephesus around the spring of AD 56. Acts 19:23 reports that *"about that time there arose no small disturbance concerning the Way."* The businesses of the silversmiths who made and sold the idols of Artemis (*Latin:* Diana) were in financial trouble because so many of the citizens of Ephesus were turning to the Lord. Demetrius, a silversmith, incited the craftsmen, workmen, and several others to protest the work of Paul (19:24–29). Paul was in danger for his life, and the disciples wisely kept him from going into the theater (i.e., stadium; 19:30–31).

Acts 20:1 records that Paul then left for Macedonia (around June of 56), the first stop on his four-stop itinerary. While in Macedonia he wrote *2 Corinthians*

Did You Know?

ARTEMIS OF THE EPHESIANS

Artemis of the Ephesians (also known to the Romans as Diana [Latin]) was the daughter of the Greek gods, Zeus and Leto. Artemis, the goddess of the moon and of nature (including wild animals, hunting, and fertility) was the chief deity of Ephesus. Her image was housed there in a massive temple measuring 425 feet by 220 feet, reaching a height of 60 feet, with 127 columns surrounding it. This temple, a structure four times the size of the Parthenon in Athens, was one of the Seven Wonders of the Ancient World. Acts 19 details a riot induced by the silversmith, Demetrius, whose business of selling silver statues of the temple and goddess was being hurt by Paul's preaching of the gospel of Christ. This riot may have occurred near or in conjunction with the annual festival devoted to Artemis on May 25.

Romans 1:10 shows us that the will of God includes God's perfect timing *("if perhaps now")*, our patient waiting *("at last")*, and God's loving purpose *("by the will of God")*.

(around the autumn of AD 56) in which he dealt with the offering for the needy saints in Jerusalem (2 Corinthians 8–9) and urged them to give like the saints in Macedonia had given. Paul had written *1 Corinthians* from Ephesus in the spring of 56 and talked about his plans to come to Corinth after his stay ended in Macedonia (1 Corinthians 16:1–9). Around January of 57, Paul left Macedonia and went to his second stop, Achaia. He spent the winter in Corinth (three months—Acts 20:3), and during those three months he wrote the *Epistle to the Romans*. Let's look at Romans for a better understanding of Paul's heart concerning the will of God and how God led Paul on his journeys.

📖 Read Romans 1:8–15. What do you see about Paul's prayers (1:8–10)? For what was Paul praying?

_____

_____

_____

What do you see about God's will and Paul's understanding of God's will (1:10)?

_____

_____

_____

What do you find out about Paul's plans (1:11–15)?

_____

_____

_____

Paul continually prayed for the believers in Rome and often requested that God would send him to Rome. Paul's prayer came from the depths of his surrendered heart—a heart that only wanted the will of God. But Paul's prayer also came from a compelling desire to see those in Rome. He wanted to be used by God to impart truth, to build up the saints, and to see more Jews and Gentiles come to Christ. Because he had such a longing to see the people of Rome, Paul had often planned to go there but had been hindered in doing so. Regardless of all his praying and planning, Paul submitted to God's plans, designs, and timing. It was February of 57 when he penned the words of Romans 1:11–15. How long would it be before Paul's requests and plans to go to Rome would be fulfilled?

Read Romans 15:22–33. What were Paul's plans (15:22–29)?

_____

_____

_____

What were Paul's prayers (15:30–33)?

_____

_____

_____

> "I urge you, brethren, by our Lord Jesus Christ and by the love of the Spirit, to strive together with me in your prayers to God for me."
>
> **Romans 15:30**

Paul had finished his work in Corinth and was now ready to go to Rome and then to Spain. He planned to first take the offering from Macedonia and Achaia to the saints at Jerusalem. He asked the Romans specifically to *"strive together with me in your prayers to God for me,"* and then he listed three prayer requests. The first request was for deliverance from those who were disobedient in Jerusalem (15:31a). Secondly, he asked the believers in Rome to pray for the acceptance by the saints of his gifts and his service (15:31b). His third request was for the church in Rome to pray that he might be able to come to Rome *"in joy by the will of God and find rest in* [their] *company"* (15:32). Paul was always concerned for the will of God in his life.

It appears from these passages in Acts and Romans that Paul was not a "self"-initiated man who continually came up his own agenda and plans. He sought to walk by the direction and guidance of the Holy Spirit, wanting only to walk with God wherever He led. I believe that the best translation of Acts 19:21 is *"Paul purposed in the Spirit to go. . . ."* In other words, he *"purposed"* or "set out in order" to get to where he was to minister (4 areas). He did so under the influence, guidance, and direction of the Holy Spirit. Paul was praying and seeking the will of God and was submitted to the Holy Spirit and His direction. Where would that lead him? We will see that in Day Two.

> *Paul was not a "self"-initiated man. He never came up with his own agenda and plans, but sought to walk by the direction and guidance of the Holy Spirit.*

THE ADVENTURES OF GOD'S WILL

Paul **DAY TWO**

After Paul sent his letter to Rome, he prepared to sail for Syria and then travel to Jerusalem. But, that did not happen. Acts 20:3 says, *"And there* [in Greece] *he spent three months, and when a plot was formed against him by the Jews as he was about to set sail for Syria* [East]*, he determined to return through Macedonia* [North]*."* In the midst of his plans (those plans which Paul *"purposed in the Spirit"*), a plot was formed against Paul. It caused him to take a detour. Instead of sailing south and then east to Syria, he went north to Macedonia. (**Stop and look** at the map of Paul's Journeys on p. 116, and note where Paul traveled.) Paul went first to Philippi and from there sailed to Troas where he stayed for seven days.

📖 Read Acts 20:7–12, and record what happened.

_____

_____

_____

The believers gathered together on Sunday, and Paul talked to them so much that he *"prolonged his message until midnight."* In that upstairs room with the many lamps and their warmth, a young man named Eutychus fell asleep while sitting in a windowsill, fell out of that window, and died from the fall. Paul went down, and God worked miraculously through him to raise Eutychus from the dead. After that Paul talked with the believers until daybreak (I doubt anyone fell asleep!), and then he departed. That meeting had lasted all night but the effects of that meeting went beyond that night into eternity. What an impact Paul had on the people of Troas, especially on Eutychus!

> *" . . .that I may finish my course, and the ministry which I received from the Lord Jesus."*
> **Acts 20:24**

📖 Read Acts 20:17–38. What do you discover about Paul's understanding of God's will in Acts 20:19–24?

_____

_____

_____

From Troas Paul sailed to Miletus, a port south of the city of Ephesus. When he arrived there he called for the elders of the church to meet with him in Ephesus, where he had lived earlier for three years (Acts 20:31). There he had a wonderful meeting with the elders, a time of pouring out his heart and sharing how God was leading him in His will as he proclaimed the message of Christ. Paul saw his life as a race, a course set by God, in which he sought to faithfully follow His Lord, Jesus Christ. *"The gospel of the grace of God"* (Acts 20:24) was at the heart of the will of God for Paul. This was also a time of instructing and exhorting the elders in their leadership of the Ephesian church. Paul was praying for the will of God in his life, and he asked others to pray. It is evident that the meeting with the elders from Ephesus was in the will of God. Where does the plot of the Jews in Acts 20:3 fit? Does God use dangers and detours in fulfilling His will? We will see the answers to these questions as we continue to study Paul's adventure of following God.

APPLY Are you facing any detours in your life? Any different directions? None of these things are a surprise to the Lord, and He is not worried. Remember that as you talk to Him about these things.

From Miletus, Paul and his companions sailed to Syria. They stayed at Tyre for seven days, then stayed in Ptolemais for a day, and then traveled to Caesarea and the home of Philip the evangelist. In Tyre and in Caesarea, Paul was cautioned, even urged, not to go to Jerusalem because of the dangers that awaited him.

📖 Read Acts 21:4, 8–14. Note here that the issue is not whether Paul is out of the will of God, but how God has been directing him in His will.

Read Acts 21:12–14 once again. What are the believers learning about the will of the Lord?

_____

_____

_____

What is Paul's understanding about the will of the Lord? (You may want to also re-read Acts 20:22–24.)

_____

_____

_____

In this situation it does not seem that the Holy Spirit was warning Paul not to go to Jerusalem. Rather, He was preparing Paul for what he would face as he carried on the ministries God had given him. It appears that his companions and friends were on the verge of discovering a new level of trust in the Lord and in His ways. This experience certainly could have brought them to more fervent prayer for Paul. Their concern for him grew as they

Paul saw his life as a race, a course set by God, in which he sought to faithfully follow His Lord, Jesus Christ.

"The will of the Lord be done."
Acts 21:14

became aware of the potential dangers involved. Difficulties do not mean that one is out of the will of God, and the conclusions of other believers may not always clearly match the will of God. Paul knew that God had been speaking to him about the difficulties ("*bonds and afflictions*" [Acts 20:23]) that he would face as he valiantly endured the course God had set.

When Paul arrived in Jerusalem, he went to the Temple. There some Jews from Asia Minor (modern Turkey) falsely accused Paul of bringing Greeks into the Temple. A crowd became enraged; several grabbed Paul and began beating him with the intent to kill him. Roman army officials and soldiers came and rescued Paul and promptly arrested him thinking that he was the cause of the uproar (see Acts 21:27–40). At that point Paul asked permission to speak.

Read Acts 21:39–40 and 22:1–22. What advantage came from this uproar? What was Paul able to share as recorded in Acts 22?

_____

_____

_____

_____

_____

The false accusations gave Paul an opportunity to speak of Jesus Christ. Though Paul was falsely accused and arrested, he had the privilege of sharing his testimony with a considerably large crowd, especially when you consider how many curious onlookers might have gathered because of the uproar. According to God's will, these events became an opportunity to speak the message of Christ.

In Acts 23 Paul had an opportunity to speak to the Council (Sanhedrin). His stance on the resurrection divided the Council between the Pharisees and the Sadducees to the point that they began fighting one another with Paul between them. The Roman commander ordered Paul taken away to the barracks, thus assuring Paul's protection from the Jews.

📖 Read Acts 23:11. What does this verse tell you about Paul being in the will of God?

_____

_____

_____

_____

_____

Often the paths along which the Lord takes us are designed to provide a witness to others.

Often the paths along which the Lord takes us are designed to provide a witness to others. The Lord was certainly concerned with getting his message out wherever He took Paul. After the arrest and the Council meeting, the Lord came and stood at Paul's side as a true Friend. He encouraged him in his witness in Jerusalem and reaffirmed his call to go to Rome (which would be stop number four on the original itinerary). Paul was walking in the will of God.

GOD'S WILL—RIGHT RELATIONSHIPS

As we walk through Paul's journey in the will of God we must not miss the main point. God's focus is always on relationships. Walking in the will of God is more than location or destination; it is a righteous walk in primarily two relationships—our relationship with God and our relationship with men. How do we see this righteous walk exemplified in the life of Paul? A look at the continuing journeys of Paul will help us better focus on where God is focused—bringing people to a right walk with Himself and with one another.

📖 Read Acts 23:12–35. Summarize the main events of this part of Paul's journey.

_____

_____

_____

_____

_____

What connections do you see between God's will worked out in Acts 23:12–35 and God's promise from the night before (Acts 23:11)?

_____

_____

_____

_____

Did You Know?
THE ROMAN ARMY

The Roman Army was known for its organization. A legion consisted of six thousand soldiers, divided into ten cohorts or battalions of 600 each. Over every one hundred soldiers was a centurion. A *chiliarch* (translated "commander" in Acts 21:31; 22:24-29) led one thousand soldiers. Included in the garrison commanded by Claudias Lysias, the chiliarch in Jerusalem, were 240 horsemen and 760 soldiers (foot soldiers and spearmen). The spearmen could refer to javelin throwers, slingers, or bowmen.

The Jews formed a plot to ambush and assassinate Paul. God in His sovereign plan provided a way for Paul's nephew to hear about the plot. He informed Paul about the plot and also informed the Roman official, a *"chiliarch,"* or commander of one thousand soldiers. The official provided two hundred soldiers, two hundred spearmen, and seventy horsemen to escort Paul out of the city under cover of night. Note that the protection for Paul far outnumbered those plotting against him by about ten to one (470 to over 40). They also provided Paul with a ride and an official letter to Felix the governor, giving even further protection. It was God's will for Paul to be in Jerusalem to witness on behalf of Jesus Christ, and it was also God's will for him to go to Rome. The Lord had promised that Paul would go to Rome, and here we see part of that promise being fulfilled. This apparent detour and delay provided yet more opportunities to share the message of Christ. Think of the 470 soldiers being called out to a night march to Antipatris. Certainly they would ask why, and certainly Paul would share with all who would listen as they traveled. The message of Christ continued to spread to more and more people. Scores of people were discovering God's will for them—a right relationship with the Lord and with one another.

 Are you facing any detours or delays in your journey? Are there relationship problems that God is bringing to your attention? Are there any opportunities to bring others into a right relationship with God? Talk to the Lord about these things.

📖 Read Acts 24. What benefit was there in Paul going to Caesarea?

_____

_____

_____

What was at the heart of Paul's defense (24:15–16)?

_____

_____

From God's point of view, what was at center stage in this imprisonment (24:24–25)?

_____

_____

_____

In going to Caesarea, Paul was better protected than he would have been in Jerusalem. There he also had the opportunity to appear before Governor Felix for the preliminary hearing. Felix ascertained that Paul was innocent, but delayed his trial. He also granted Paul a measure of flexibility while he remained in custody so that his friends could minister to him (24:22–23). Though this was yet another delay for Paul, it provided an opportunity for him to share his faith in Christ Jesus with both Felix and his wife, Drusilla (24:10–21, 24–25). Paul had lengthy conversations with Felix and with those in attendance, taking full advantage of the tremendous opportunities presented to him to deliver the gospel message. At the heart of Paul's message was the certainty of the resurrection of the **righteous** and the **wicked**—those **with** and those **without** a right relationship to Jesus Christ. As for Paul, his life was a walk of seeking to do the will of God moment by moment, seeking to maintain a blameless conscience before God and before man, all in light of what God had taught him about _"righteousness, self-control and the judgment to come"_ (24:25). Paul sought to walk in a righteous fellowship with His Lord and with his fellow man. Paul's close relationship with God was at the heart of the will of God and central to all God was doing in and through Paul.

Acts 24:27 mentions that Paul stayed in prison over two years, and when Portius Festus succeeded Felix as governor, Paul was still in prison. What benefit could possibly come for Paul in this lengthy delay? Does it appear to you that this delay might have been part of God's will for Paul?

_____

_____

_____

Paul's imprisonment of more than two years at first glance seems like a waste of time. The Lord had promised Paul that he would also witness in Rome. It is easy for us to question Paul's circumstances, but we don't always see the whole picture. We know that Paul had several opportunities to speak to people while in Caesarea for those two-plus years. God's timing is not always in harmony with our timing, and we must trust the Lord in what He allows and doesn't allow.

Did You Know?

LUKE IN CAESAREA

From passages in Acts, we know that Luke (who wrote the Book of Acts) was one of the companions of Paul during his stay in Caesarea (Acts 27:1–2). What did he do during this time? How was this detour and delay beneficial to him? Many believe it was during this time that Luke penned the Gospel of Luke, part of the Luke–Acts historical record the Spirit of God led him to write (Luke 1:1–4; Acts 1:1–2). This is yet another example of the many ways that God works to spread His message throughout the world.

Read Acts 25 and 26. What advantages do you see in the delays Paul faced?

_____

_____

_____

Who were some of those touched by Paul's message (25:23)?

_____

_____

What was at the heart of Paul's testimony to those assembled (26:12–20, 22–23)?

_____

_____

_____

Again, the advantage of the delay is found in more opportunities for Paul to share his testimony and to speak about his faith in Christ. Festus even arranged for a special meeting with Paul for himself, King Agrippa and his sister Bernice, the commanders, and prominent men of the city (25:23). This was no trial. This was an opportunity to freely share the testimony of his walk with Christ—how Christ met and called him on the Damascus Road and commissioned him with the message of forgiveness of sins through faith in Christ. Paul clearly spoke of how Christ sent him to bring others out of darkness and the dominion of Satan into the light and life of the kingdom of God. God's will is to get the message of His heart—the message of His Son—out to the world. Through Paul, God sent this message to many people, using what we would consider frustrating detours and delays to accomplish His will.

"*I would pray to God, that whether in a short time or long time, not only you, but also all who hear me this day, might become such as I am, except for these chains*"

Acts 26:29

SEEING THE DETOURS AND DELAYS GOD'S WAY

In Acts 27, Paul was finally sent as a prisoner to Rome (after he appealed to be judged by Caesar), and then there was yet another detour and ensuing delay. This time the diversion came through a raging windstorm, known as a *Euraquilo* or "Northeaster." It drove the ship and its 276 passengers out to sea for fourteen days, eventually causing the battered ship to run aground on the island of Malta. The ship was destroyed, but the crew was unharmed, and they stayed there for three months.

Read Acts 27 and 28:1–11. What benefits do you see in this journey marked by incessant detours, delays, and even dangers?

_____

_____

_____

What significance do you see in the report of Acts 27:22–25?

_____

_____

_____

The storm detour brought Paul to the surface as a man of integrity and a man of God. The detour and delay on Malta gave opportunity for the other 275 people on board ship to fully hear the gospel and to see the power of God at work. For example, the Lord used the bite of a viper to show God's power to the ship's crewmembers and to the people of Malta. The three-month delay was an opportunity for people from all over the island to hear the gospel and to see the almighty power of Jesus Christ. Acts 27:22–25 gives us the heartbeat of God for Paul and for the ministry He had given to him. Paul knew he belonged to God and was available to serve Him. God comforted Paul ("_Do not be afraid_") through reminding him of his mission to Rome and promising him that He would get him there. God also impressed upon Paul the tremendous opportunity he would be given to get the message to the 275 passengers ("_God has granted you all those who are sailing with you_").

📖 Read Acts 28:11–31. What is the focus of this passage (28:17–29)?

_____

_____

_____

What is emphasized in verses 28, 30–31?

_____

_____

_____

The opportunity to get the message of Christ to the Jews is the focus in verses 17–27, 29. Paul spoke of the "_hope of Israel,_" which centered around the Messiah and His coming kingdom, a kingdom in which the righteous King would reign supreme and relationships would be made right. The emphasis of verses 28, 30–31 is the message of Jesus Christ—His life, death, resurrection, ascension, and return—going out unhindered.

📖 Look back at Romans 1:10–17 and 15:26–33 (passages studied in Day One). Did Paul have his prayers answered? Did he come to Rome in the will of God?

_____

_____

_____

Paul's prayers were answered, but not exactly as he had anticipated (about three years later than he first expected). Note the time sequence. Paul wrote to the Romans around February of 57 expecting to be in Rome by the summer of 57. He arrived in Rome around February of 60. He was delivered from those who were disobedient in Jerusalem, his service and gifts were accepted by the elders and church in Jerusalem, and he came to Rome in joy

"... the God to whom I belong and whom I serve...."
Acts 27:23

Doctrine
THE HOPE OF ISRAEL

The "Hope of Israel" was that the Messiah would bring salvation to His people and reign in His Kingdom over all the nations in fulfillment of the many Old Testament prophecies. Paul made it clear that the Hope of Israel is the Lord, Jesus Christ.

(see Acts 28:15) by the will of God. Paul had also prayed to be able to impart some spiritual gift and to be able to preach the gospel in Rome (Romans 1:11–15). He had two years in Rome to do just that, though it was while he was under house arrest.

Was it necessary for Paul to appeal to Caesar? It meant that Paul would have to stay in prison for two more years. What advantages could possibly come from imprisonment? Consider this fact. Just before Paul was released from this Roman incarceration, he wrote a letter to the believers in Philippi. We can discover some answers to our questions in that letter.

📖 Read Philippians 1:12–20, and note what you find.

_____

_____

_____

📖 Look at Philippians 4:22. What additional insights do you find?

_____

_____

Did You Know?
THE PRAETORIAN GUARD

A *"praetorian"* referred to any official residence or palace. In Philippians 1:13, it most likely refers to the imperial guard ordered to watch Paul day and night for the two years he was under house arrest in Rome. Each day and each night presented an opportunity for these guards to hear the message of life in Christ as Paul taught those who came to him (Acts 28:16, 30–31).

These two years were years of protection for Paul, provided by the Roman army. Paul had continual contact with many soldiers including the Praetorian Guard. Visitors were able to come and go in Paul's rented quarters, and he was able to preach and teach *"concerning the Lord Jesus Christ with all openness, unhindered"* (Acts 28:31b). Also during this time, Paul wrote four small letters: **Ephesians**, **Colossians**, **Philemon** and **Philippians**—all small in size but immensely deep in eternal truth. Through Paul's writing and through his daily contact with soldiers and visitors, many were brought to faith in Christ. Philippians 1:12 says his circumstances *"turned out for the greater progress of the gospel."* In 1:14, Paul says *"most of the brethren"* in Rome had *"far more courage to speak the word of God without fear."* In Philippians 4:22 Paul even sends greeting from all the saints *"especially those of Caesar's household."* If Paul had not appealed to Caesar, he would probably not have had the connections to the Roman army and to Caesar's household. How awesome are the ways of God!

How awesome are the ways of God!

Think back over what happened in Paul's life and what we can learn about the will of God in his life. Think of the people who were touched and changed because of what seemed like endless detours and postponements. Consider the people that Paul touched and the circumstances he faced in Troas, Miletus, Tyre, and Jerusalem—at the Temple area, in the Sanhedrin, and in the Roman barracks. Then consider the impact of the journey to Antipatris and Caesarea and the two years of imprisonment in Caesarea, the perilous voyage at sea aboard the prison ship that resulted in shipwreck. We certainly see God's hand upon Paul's ministry to the inhabitants of Malta. In Rome—in Paul's rented quarters, in the Praetorian guards' lives, in Caesar's household—again, we see the will of God being fulfilled. Then, in Ephesus, Colossae, Philippi and the surrounding cities, we know that God touched numerous lives through the letters that Paul wrote to these regions.

 Now, think of your own life. Have the things that are written in Acts 19–28 touched you or others you know? As you meditate on these things, think about what the Lord might be saying to you about His will for your life. Do you see that it is God's will for the message of His heart to spread throughout the world, using all kinds of people, in all kinds of circumstances, and in all kinds of places? Do you see He even uses dangers, detours, and delays to get the message to more people? Finally, do you see that He wants **you** to walk in His will as a living example to others of what a relationship **in the will of God** looks like?

FOR ME TO FOLLOW GOD

There are some conclusions and applications we can draw concerning the will of God in Paul's life and in our lives . . .

1.) Paul **definitely** wanted to **do the will of God**. He was surrendered to the Lord and His will. He read the Scriptures and obeyed what he knew to do.

2.) The **dangers** and conflicts that Paul faced were used by God to direct Paul in His will.

3.) The **detours** were actually God's well-chosen paths to get the message out—the message of truth that leads to a right relationship with God and with man. The detours were also used to minister to Paul in unexpected ways.

4.) The **delays** were part of God's wise timing in getting the message to more people because they opened added doors of opportunity for him to speak that message.

5.) The **difficult** and **dark** circumstances were actually God's opportunities to more clearly reveal the light, the truth about who God is and what He has done to bring grace and salvation through the Lord Jesus Christ. Through Paul's life the Lord gave the opportunity for many to place their faith in Christ and begin their walk with Him. In the difficult and dark circumstances God made sure the light of truth shone brightly.

What about His will in your life? Are you facing some detours or delays today? Do you have a heart that is seeking God's will for your life? In most cases, the will of God is as clear as the noonday sun, because it is written in the Scriptures. Concerning the areas that aren't as clear, God gives enough light to take the next step in following Him. Paul made it clear that the foundation for a clear knowledge of the will of God is a personal relationship with Jesus Christ. Upon that foundation we can build a greater knowledge of His will. He wrote to the Colossian believers,

> *"We have not ceased to pray for you and to ask that you may be filled with **the knowledge of His will** in all spiritual wisdom and understanding, so that you may walk in a manner worthy of the Lord, to please Him in all respects, bearing fruit in every good work and increasing in the knowledge of God; strengthened with all power, according to His glorious might, for the attaining of all steadfastness and patience;*

Did You Know?
CAESAR'S HOUSEHOLD

In Philippians 4:22, Paul says, *"All the saints greet you, especially those of Caesar's household."* Caesar's household included all those involved in the day-to-day administration of the palace—servants, cooks, army officers and soldiers, and government officials, as well as Caesar's family members. The message of salvation in Jesus Christ reached into Caesar's palace as well as into Paul's prison.

Romans 12:1–2 tells us that the will of God is "good (beneficial) and acceptable (well-pleasing) and perfect (reaching the right goal)."

joyously giving thanks to the Father, who has qualified us to share in the inheritance of the saints in light." (Colossians 1:9–12)

What does this walk in the will of God look like? What does it not look like? The answers to these two pertinent questions are found in several passages of Scripture.

📖 Look at each of the Scriptures given below. These verses unmistakably identify the will of God. Write what is **clearly the will of God** and what is **clearly not** the will of God.

Scripture	What IS the will of God?	What IS NOT the will of God?
Romans 12:1–2		
Colossians 1:9–12		
1 Thessalonians 4:1–8		
1 Thessalonians 5:17–21		
Ephesians 5:17–21		
1 Peter 2:13–17		
1 Peter 3:13–17?		

APPLY From what you have seen in these Scriptures, are many aspects of God's will clearer to you now? What application is the Lord making to your life today? Write down any specific application that the Lord has given to you.

_____

_____

_____

"Thou hast taken hold of my right hand. With Thy counsel Thou wilt guide me."

Psalm 73:23b-24a

📖 What about the **dangers** you may have faced (or are facing) in your life? Has the Lord used, or is He still using these difficulties to call you to a more complete surrender to Him or to give you direction in His will? Is He giving you a better knowledge of Himself and His ways? Ponder these questions as you read Psalm 27:1–14. Write any personal applications.

_____

_____

_____

_____

What about the **detours** in your life (even those caused by the sins of others or of yourself)? What are you learning about the paths God chooses for His children? Read Psalm 23:1–6 and Psalm 73:23–24, and write any personal applications.

_____

_____

_____

_____

What about the **delays** in your life? What is God teaching you about His timing? Read Psalm 31:14–15, and note what you discover.

_____

_____

_____

_____

What about the **difficult days** in your life when things seem a bit cloudy or dark? What information is God giving you about the next step? Read Psalm 36:5–9 (note verse 9) and 119:105. As you read these psalms, consider God's ways in your life.

_____

_____

_____

_____

As you think of any difficult circumstances, detours, delays, or even dangers in your life, do any of these circumstances seem like a denial of the promises of God to you? You may not have all the answers to these questions but you can trust the One who does have the answers. He is carrying out His will. He is getting His message out to others. Are you following Him in the areas where you know for sure what His will is, the areas we have read about in the Scriptures and of which there is no doubt? Offer yourself to do His will, and join Him in what He wants for you.

 Lord, thank You for calling me to walk with You in Your will, that which is good, acceptable, and perfect. Thank You for the loving and wise design You have for my life and for all Your children. I admit I have questions sometimes, but I thank You that You are a patient Father and Teacher to me. Thank You for the way You come alongside to encourage me by Your Spirit and for the continual encouragement of Your Word. You know we are all like dust, frail and weak, but I thank You that You are always present to strengthen us and to give us the grace and wisdom to do Your will. I also thank You that you give us enough time to do Your will. Teach me how to better use and more carefully guard the time You give me rather than wasting it (like I have so many times). Show me how to invest my time in relationships—with You and with others. Teach me to trust You more completely in

Offer yourself to God to do His will, and join Him in what He wants for you. Surrender to the adventure of the will of God.

what looks like a detour or a delay. Thank You that You are always working **all things** together for good to those who love You and are called according to Your purpose (Romans 8:28). May I more and more be filled with the knowledge of Your will in all spiritual discernment and understanding so that I may truly walk in a way that is pleasing to You in all things (1 Thessalonians 2:12). In Jesus' Name. Amen.

In light of all you have learned about the will of God, write a prayer to the Lord expressing your surrender to Him and His will.

_____

_____

_____

_____

_____

_____

_____

_____

_____

_____

_____

_____

An Outline of the Life and Ministry of the Apostle Paul

DATE	EVENTS	SCRIPTURE
Birth—Schooling—Direction Set		
AD 2?	Paul born in Tarsus of Cilicia	Acts 9:11; 21:39; 22:3 Galatians 1:15; Philippians 3:5–6
	Schooled under Gamaliel in Jerusalem	Acts 22:3
	Zealous Pharisee and persecutor of Christians	Acts 7:60; 8:1–3; 9:1–2; 22:3–4; 26:4–5, 9–11
New Birth—New Schooling—New Direction Set		
c.a. AD 35	Paul "born from above" on the road to Damascas	Acts 9:1–7; 22:3–16; 26:4–18
35	Early growth and revelation from the Lord	Acts 9:8–25; 26:19–20
35–37	In Damascus and in Arabia	Acts 9:23; Acts 9:24–25, 27 Galatians 1:16–17
37	Jerusalem (First Visit)	Acts 9:26–29; Acts 22:17–21 Galatians 1:18
Tarsus Time (AD 37–43)		
37	Paul went to Tarsus.	Acts 9:30
37–43	Into regions of Syria and Cilicia	Galatians 1:16–17
Homebase and Proving Grounds (AD 43–48)		
43	From Tarsus to Antioch of Syria with Barnabas	Acts 11:19–26
47	Jerusalem (Second Visit)	Acts 11:27–30; Galatians 2:1
47–48	Ministry in Antioch	Acts 12:25—13:1–3
First Missionary Journey and Battle Grounds (AD 48–50)		
Spring 48	From Antioch of Syria to Cyprus	Acts 13:2–12
	In Perga and Pamphylia—John Mark left Paul, Barnabas, and their companions and returned to Israel.	Acts 13:13
	In Antioch of Pisidia	Acts 13:14–52
	In Iconium	Acts 13:51; 14:1–6
	Into Lystra (Galatian area) and Derbe (Galatian area)	Acts 14:6–20
	Return to Lystra, Antioch of Pisidia, Pamphylia, Perga, Attalia	Acts 14:21–25
Autumn 49	Back to Antioch of Syria (Homebase)	Acts 14:26–28; 15:1–2
	Paul confronted Peter and Barnabas at Antioch.	Galatians 2:11–16
49	Jerusalem (Third Visit)	Acts 15:2–4
49	Jerusalem Council	Acts 15:4–29
49	Paul and team were sent to Antioch with letter from Jerusalem Council.	Acts 15:22–23
49?	Paul wrote *Galatians*.	Galatians 1:1–6
49-50	Ministry in Antioch of Syria—Paul, Barnabas, and Silas	Acts 15:34–35

DATE	EVENTS	SCRIPTURE
Second Missionary Journey and New Grounds (AD 50–52)		
Spring AD 50	Disagreement between Paul and Barnabas. Barnabas went with John Mark to Cyprus. Paul and Silas departed towards Syria and Cilicia.	Acts 15:36–40; 15:39–41
	Derbe and Lystra. Timothy began to minister with Paul and Silas.	Acts 16:1–3
	Paul delivered the decrees of the Jerusalem Council in several cities.	Acts 16:4–5
	Paul traveled through the Phyrgian and Galatian region to Troas (as led by the Holy Spirit).	Acts 16:6–8
	Troas and the Macedonian Vision	Acts 16:9–10
Summer through early Autumn 50	In Philippi and Macedonia	Acts 16:11–40; Philippians 1:5; 1 Thessalonians 2:2
November 50 through January 51	In Thessalonica	Acts 17:1–9 1 Thessalonians 1:5–10; 2:1–2
February 51	To Berea	Acts 17:10–14
March 51	To Athens (Paul sent Timothy back to Thessalonica.)	Acts 17:15–34 1 Thessalonians 3:1–2, 5
March 51	To Corinth	Acts 18:1–18
May 51	Silas and Timothy came from Macedonia to Corinth.	Acts 18:5
Summer 51	Paul wrote *1 and 2 Thessalonians* from Corinth.	1 Thessalonians 1:1 2 Thessalonians 1:1
Autumn 52	To Ephesus	Acts 18:18–21
Autumn 52	To Jerusalem (Fourth Visit)	Acts 18:22b
Autumn 52	To Antioch of Syria	Acts 18:22c
Third Missionary Journey—Building Grounds (AD 53–57)		
53	Galatian region and Phyrgia	Acts 18:23
53–56	Ephesus—Three-year ministry which included work in the Synagogue, the School of Tyrannus, and the community	Acts 19:1–20
	Plans ministry for Macedonia, Achaia, Jerusalem, and Rome	Acts 19:21–22
Spring 56	Paul wrote *1 Corinthians* from Ephesus.	1 Corinthians 16:8
May 56	Disturbance in Ephesus	Acts 19:23–41
June 56	To Macedonia	Acts 20:1–2
Autumn 56	Paul wrote *2 Corinthians* from Macedonia.	2 Corinthians 8:1, 16–24; 9:1–5; 13:1–10
December 56	To Greece (Achaia), specifically Corinth (3 months)	Acts 20:2–3
February 57	Paul wrote *Romans* from Corinth. Paul sent the Romans epistle with Phoebe from Cenchrea, the port area of Corinth.	Romans 16:1–2
Spring 57	Journey to Philippi, Troas, Miletus, Tyre, and Caesarea	Acts 20:3–38; 21:1–14
May 57	To Jerusalem (Fifth Visit)	Acts 21:15–17
May 57	Meeting with James and the elders	Acts 21:18–25

DATE	EVENTS	SCRIPTURE
In the Temple, in Prison and in Trials—Prison Grounds (AD 57–60)		
May/June AD 57	Beginning of the "Seven Days of Purification" for four men under a Nazirite vow	Acts 21:23–26; Numbers 6:9–21
June 57	Seventh day of Purification, ensuing riot in the Temple area, and Paul arrested	Acts 21:27–40
Same day	Paul's testimony to the Jews in the Temple area	Acts 21:40; 22:1–22
Same day	Paul's imprisonment and defense in the barracks	Acts 22:22–29
Day after arrest	Paul placed on trial before the Sanhedrin and sent to prison	Acts 22:29; 23:1–10
That night	Paul in prison, visit and promise from the Lord at night	Acts 23:11
Next day	Conspiracy by over 40 Jews to kill Paul	Acts 23:12–22
That night	Journey to Antipatris with 470 Roman soldiers	Acts 23:23–31
Next day	Journey to Caesarea with 70 horsemen and imprisonment in Herod's Praetorium	Acts 23:32—35
5 days	Waiting for Trial. After 5 days, the Jews arrived.	Acts 24:1
Fifth day	Trial before Felix	Acts 24:2–22
June 57	In custody under a Roman centurion, and granted a measure of flexibility	Acts 24:23
June 57	Paul testified to Felix and Drusilla.	Acts 24:24–25
57–59	Paul often conversed with Felix. Felix hoped for a bribe.	Acts 24:26
	Paul in Prison for two years under Felix, then left in prison when Felix was succeeded by Portius Festus	Acts 24:27
July 59	In prison under Portius Festus in Caesarea	Acts 24:27; 25:1–5
July 59	Trial before Festus and appeal to Caesar	Acts 25:6–12
August 59	Arrival of King Agrippa and Bernice	Acts 25:13–22
August 59	Preparation for investigation of Paul before Festus, Agrippa, Bernice, commanders and prominent men of the city	Acts 25:23–27
August 59	Paul's defense and testimony	Acts 26:1–32
Journey to Rome—Promise Grounds (AD 59–60)		
August 59	Paul delivered to Julius, centurion of Augustan cohort	Acts 27:1
Aug./Sept. 59	Out to sea	Acts 27:2–8
Sept./Oct. 59	Warnings of Paul not to sail and the crew's decision	Acts 27:9–13
October 59	Winds of the Storm (*Euroquilo* or "Northeaster")	Acts 27:14–20
October 59	After several days . . . God's promise of completion of the journey to Rome, and safety for all on board	Acts 27:23–24
October 59	Encouragement by Paul for all crewmembers	Acts 27:21–26
October 59	After 14 days . . . shipwreck on the island of Malta. All crewmembers made it safely to shore.	Acts 27:27–44; 28:1
October 59	Paul bitten by a viper, presenting an open door for ministry	Acts 28:1–6
Oct. 59–Jan. 60	Ministry to the father of Publius and to the people of Malta	Acts 28:7–11
February 60	Conclusion of the journey, by sea and land to Rome	Acts 28:11–16

DATE	EVENTS	SCRIPTURE
First Imprisonment in Rome **Ministry and Message Released; Protection for Paul and the Message Of Christ (AD 60–62)**		
February 60– Spring 62	Paul in his own rented quarters with *"the soldier who was guarding him"* A time of protection for Paul, for churches, and for Christians	Acts 28:16–21
Autumn 60	Paul wrote *Ephesians* (written from Rome to the church at Ephesus).	Ephesians 3:1; 4:1; 6:19–22
Autumn 61	Paul wrote *Colossians* (from Rome to Colossae, Laodicea, and Hierapolis).	Colossians 1:24; 4:3–4; 7–9, 18
Autumn 61	Paul wrote *Philemon* (from Rome to Philemon in the city of Colossae).	Philemon 1, 9, 10, 13, 23
Early 62	Paul wrote *Philippians* (from Rome to Philippi).	Philippians 1:7; 12–14, 19–20; 25–27; 2:17, 19, 25–30; 3:9–14, 18, 22
Acquittal and Release—Mission/Ministry/Message Expansion (AD 62–67)		
Spring 62	Acquittal and release from imprisonment in Rome	Philippians 2:24
Spring 62	To Colossae, then to Ephesus (left Timothy there), then to Philippi (in Macedonia)	Philemon 22; 1 Timothy 1:3; Philippians 2:24
Autumn 62	Paul wrote *1 Timothy* from Macedonia to Timothy in Ephesus.	1 Timothy 1:3
63–66	Possibly went to Spain (AD 63–65); Arrived in Crete (AD 65/66) Paul may have also journeyed to Asia Minor.	Romans 15:24, 28; Titus 1:5
Summer 66	Paul wrote *Titus* from Asia Minor to Titus in Crete.	Titus 1:5; 3:12
Autumn 66	To Nicapolis, Achaia (Greece) to spend the Winter	Titus 3:12
Winter 66, 67	In Nicapolis	Titus 3:12
Second Imprisonment in Rome (AD 67–68) **Release of the Message of Christ and Release of Paul through Martyrdom (AD 68)**		
Autumn 67	Possibly arrested in Troas, "[He] *left his cloak, books, and parchments there*" (2 Timothy 4:13). Taken to the Mamertine Prison in Rome	2 Timothy 1:8, 16; 2:9
Autumn 67	Paul wrote *2 Timothy* in Rome to Timothy in Ephesus.	2 Timothy 1:2, 18
Autumn 67	Trial/defense before Roman court	2 Timothy 4:16–17
Spring 68	Paul was executed during Nero's rule . . . a martyr's death.	2 Timothy 4:6–8, 18

"The Word of God is not imprisoned" (2 Timothy 2:9b).

"For I am already being poured out as a drink offering, and the time of my departure has come. I have fought the good fight, I have finished the course, I have kept the faith; in the future there is laid up for me the crown of righteousness, which the Lord, the righteous Judge, will award to me on that day, and not only to me, but also to all who have loved His appearing" (2 Timothy 4:6–8).

"The Lord will deliver me from every evil deed, and will bring me safely to His heavenly kingdom; to Him be the glory forever and ever. Amen" (2 Timothy 4:18).

Notes

Notes

Paul's Companions

FOLLOWING GOD TOGETHER

When we look at the life of Paul we find it hard to grasp how one man could do so much. We stand amazed at the impact of his life, his ministry, and his writings. However, when we consider his life and ministry we must see it in the context of the overall ministry of the early Church. We must look at the full picture which includes many believers. One of the mysteries God revealed through Paul was the mystery of the Body of Christ, the Church, of which Christ is the Head (Colossians 1:18). When we look at that Body in the New Testament, we see many gifted members, each serving where the Lord placed them with the gifts given by Him *"for the common good"* (1 Corinthians 12:7, 12–14, 18). We will also see this principle of gifted laborers correctly using their gifts as we study the companions and co-laborers of the apostle Paul. As part of the Body of

The New Testament lists the names of seventy men and women who served alongside Paul in one way or another.

PAUL AND SOME OF HIS COMPANIONS

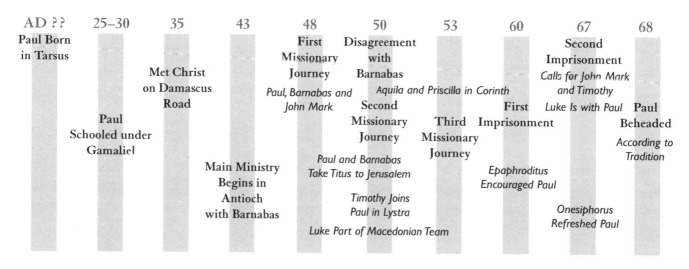

AD ??	25–30	35	43	48	50	53	60	67	68
Paul Born in Tarsus		Met Christ on Damascus Road		First Missionary Journey	Disagreement with Barnabas			Second Imprisonment	
	Paul Schooled under Gamaliel			Paul, Barnabas and John Mark	Aquila and Priscilla in Corinth		First Imprisonment	Calls for John Mark and Timothy	Paul Beheaded
					Second Missionary Journey	Third Missionary Journey		Luke Is with Paul	According to Tradition
			Main Ministry Begins in Antioch with Barnabas		Paul and Barnabas Take Titus to Jerusalem		Epaphroditus Encouraged Paul		
					Timothy Joins Paul in Lystra			Onesiphorus Refreshed Paul	
					Luke Part of Macedonian Team				

Christ, Paul's companions followed Christ **together**. In this lesson we want to see how God used many of these who at one time or another served alongside the apostle Paul. A look at their lives will give each of us encouragement as we follow Christ individually and as we follow Him together with others in the Body of Christ.

Paul's Companions   DAY ONE

JOHN MARK AND SILAS— COMPANIONS ON THE JOURNEY

John Mark, sometimes called Mark, is one of the more noted companions of the apostle Paul. The first mention of John Mark occurs in Acts 12:12 (though some think he is the *"certain young man"* at the arrest of Jesus in Mark 14:51–52). The incidents of Acts 12 occurred around AD 47. Herod had put James the brother of John to death. Peter had been arrested, and an angel delivered him while a prayer meeting was taking place at the home of Mary, the mother of John Mark. John Mark was certainly able to see the hand of God at work in Jerusalem. Soon after the events of Acts 12:1–19, Barnabas and Saul, who had gone to Jerusalem to deliver an offering for the needs of the saints in Judea, returned from Jerusalem *"taking along with them John, who was also called Mark"* (12:25b).

📖 Read the account of the eve of Barnabas and Saul's first missionary journey in Acts 13:1–5. Where does John Mark fit in?

_____

_____

_____

What do you find out about John Mark in Colossians 4:10? Why do you think he is part of this journey?

_____

_____

_____

The Holy Spirit set apart and sent out Barnabas and Saul from the church at Antioch to take the gospel to other areas. John Mark went along as their *"helper"* (13:5). One of the reasons he went along could have been his kinship with Barnabas since Colossians 4:10 points out that he was Barnabas' cousin. Along with that was Barnabas' desire to encourage the young John Mark.

📖 Read Acts 13:13 and 15:36–40. (The date is around AD 50.) What do you discover about John Mark?

_____

_____

_____

Word Study
"SENT OUT BY THE HOLY SPIRIT"—

The Holy Spirit *"called"* and *"sent out"* Barnabas and Saul on their first missionary journey. The Greek word for "sent" by the Holy Spirit is *"ekpempo,"* meaning "to send out." The church at Antioch *"set apart"* and *"sent"* them on their way (Acts 13:2–4). The word for "sent" by the church is *apoluo* meaning "to release or let go." The Holy Spirit sent them out on His mission, while the church, in worshipful surrender to the Lord, released them to that calling.

John Mark left *"Paul and his companions"* when they reached Pamphylia, and he returned to Jerusalem. Paul labeled this act as desertion. John Mark had withdrawn from them and the mission. He *"had not gone with them to the work"* (15:38), and Paul saw this as a serious problem. Paul did not want John Mark along on the second journey, but Barnabas, the *"son of encouragement,"* desired to take his cousin along. Barnabas' desire caused such a sharp disagreement between Paul and him, that Barnabas took John Mark and sailed to Cyprus. Paul chose the prophet Silas, and from Antioch they began what is known as the second missionary journey.

📖 Colossians was written around AD 61, eleven years after the events of Acts 15:36–40. Read Colossians 4:10–11, and record what you learn about John Mark.

_____

_____

_____

_____

Second Timothy was written in AD 67. Read 2 Timothy 4:11, and note what you discover about Paul and John Mark.

_____

_____

_____

_____

What conclusions and applications do you see in these passages?

_____

_____

_____

John Mark was with Paul in Rome when he wrote to the Colossians (around AD 61), perhaps preparing to come to Colossae. If he came to Colossae, Paul encouraged them to welcome him. John Mark was noted as part of the group of *"fellow workers for the kingdom of God who are from the circumcision"* and was *"an encouragement"* to Paul. In 2 Timothy (AD 67), Paul desired John Mark to be with him in Rome where he was imprisoned. Paul considered him *"useful . . . for service"* (4:11). Over time John Mark had proven himself faithful and useful in the kingdom of God. His life and example are an exhortation not to give up on someone. No one is ever beyond being better equipped, growing in grace, or beyond forgiveness and restoration in the Body of Christ.

 Can you think of someone (perhaps yourself) who has made some immature or even hurtful choices? Is there something you could do to help restore them, perhaps a prayer, a phone call, a visit, or maybe a letter? Remember maturity in the Body of Christ is a process that takes time.

Silas was another noted companion of the apostle Paul. What do we know of this man? We first meet Silas at the Jerusalem Council in Acts 15. That council met to settle what did and did not constitute the gospel. Was circumcision

Put Yourself In Their Shoes
TIMES OF NEED

When Paul was in the Mamertine prison in Rome, he called for Timothy and John Mark. We all have times of need and Paul was no different. Paul told Timothy to *"pick up [John] Mark and bring him with you."* Paul needed John Mark there, *"for he [was] useful . . . for service"* (2 Timothy 4:11). In 2 Timothy 4:13, Paul tells Timothy to *"bring the cloak [for winter was coming] . . . and the books, especially the parchments."* The *"parchments"* were perhaps the Old Testament Scriptures needed for Paul's personal use or for ministry. In 2 Timothy 4:21, Paul pleads with Timothy to *"make every effort to come before winter."* Paul had a sense of urgency, knowing his *"departure"* was at hand (2 Timothy 4:6).

necessary? They decided it was not. Having heard testimony of the work of God among the Gentiles and applying what they knew from the Scriptures, they became of one mind and issued a letter to be read in the Gentile churches in Antioch, Syria, and Cilicia. That letter is given in Acts 15:23–29. The first mention of Silas reveals that he was one of the *"leading men among the brethren"* in the church at Jerusalem (15:22).

📖 Looking at Acts 15:30–35, what do you discover about Silas?

_____

_____

_____

Silas was a prophet, one who was equipped and gifted of God to handle the Word and to preach the message of Christ. Along with Judas Barsabbas, he encouraged and strengthened the brethren in Antioch with a lengthy message. Silas and Judas stayed for a time with the congregation in Antioch. Acts 15:33–34 notes that when they were sent back to Jerusalem, Silas thought it was good to remain in Antioch. There he ministered in teaching and preaching alongside Paul and Barnabas.

We previously learned in Acts 15:36–41 that, as a result of the disagreement between Paul and Barnabas over John Mark, Paul chose Silas to go with him on the second missionary journey. Acts 16:4–5 and 16:11–40 reveal that Silas had a significant part in these events (note *"they," "them," "these men"*). In Acts 16:4–5 we find Silas carrying out his commissioned task of delivering the decrees of the Jerusalem Council, resulting in the churches being strengthened in the faith and expanded in numbers. In Philippi (Acts 16:11–40) it appears that Silas proclaimed the message with Paul since, after the incident with the slave-girl, her masters grabbed Paul and Silas. Consequently, Paul and Silas were arrested, beaten, and imprisoned. Luke and Timothy were also in Philippi but were not arrested with them. The faith of Paul and Silas is seen in their response. At midnight they were singing hymns, and later, both shared the message of salvation with the jailer and his family (16:31–32). Both were also recognized as Roman citizens (16:37–39).

📖 It is evident that God used **both** Paul and Silas. What other things do you see about Silas in Acts 17:1–4 and 17:10–15.

_____

_____

_____

"For they received the word with great eagerness, examining the Scriptures daily, to see whether these things were so. Many of them therefore believed, along with a number of prominent Greek women and men."

Acts 17:11–12

Silas had a part in the proclamation in Thessalonica as believers there *"joined"* Paul and Silas (17:4). To protect them, both were then sent away from Thessalonica to Berea. When they arrived **"they** *went into the synagogue,"* and the people *"received the Word with great eagerness."* It appears that Paul was the chief spokesman, but Silas also taught. Paul then left Silas and Timothy in Berea and traveled to Athens. At some point while in Athens, Paul requested that Silas and Timothy come to join him there. Acts 18:5 tells us that Silas and Timothy finally joined Paul, who was now in Corinth. In First and Second Thessalonians (both written from Corinth in the summer of AD 51) we find that Paul considered Silas and Timothy as partners in ministry. They also preached among the Corinthians alongside Paul (2 Corinthians 1:19). These were two faithful men following Christ and serving where He led them.

APPLY We often forget that God uses **many** members of the Body of Christ to do His work and to get His message out. He wants to use **all** the members of His Body. Talk to Him about where you are on the journey with Him, where you fit, and how He wants you to join with Him.

Titus—Fellow Worker, Epaphras—Fellow Bondservant

 *Paul's Companions* **DAY TWO**

In Matthew 28:19–20, Jesus told His followers to *"make disciples"* throughout the world. In the lives of Titus and Epaphras, that command was a life-long reality. As you read about their lives, look for application points to your own life. God works in many different ways and with all kinds of people. Watch for how He worked in these lives, and you may see some ways God wants to work through your life.

We find the first mention of **Titus** in Galatians 2:1, where Paul reports that he (Paul) and Barnabas went up to Jerusalem to discuss the message of the gospel (what it is and what it is not) with the leaders there. That was around AD 49. They took Titus with them. That means that Titus was with them in Antioch for some period of time and had achieved some level of leadership or leadership training. Galatians 2:1–5 reports that Titus was an uncircumcised Greek and a believer in Jesus Christ. He was not required to be circumcised, a point Paul emphasized to the law-laden Galatians. Titus was one who was free with the *"liberty which we have in Christ"* (Galatians 2:4).

The next time we see Titus is in 2 Corinthians (around AD 56). Paul had written 1 Corinthians a few months before. In that letter he sought to clear up several problems in the Corinthian church. After writing the letter he made a quick visit to Corinth to address the problems (2 Corinthians 2:1; 12:14) and subsequently wrote a sorrowful second letter to Corinth (2:4). Titus delivered that letter (2 Corinthians) to the church at Corinth. Later, Paul went to Troas, expecting to find Titus and to see how the Corinthian believers had received his letter. Titus was not there, so Paul sailed to Macedonia (2 Corinthians 2:12–13).

📖 Read 2 Corinthians 7:5–8, 13–16. What do you learn about Paul?

_____

_____

_____

What do you learn about Titus?

_____

_____

_____

PAUL'S COMPANIONS

For Paul, his companions and co-laborers were a family. Many times throughout Paul's epistles, he uses beautiful phrases to describe his appreciation for his friends such as, *"my beloved," "my kinsmen,"* referring to a household, *"fellow bondservants,"* with reference to an army, *"fellow soldier," "fellow prisoners"* and *"fellow workers"* as those in a vineyard or a harvest field.

Paul reveals in 2 Corinthians that he faced the same struggles that everyone faces; he encountered many pressures as well as *"conflicts without"* and *"fears within."* However, he found comfort in the coming of Titus with news from Corinth. Paul was confident that God was at work among the Corinthians and that they would receive the truth (7:14). Titus found comfort in the right response of repentance by these Corinthian believers. *"His spirit"* was *"refreshed"* by the Corinthians. He had a deep affection for them. Clearly his ministry was marked by the work of the Spirit of God among the Corinthians as seen in Paul's encouragement concerning their *"obedience"* and their receiving Titus in *"fear and trembling"* (7:15).

In 2 Corinthians 8:1–5, we learn that Paul was collecting an offering for the needy saints in Jerusalem, and the churches in Macedonia had given generously. In 2 Corinthians 8:6, Paul notes that Titus had made initial preparations for this offering in Corinth, and Paul and his team urged Titus to complete that work. Therefore, Paul sent Titus back to Corinth along with some other men.

📖 Read 2 Corinthians 8:16–23, and record what you find about Titus.

_____

_____

_____

Titus had an earnest heart for the Corinthians and wanted to see them. He desired that they complete the ministry of giving that they had begun. Therefore he went to Corinth *"of his own accord"* along with a team of men whom Paul recognized as *"honorable"* and *"diligent"* men. Paul viewed Titus as his *"partner and fellow worker"* among the Corinthians. He was a man of integrity and a strong spiritual leader.

📖 About ten years later we meet Titus once again. There are three references to Titus in Paul's last two letters. Read Titus 1:4–5 (with 6–9) and 3:12, and list what you find about Titus.

_____

_____

_____

_____

📖 Looking at 2 Timothy 4:10 what do you discover?

_____

_____

_____

_____

Extra Mile

PAUL AND TITUS

Read Titus 1—3 to see the full context of the ministry Paul entrusted to Titus. Note particularly 2:1,15 and 3:1–14.

Paul considered Titus as *"my true child in a common faith"* (1:4) and left Titus in Crete with the assignment of setting *"in order"* what was left to be done to firmly establish these new churches. Titus had ministered with Paul on the island of Crete and proved to be a capable leader who could finish establishing the work there. Paul told him to *"appoint elders in every city as I direct*[ed] *you."* It is evident that Titus was a man of integrity, faithful to the Word, and an example of the qualities of an elder given in Titus 1:6–9. Paul's desire for

Titus to come to Nicopolis shows that Paul saw Titus as a genuine help to him (3:12). Second Timothy 4:10 reveals that Titus went from Rome to Dalmatia (modern Albania), where, according to tradition, he died as a martyr in a Roman amphitheater. Titus proved in many ways that he was a trustworthy, faithful, and capable servant in the kingdom of God.

📖 Late in Paul's ministry we read of another who faithfully proclaimed the message and then joined Paul in Rome (sometime during AD 60–62). Read Colossians 1:3–8 and 4:12–13. What do you learn about Epaphras?

_____

_____

_____

Epaphras preached and taught the gospel to those in Colossae, a city in western Asia Minor (modern Turkey). He was a *"beloved fellow bondservant"* and a *"faithful servant of Christ,"* always *"laboring earnestly in prayer"* for the believers in Colossae and praying that they would *"stand perfect and fully assured in all the will of God."* Epaphras had a deep concern for them as well as for those in Laodicea and Hierapolis.

In the lives of Titus and Epaphras we see clear examples of faithfulness, integrity, and trustworthiness. Paul's gladness over the work of each of these companions and over the personal encouragement they were to him should be a call to each of us to be marked by that same faithfulness and trustworthiness. Dependability and trust are two elements that help relationships thrive and are among many elements needed for serving and leading others in the Body of Christ.

AQUILA AND PRISCILLA– EQUIPPING THE SAINTS

I n Acts 17 Paul told the Athenians that God determined their appointed times and the places where they lived (17:26). The Greek word for God is *"theos,"* the root idea being "the one who places." It is God who places things and people as He wills to accomplish His purpose. When we come to Acts 18 we find Paul being placed with a new couple, new companions in ministry.

📖 In Acts 18:1–3, we are introduced to **Aquila** and **Priscilla** (around AD 51). How did they get to Corinth?

_____

_____

_____

_____

What did God have waiting for them there (18:2–3)? Consider what this says about the ways of God as you look at these verses.

_____

_____

_____

The Roman Emperor Claudius reigned from AD 41 to 54. His decree for all Jews to leave Rome was issued around AD 49. That decree brought Aquila and Priscilla to Corinth, where they met the apostle Paul around the spring of AD 51. God turns the heart of the king like channels of water (see Proverbs 21:1). The Greek word for God is *"theos."* It is rooted in the word *"theo,"* meaning "to put in place," the idea being that whoever puts things in place is by definition God. God is "The Placer" not only in the lives of Aquila, Priscilla, and Paul, but in our lives as well.

Aquila, a native of Pontus in Asia Minor, and Priscilla, his wife, were in Corinth when Paul arrived. They had recently moved from Italy because of an order by Emperor Claudius for all Jews to leave Rome (around AD 49). They were tentmakers like the apostle Paul, and the three of them began working together. Apparently, at this point, Paul had no other financial support, so he worked his trade during the week and taught in the synagogue on the Sabbath. When Silas and Timothy joined him, he devoted himself to his ministry full-time. Evidently, they had brought along financial support for the ministry.

In Acts 18:18–19 we find Aquila and Priscilla with Paul sailing from Corinth to Ephesus. Paul left for Antioch, but they stayed in Ephesus. What ministry did God give them in this new location?

_____

_____

_____

_____

_____

What do you find significant in Acts 18:24–28?

_____

_____

_____

_____

_____

Did You Know?

TENTMAKING

Paul and Aquila and Priscilla worked together making tents (Acts 18:3). Jewish children were taught a trade from childhood, and Paul's trade was tentmaking. Cilicia, where Paul was born, was known for the high quality of its cloth woven from black goat hair. This cloth was so well known that it was exported from Cilicia as *"Cilician cloth"* and widely used in tentmaking. Tentmaking consisted of sewing these cloths together along with the needed ropes and connecting loops. Paul doubtless knew this trade well since he grew up in Tarsus of Cilicia.

When Aquila and Priscilla heard the eloquent Jew, Apollos, they realized that he did not understand the full revelation of God about Christ. Therefore, they *"took him aside and explained the way of God more accurately"* (Acts 18:26). As a result, Apollos was better equipped in the Scriptures, and when he went to Achaia (southern Greece) and most likely to the city of Corinth, he *"helped greatly those who had believed through grace"* (18:27).

The next time we see Aquila and Priscilla is around AD 56 (about 4 years later). In concluding his first letter to the Corinthians, Paul mentions this couple (1 Corinthians 16:19). Aquila and Prisca (Priscilla) sent greetings to the church in Corinth as part of the greetings of the churches of Asia (modern-day Turkey). Paul included *"the church that is in their house,"* implying that they were leaders of a house-church that was most likely in the city of Ephesus. A year later (AD 57), Paul wrote to the Romans, and in Romans 16:3–5 he sent his greetings to them again. From this we conclude that they were back in Rome at this point.

📖 In light of these facts and with what you have seen of Aquila and Priscilla thus far, read Romans 16:3–5. What do you see about their walk with God and their ministry in the kingdom?

_____

_____

_____

Paul considered Aquila and Priscilla *"fellow workers in Christ Jesus"* (16:3). At some point they had even *"risked their own necks"* for Paul's sake (perhaps at the riot in Ephesus about nine months before—May, AD 56). They were equipped to minister to others, and again, we find a church in their house. Now in Rome, as usual, they were faithfully ministering where they were.

📖 Ten years later (AD 67) we find Paul writing from his prison cell in Rome his final letter to Timothy (who was in the city of Ephesus). Read 2 Timothy 4:19, and record your insights and any conclusions you see about Aquila and Priscilla.

_____

_____

_____

In 2 Timothy 4:19, we find that Aquila and Priscilla have moved once again. This time they are living back in Ephesus and ministering with Timothy. Though they lived in at least three different cities (Rome, Corinth, Ephesus), they were faithful through the years wherever they were in ministering to others and equipping the saints.

 Take some time to consider what you have seen in the lives of John Mark, Silas, Titus, Epaphras, and Aquila and Priscilla. Consider the ways they followed God and the ways they served alongside Paul. How are you serving? What is God saying to you through their lives and ministries?

Luke–"The Beloved Physician"

In Luke 1:1–4 we find that **Luke** set out to write *"in consecutive order"* the things that happened concerning the Lord Jesus. He was not an *"eyewitness"* from the beginning, but the account of eyewitnesses was *"handed down"* to him and others. Luke *"investigated everything carefully from the beginning"* in order to write an accurate account so that Theophilus and others *"might know the exact truth about the things* [he had] *been taught."* Acts 1:1 reveals that the Gospel of Luke was *"the first account . . . about all that Jesus began to do and teach."* Luke compiled Acts as volume two on the work of Christ. In that account, Luke was an eyewitness to some of the events. We find his trademark *"we"* beginning in Acts 16:10. There he says *"we sought to go. . . ."* This indicates that Luke joined Paul probably in Troas. From there he traveled with Paul to Philippi and beyond. What can we learn from the Scriptures about this companion of Paul?

"LUKE, THE BELOVED PHYSICIAN"

Luke traveled with Paul for many years ministering both spiritually and physically. The Greek word for "physician" is *"iatros,"* from the root word *"iaomai,"* meaning "to heal or to cure." Medicines in Paul's day included olive oil, wine, and various plants and herbs. Luke would have been knowledgeable of all of these medicines. Paul's needs may have included attention to wounds incurred along the way—perhaps Paul needed some treatment of his *"thorn in the flesh"* (2 Corinthians 12:7). Paul's other companions may have had medical needs as well.

"The will of the Lord be done."

Acts 21:14

📖 Read Acts 16:10–18, and record your insights into the life and character of Luke. Note each use of *"we"* or *"us"* in your search. (The events occurred around August to October of AD 50.)

_____

_____

_____

_____

_____

Luke was part of the team seeking to go to Macedonia with Paul, and he considered himself called to preach the gospel there. He sailed with Paul to Macedonia and stayed with him in the city of Philippi several days. He also went with Paul to the riverside place of prayer and was one of the men speaking to the women assembled there. After Lydia responded to the message, she and her household were baptized, and she invited everyone, including Luke, to stay at her house. Apparently, for many days they went to the place of prayer, and each day a slave-girl kept annoying them with her mockery of their message. Luke was there when Paul commanded the evil spirit to come out of the girl, and he was there (along with Timothy) when Paul and Silas were seized and imprisoned. Apparently Luke and Timothy were left unharmed.

The next time we see Luke is in Acts 20:5–15 (around Spring, AD 57) with Paul on his journey from Corinth to Philippi and Troas. Luke was with him at Miletus as well (20:15–16), where he heard his exhortation to the elders from Ephesus (Acts 20:17–38).

📖 Read Acts 21:1–18, noting each use of *"we," "us,"* or *"our."* How did Luke participate in this journey?

_____

_____

_____

_____

_____

_____

Luke was a constant companion during the journey to Jerusalem. In Acts 21:12, Luke joined the others in *"begging"* Paul not to go to Jerusalem because of the dangers. Perhaps he was one of the ones *"weeping"* over this matter and certainly was one of the ones who declared *"the will of the Lord be done"* (21:14). Luke, a faithful follower of Christ and a faithful companion of Paul, arrived with Paul in Jerusalem around May of AD 57.

The next time the word *"we"* is used is in Acts 27:1 as Paul, Luke, and perhaps some other companions of Paul were getting ready to sail for Italy. The narrative from Acts 21:19 through 26:32 covers over two years of imprisonment. It appears that Luke was with Paul in some way during this time. He would not have been in the Jerusalem jail but could have traveled to Caesarea when he and Paul's other companions found out about the move. It appears that Luke stayed in Caesarea during this time. Some believe that it was during these two years (June, AD 57–August, AD 59) that Luke wrote his Gospel. According to Acts 27 and 28:1–16, Luke was with Paul for the entire journey to Rome—the shipwreck, the time on Malta, and the remaining voyage to Rome. Luke summarized Paul's stay in Rome, *"And he stayed two full years in his own rented quarters, and was welcoming all who came to him, preaching the kingdom of God, and teaching concerning the Lord Jesus Christ with all openness, unhindered"* (Acts 28:30–31).

During the two years in Rome, Paul wrote the following epistles: Ephesians, Philippians Colossians, and Philemon. Colossians and Philemon were written and sent to the city of Colossae around the autumn of AD 61.

📖 Read Colossians 4:7–14 and Philemon 23–24. Note what Paul says about Luke in Colossians 4:14 and Philemon 24. What conclusions can you draw from these two verses?

_____

_____

_____

_____

_____

In Colossians, Paul lists Tychicus, Onesimus, Aristarchus, Barnabas' cousin Mark, Jesus called Justus, Epaphras, Luke and Demas; while in Philemon, we find the names of Epaphras, Mark, Aristarchus, Demas, and Luke. In Colossians 4:14; Paul calls Luke *"the beloved physician,"* a title rich in meaning, revealing the love Paul and many others had for Luke. Luke stayed close to Paul as a *"fellow worker"* according to Philemon 24. A man of loyalty, humility, and loving service, Luke was faithful to the Lord and to Paul. Luke is mentioned once more in the year AD 67. In the letter of 2 Timothy, we find Paul in the Mamertine prison in Rome approximately six months before his execution at the hands of the Roman government.

📖 Read 2 Timothy 4:9–13, 21. Record what you see about Luke. Note the contrast with the others mentioned.

_____

_____

_____

_____

_____

Paul greatly desired Timothy to come to Rome and to do so *"soon"*—*"make every effort to come before winter"* (4:9, 21). Demas, *"having loved this present world,"* deserted Paul and went to Thessalonica. Crescens and Titus had gone to Galatia (Asia Minor) and Dalmatia (Albania) respectively, and Paul sent Tychicus to Ephesus. *"Only Luke"* was with Paul, staying with him to the end. We see here a marked example of working together as brothers, as fellow workers following Christ whatever the cost.

 Look back over what you have read about Luke. What is the message to your heart? Spend some time in prayer. Let God apply these truths to your life.

FOR ME TO FOLLOW GOD

W hat does it mean to be a loving servant of God? Perhaps no better examples of Christian service can be found in Scripture than the stellar examples of two men who are found in the books of Philippians and 2 Timothy. These two men are Onesiphorus and Epaphroditus. Let's look at their lives.

📖 In 2 Timothy we have a brief glimpse of Onesiphorus who lived in Ephesus where Timothy served. Read 2 Timothy 1:15–18 and 4:19, and record what you find about this man.

_____

_____

Onesiphorus often refreshed Paul, probably when he was in Ephesus as well as when he was in Rome. He was not ashamed to be associated with Paul even though he was in prison. Instead, he *"eagerly searched"* for Paul and found him in prison where he refreshed and encouraged him. Paul reminded Timothy of the *"services* [Onesiphorus] *rendered at Ephesus."* It is possible that Paul and Timothy were in Ephesus together nearly the entire three-year period of Acts 19 (note 19:22, AD 53–56) and would have had ample opportunity to observe the service of Onesiphorus.

📖 Is everyone supposed to be a "servant?" Are a servant's heart and good deeds part of the Christian life all the time? Read each of the Scriptures given below, and record what you find.

Ephesians 2:8–10

_____

_____

Ephesians 4:12

_____

_____

Titus 2:14

_____

_____

Titus 3:8

_____

_____

SUPPORT FOR MINISTRY

Some of the companions of Paul never traveled even a mile with him. Some supported him through fervent **prayer** (2 Corinthians 1:10–11), some through material and financial **gifts** (Philippians 4:14–19), and still others through **food and lodging** (Acts 16:15).

 Who is there that you can *"refresh"* along the way, someone who is a *"fellow worker"* in ministry? This does not have to be a "full-time" pastor, but could certainly include any involved in vocational ministry. It could be any believer, since all believers are "servants" of the kingdom being equipped for the *"work of service,"* as Ephesians 4:12 explains. In what practical way can you encourage that person (or persons)?

___Write a note to them.
___Give them a call.
___Sit and talk with them.
___Help them in some practical way.
___Give something to help fill a particular need.
___Other

📖 Epaphroditus is yet another of Paul's companions who rendered great service. Read Philippians 4:18 and 2:25–30 (along with the context of 2:3–5), and record what you learn about Epaphroditus.

_____

_____

_____

_____

The church in Philippi sent Epaphroditus to Paul in Rome with an offering for his needs. Paul considered it an abundant supply and as *"a fragrant aroma, an acceptable sacrifice, well-pleasing to God"* (4:18). Paul saw Epaphroditus as a *"brother and fellow worker and fellow soldier"* as well as the *"messenger"* from Philippi who served as *"minister to [Paul's] need"* (2:25). In carrying out the ministry given to him, Epaphroditus became sick in Rome even *"to the point of death,"* but *"God had mercy on him"* (2:26–27). Epaphroditus was very concerned for the Philippian believers and longed for them, and he was distressed that they had heard that he was sick. Paul considered him a man of honor and exhorted the Philippians to *"hold men like him in high regard, because he came close to death for the work of Christ, risking his life to complete what was deficient"* in their service for Paul (2:29–30). Epaphroditus was a true example of Philippians 2:3–4.

APPLY Read Philippians 2:3–11. What does it take to be an *"Epaphroditus"*? List four or five (or more) clear statements of what it means to have the mind or attitude of Christ (note especially verses 3–4).

_____

_____

_____

_____

We see in the life of the apostle Paul and in the life of the early Church many who served. The list of those with whom Paul served in one way or another numbers some seventy individuals. Serving alongside one another is the way God has designed the Body of Christ.

APPLY What have you learned about serving others? What insights have you received about Paul and how God worked through him and through the people who served with him? Evaluate where you stand in serving God and others. What applications do you see for your life?

Remember that He has a place for each member of the Body of Christ, and He has gifted you for that place. Spend some time talking to the Lord about these things, and follow Him where He is leading. Let's follow Him **together!**

"Do nothing from selfishness or empty conceit, but with humility of mind let each of you regard one another as more important than himself."

Philippians 2:3

Lord, I thank You for the Body of Christ, for the gifts You have given to the members of Your Body, and for the way You use each of us uniquely for Your purposes. Thank You that we are not left alone as believers. You are always with us, and You have placed us in a Body of believers to encourage and be encouraged. As I follow You, may I be a faithful fellow worker for the truth and an obedient and loyal fellow soldier. Help me understand the gifts You have given me, and empower me to use them under Your direction. May I make the most of every opportunity to share the message of life in Christ, and may I be the encouragement I need to be to others in the Body of Christ. Thank You for placing me where I am in this Body.

In light of all you have seen about Paul's companions and the ways of God in the Body of Christ and in ministry, write a prayer expressing your heart to the Lord, the Head of the Body.

_____

_____

_____

_____

_____

_____

_____

_____

_____

_____

_____

_____

THE COMPANIONS OF THE APOSTLE PAUL

NAME	CITY	SCRIPTURE	NAME	CITY	SCRIPTURE
Achaicus	Corinth	1 Corinthians 16:17	Luke	Antioch	Colossians 4:14
Ampliatus	Rome	Romans 16:8	Mary	Rome	Romans 16:6
Andronicus	Rome	Romans 16:7	Narcissus	Rome	Romans 16:11
Apelles	Rome	Romans 16:10	Nereus	Rome	Romans 16:15
Apphia	Rome	Philemon 2	Nereus' Sister	Rome	Romans 16:15
Apollos	Corinth	1 Corinthians 1:12	Nymphas	Colossae	Colossians 4:15
Aquila	Corinth	Acts 18:1–3	Olympas	Rome	Romans 16:15
Archippus	Colossae	Colossians 4:17	Onesimus	Colossae	Colossians 4:7–9
Aristarchus	Ephesus	Acts 19:29	Onesiphorus	Ephesus	2 Timothy1:16, 18
Aristobulus	Rome	Romans 16:10	Patrobas	Rome	Romans 16:14
Artemas	?	Titus 3:12	Persis	Rome	Romans 16:12
Asyncritus	Rome	Romans 16:14	Philemon	Colossae	Philemon 2, 5, 6, 7
Barnabas	Cyprus	Acts 4:36, 37	Philologus	Rome	Romans 16:15
Claudia	Rome	2 Timothy 4:2	Phlegon	Rome	Romans 16:14
Clement	Philippi	Philippians 4:3	Phoebe	Cenchrea and Rome	Romans 16:1–2
Crescens	Rome & Galatia	2 Timothy 4:10	Priscilla/Prisca	Corinth	Acts 18:1–3, 18–26
Demas	Rome	2 Timothy 4:10	Pudens	Rome	2 Timothy 4:21
Epaenetus	Achaia	Romans 16:5	Quartus	Corinth	Romans 16:23
Epaphras	Rome	Colossians 1:7, 8	Rufus	Cyrene	Mark 15:21
Epaphroditus	Philippi	Philippians 2:25–30	Rufus' Mother	Cyrene	Romans 16:13
Erastus	Corinth	Romans 16:23	Silas/Silvanus	Jerusalem	Acts 15:22, 27, 32
Eubulus	Rome	2 Timothy 4:21	Sosipater	Berea	Acts 20:4–6
Euodia	Philippi	Philippians 4:2	Sosthenes	Corinth	Acts 18:17
Fortunatus	Corinth	1 Corinthians 16:17	Stachys	Rome	Romans 16:9
Gaius	Corinth	Romans 16:23	Stephanas	Corinth	1 Corinthians 1:16
Hermas	Rome	Romans 16:14	Syntyche	Philippi	Philippians 4:2
Hermes	Rome	Romans 16:14	Tertius	Corinth	Romans 16:22
Herodian	Rome	Romans 16:11	Timothy	Derbe and Lystra	Acts 16:1
Jason	Thessalonica	Acts 17:5–9	Titus	Corinth	2 Corinthians 7:13
Jesus (called Justus)	Rome	Colossians 4:11	Trophimus	Ephesus	Acts 20:4
John Mark	Jerusalem	Acts 12:12, 25	Tryphaena	Rome	Romans 16:12
Julia	Rome	Romans 16:15	Tryphosa	Rome	Romans 16:12
Junias	Rome	Romans 16:7	Tychicus	Province of Asia	Acts 20:4
Linus	Rome	2 Timothy 4:21	Urbanus	Rome	Romans 16:9
Lucius	Cyrene	Acts 13:1	Zenas		Titus 3:13

Notes

Timothy

FOLLOWING THOSE WHO FOLLOW GOD

Two especially important things stand out when one looks at the New Testament character Timothy. **First,** it is evident that he was the apostle Paul's key disciple. Of all the men who are identified with Paul, Timothy is mentioned the most. Not only is he the recipient of two of Paul's epistles, but he is also listed by Paul as co-author of six of his epistles (2 Corinthians, Philippians, Colossians, 1 and 2 Thessalonians, and Philemon). **Second,** of all those mentioned in the New Testament who were not a part of Christ's earthly ministry, Timothy is by far the most prominent. Like us, he learned everything he knew about Christ from other people. His walk with God had to be learned from others who followed God. As we look at his life we will see both his weaknesses and his growth into the senior pastor of one of the most renowned churches of his day. His relationship with Paul was so close that Paul often referred to him as his son in the faith. From studying Timothy and the process of Paul's mentoring of him, we should obtain some valuable lessons about how to grow in Christ by following those who follow God.

FACTS ABOUT TIMOTHY

Timothy probably came to Christ through family members converted through the ministry of Paul. Timothy was taken on as a ministry apprentice by Paul on the second missionary journey and served alongside of Paul for the rest of the apostle's life. Eventually Timothy took over Paul's ministry at Ephesus and continued Paul's work after his death. Tradition holds that Timothy died as a martyr during the persecution by the Roman Emperor Domitian while attempting to stop an indecent heathen procession during the Festival of Diana.

THE MINISTRY OF TIMOTHY

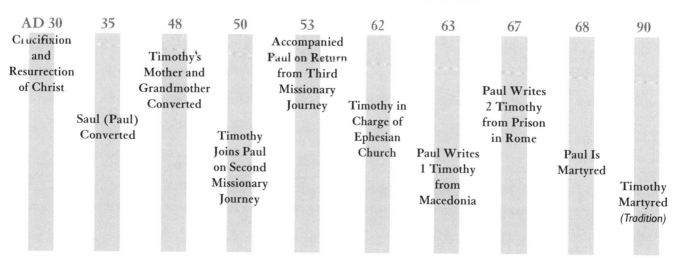

AD 30	35	48	50	53	62	63	67	68	90
Crucifixion and Resurrection of Christ	Saul (Paul) Converted	Timothy's Mother and Grandmother Converted	Timothy Joins Paul on Second Missionary Journey	Accompanied Paul on Return from Third Missionary Journey	Timothy in Charge of Ephesian Church	Paul Writes 1 Timothy from Macedonia	Paul Writes 2 Timothy from Prison in Rome	Paul Is Martyred	Timothy Martyred *(Tradition)*

COMING TO CHRIST

As far as our families are concerned, if we do not teach our children and their generation about the Lord, then our faith may end with us.

Christianity will never become extinct! God's message will continue to be proclaimed even in the darkest and most wicked times. But as far as our families are concerned, if we do not teach our children and their generation about the Lord, then our faith may end with us. All that is required for the worship and work of God to die out in a family is for the faith to not be passed on to the next generation. In Timothy we see a living, vibrant and personal glimpse of the God-honored process of passing that faith on to the next generation. Timothy may not have even been born when Christ walked the dusty streets of Jerusalem or taught on the hillsides of Galilee. He probably did not hear the gospel until 18 years after the resurrection. He was a part of that "second generation" of the first century Church. Yet his faith was no less real or sincere. Though the apostle Paul started the church at Ephesus through his evangelistic efforts, it was Timothy who kept the ministry going. He was the next link in the chain of faith that went from the apostles to men and women of today. We want to begin our consideration of Timothy by focusing on what we know about the "when" and "how" of his conversion and spiritual development.

📖 Take a few minutes, and read thoroughly 2 Timothy 1:5 and 3:14–15, and write down all you learn there about Timothy's faith.

2 Timothy 1:5:

_____

_____

2 Timothy 3:14–15:

_____

_____

_____

PAUL'S NEW DISCIPLE

It was during the second missionary journey when Paul returned to Derbe and Lystra that he recruited Timothy as a disciple. Acts 14 records the circumstances of the first missionary journey, when Paul and Barnabas *"made many disciples"* in that area (Acts 14:21) and established churches there (Acts 14:23). It is possible that Timothy's Jewish grandmother and mother (2 Timothy 1:5) were led to Christ by Paul and Barnabas, and then these two ladies led Timothy to Christ. It is apparent from Acts 16:1 that Paul had no previous relationship with Timothy.

Second Timothy 1:5 records that both Timothy's mother and grandmother were believers, and the word *"first"* implies that they believed before Timothy. Second Timothy 3:14–15 tells us that Timothy was taught the *"sacred writings"* from childhood. This does not necessarily suggest that he became a believer as a child, but it does mean that he was taught the Word of God at a very young age. Most likely, his mother and grandmother were devout Jews and even before they trusted Christ, had taught him the Old Testament, which at this early date was all the Scripture that was recognized.

📖 Look at Acts 16:1–3, and identify what else you can learn about Timothy's coming to Christ.

_____

_____

_____

_____

_____

We see that by the time of the second missionary journey, Timothy is identified as a *"disciple"* and that his mother was a Jewish believer. His father was Greek and apparently not a believer. Although his father allowed Timothy to be taught the Scriptures as a child, apparently he drew the line at circumcision. Paul made sure that the subject of circumcision was addressed while Timothy was an adult so that in ministry this subject would not be a hindrance. Had Timothy been a full-blooded Gentile, circumcision wouldn't have been necessary. The only commentary Luke makes on Timothy is that he was *"well spoken of by the brethren who were in Lystra and Iconium."*

Acts 16:3 tells us that Paul wanted Timothy to go with him on his missionary journey. Write your thoughts on what that says about Timothy.

_____

_____

_____

_____

The most obvious thing here is that Paul placed his stamp of approval on Timothy not only as a believer, but also as one with great potential as a minister. Just as Barnabas had mentored Paul, Paul mentored Timothy. (Acts 9:27; 11:22, 25). As we will see later, Paul's goal for Timothy was that he would mentor others who would in turn teach even more people to continue the chain of mentoring (2 Timothy 2:2).

📖 Now read Acts 15:36–41.

What circumstances had just transpired in Paul's life?

_____

_____

_____

What impact does that have on his desire to take Timothy with him?

_____

_____

_____

Paul and Barnabas had just parted company because of their disagreement over John Mark. Paul's intense personality may have been too much for Mark to handle. Regardless, the departure of Barnabas and Mark left a void for Paul and may have served as a reminder to him of his need to be investing himself in others. It would seem that Timothy replaced the role Mark played on the first journey, the role of apprentice in ministry. Apprenticeship was Paul's method to raise up new ministers.

Apparently Timothy came to Christ after the first missionary journey, for there is no indication in the text that Paul met him on that first trip. He probably came to Christ through his mother and grandmother, believers who would have been involved in the church that Paul established in Lystra and who may have been converts of Paul. It was approximately two or three years later that Paul returned to Lystra and took on Timothy as an apprentice in the work of God.

Did You Know?
WHY WAS TIMOTHY CIRCUMCISED?

Why was Timothy circumcised after the Jerusalem Council had concluded that Gentile converts did not need to be? After all, Paul insisted that Titus not be circumcised (Galatians 2:3). Acts 16:3 gives us Paul's reasoning: *"…because of the Jews who were in those parts, for they all knew that his father was a Greek."* Timothy was an unusual case, since he was half-Jewish. Since his Greek paternal heritage was common knowledge, Jews would assume that he was not circumcised, and the subject of circumcision would be a stumbling block to them. It was Paul's practice in every city he visited to try to reach the Jews first. If Timothy were to minister alongside Paul he needed to remove this obstacle to his testimony. It was not a biblical requirement that he should be circumcised, but it was prudent to broaden his opportunities to minister. Like Paul, he became all things to all men that he might save some (1 Corinthians 9:22).

TIMOTHY'S CHARACTER

In first-century Palestinian culture, much stock was placed in the meaning of one's name. Timothy is actually a Greek name that means, "honor God" or "one who honors God." What a fitting prophecy this name is for this young understudy who would eventually take over a significant part of Paul's ministry. His life and ministry brought great honor to the Lord, and tradition tells us that his death did as well. Most of what we know about Timothy is taken from various references throughout the New Testament. Yet of those in the New Testament who were not apostles, he is mentioned more than anyone else. He is referred to by name in twelve different books of the New Testament and by implication in others. To learn what he was like, we must lean on what others said to him and about him. Today we want to search a number of references and piece together a portrait of what type of man Timothy was.

In Acts 16:1 we learn that Timothy was half Jew and half Gentile. What effect do you think this had on him as he grew up?

_____

_____

_____

The time of Christ was a time of great racial prejudice. The Jews had nothing to do with the Gentiles. In fact, they called the Gentiles "dogs." The Gentiles strongly disliked the Jews as well. Timothy was the product of a racially mixed marriage. Probably neither the Jews nor the Gentiles ever fully accepted him. Because of this, Timothy may have grown up with much insecurity and a sense of inferiority.

Read 2 Timothy 1:6–8. What do these exhortations from Paul suggest about Timothy?

_____

_____

_____

_____

In verse 6 we see that Paul is concerned that Timothy do all that he can to develop his gifts. To *"kindle afresh"* means to "fan the flames." The words convey a meaning of tending a fire and bringing it to a full blaze. There was room for Timothy's gifts to be developed and maximized. Some have seen in 2 Timothy 1:7 a suggestion that Timothy struggled with timidity. However, the Greek structure of these verses doesn't support this interpretation. Paul's exhortations here are probably more of an encouragement to excel at what he already expected rather than an indication of a concern for what Timothy would do. Paul had already seen evidence that Timothy was not ashamed of the testimony of our Lord and would join in suffering for the gospel according to the power of God (1:8).

As we read through the book of Acts, we are informed in chapter 16 that Timothy had joined Paul as an apprentice. In Acts 17:14 we are told that Paul left Timothy behind with Silas. There is no mention in these two chapters

Word Study
WAS TIMOTHY TIMID?

Many have assumed from Paul's instruction to Timothy (*"God has not given us a spirit of timidity"* [2 Timothy 1:7]) and his exhortation (*"do not be ashamed of the testimony of our Lord, or of me His prisoner"* [2 Timothy. 1:8]), that Timothy was timid and mild mannered. However, upon closer examination of the text in Greek, we see that the words *"be ashamed"* is grammatically what is known as an "aorist subjunctive." When such a verb is combined with a negative (i.e. *"do not be ashamed"*) it forms a prohibition designed not to cease an action but to never start an action in the first place. In other words, Paul is not saying, "Stop being ashamed," but rather, he is saying, "Don't ever start being ashamed."

that Timothy left or rejoined Paul, so apparently Timothy was part of the mission team in Philippi, yet only Paul and Silas were beaten and arrested.

📖 Look at Hebrews 13:23, and write what you learn there about Timothy.

_____

_____

_____

_____

We see here that Timothy had been released, indicating that he had spent some time under arrest. Hebrews was probably written just before the destruction of Jerusalem in AD 70, a time when the persecution of believers was growing greater. However timid Timothy may have been as a youth, here he took a stand firm enough to provoke the authorities to arrest him. Evidently he had learned from Paul's mentoring of him and became the man God desired.

📖 What does 1 Timothy 5:23 tell us about Timothy's physical makeup?

_____

_____

_____

_____

This verse relates that Timothy had difficulties with his stomach and also *"frequent ailments."* Wine was an accepted medicinal treatment in Paul's day. Although we don't know exactly what Timothy's ailments were, the text makes it clear that they weren't just occasional symptoms. Perhaps, like his mentor Paul, he too was a frail, sickly man. Notice that although Paul had been given the power from God to heal the sick, he never cured himself of his illnesses in a miraculous way, nor did he apply his power to Timothy, but instead, prescribed medicine.

📖 Look at 1 Timothy 4:12, and see what this verse suggests about Timothy.

_____

_____

_____

_____

The fact that Paul exhorts Timothy to *"let no one look down on your youthfulness"* tells us both that Timothy was young and that his youthfulness could have posed a hindrance to his ministry. Paul's anxiety cannot be entirely without justification. Paul would not tell his understudy to be brave half a dozen times over the course of two letters unless he had concerns about what Timothy would face in the days ahead. Rather than interpreting Paul's concern as a negative reflection on Timothy, this should be a great encouragement to us to see how God used Timothy, in spite of his humanness

"USE A LITTLE WINE"

Paul instructed Timothy to *"use a little wine"* for the sake of his stomach and frequent ailments. Some have suggested a correlation between Timothy's ailments and the unsterile state of the drinking water in that area. While poor water conditions may have contributed to Timothy's stomach problems, clearly the passage has more in view than simply wine as an alternative drink since the advice to use wine is applied to his *"frequent ailments."* While the alcohol in wine might combat germs on a minimal level, its primary benefit would be to settle the stomach and to ease pain and discomfort.

Did You Know?
"YOUTHFULNESS"

In Paul's day, a person between the ages of thirty and forty was considered to be a young person. Timothy was probably in his mid-thirties when Paul wrote the letter of 1 Timothy.

TIMOTHY'S CALLING

Timothy was not in the ministry because he chose it as his vocation. He didn't apply to study at the religious schools of his day. He didn't search the "want ads" for an available position. He was in the ministry because God had called him. We learned in Acts 16 that Paul recruited Timothy right after he and Barnabas had parted company over the subject of John Mark. All Timothy had done was walk with God, and the Lord brought Paul to him. He had earned the respect of the believers in Lystra and Iconium (Acts 16:2), and it was the apostle Paul's initiative that brought Timothy on to the missionary team. His ministry was "received" not "achieved." Today we will look at how this young man got his start, and we will also look into all that Scripture tells us about his calling and ministry.

📖 Read 1 Timothy 1:18 and 4:13–16, and record what you learn about Timothy's calling.

_____

_____

_____

_____

In 1 Timothy 1:18, we learn that *"prophecies"* had been made concerning Timothy, but it is not until 4:13–16 that we begin to understand what these prophecies were. The suggestion of 4:13 is that exhortation and teaching were Timothy's gifts. In 4:14 we see that this giftedness was bestowed through *"prophetic utterance"* as the *"presbytery"* (group of elders) laid hands on him. Paul exhorts in 4:15 that Timothy *"take pains with these things"* that his progress should be seen by all. In 4:16, Paul adds, *"pay close attention to your teaching,"* so obviously Timothy was gifted in this way.

📖 What does 2 Timothy 1:6 add to our understanding of Timothy's giftedness?

_____

_____

_____

Here we see that Timothy received his giftedness from God through the laying on of Paul's hands. Obviously Paul was part of the group of elders *("presbytery")* spoken of in 1 Timothy 4:14. There is no indication in Scripture that the laying on of hands is the only way to receive gifts from God. In fact, many see this event in Timothy's life as the origin of the modern practice of ordination, where a minister's gifts are affirmed publicly by church leaders. It may indicate as well that the gifts spoken of here are not merely apparent in Timothy's spiritual ability, but are also evident in the gift of his office.

Look at 2 Timothy 4:5, and identify what is revealed there about Timothy's ministry.

_____

_____

Did You Know?
"LAYING ON OF HANDS"

The practice of *"laying on of hands"* has its roots in the Old Testament sacrificial system. The priest would lay his hand on the head of his offering, identifying the sins with it before it was slain (Leviticus 3:2). It was also practiced by Moses when he transferred his ministry to Joshua (Numbers 27:15–21; Deuteronomy 34:9). In the New Testament it became a common practice associated with ordaining people for a particular task or ministry. The elders at Antioch laid hands on Barnabas and Paul when they sent them out on the first missionary journey (Acts 13:2–4). It would seem that in 1 Timothy 4 the presbytery ordained Timothy for his ministry. The laying of hands here served more or less as a "stamp of approval."

We see in this verse that Timothy is to *"do the work of an evangelist"* and thus fulfill his ministry. The only other man in the New Testament identified as an evangelist is Philip. Obviously, evangelism was part of Timothy's role in ministry, though at the time of Paul's letter it was not an itinerant ministry. Timothy was expected to fulfill this role in his pastoral duties at Ephesus.

📖 Take a few minutes to read Ephesians 2:11–22. Recognizing that Timothy was half Jew and half Gentile, and that he would become the chief pastor of the church of Ephesus, reflect on Paul's teaching here and how by God's sovereignty Timothy fit in to it.

_____

_____

_____

_____

In Ephesians 2:11–22 we read that God has taken the two groups in the Church (Jew and Gentile) and made them into one body in Christ. He has broken down the barrier of the dividing wall, that partition in the temple that Jews could pass but Gentiles could not under penalty of death. How fitting that the plan of God would take a man who represented such a Jewish/Gentile fusion to illustrate this beautiful truth of His intent.

THE EQUIPPING OF TIMOTHY

Timothy DAY FOUR

Often when we think about the men that God greatly used during the first century, we assume that they were somehow born righteous or that they became spiritual giants through a special encounter with God. In reality their growth and development was a process over time marked by mistakes and failures. The apostle Paul was converted on the Damascus road, but it was eight years later before his ministry really began. Moses failed greatly and spent forty years tending sheep before God made him the deliverer he was meant to be. Growth and maturity doesn't just develop overnight. Dr. A. H. Strong illustrates this well: "A student asked the president of his school whether he could not take a shorter course than the one prescribed. 'Oh yes,' replied the president, 'but then it depends upon what you want to be. When God wants to make an oak, He takes a hundred years, but when he wants to make a squash, he takes six months.'" Becoming useable to God is a process which takes a great deal of time, and Timothy is no exception to this rule. Let's try today to acquire an understanding of the process God brought Timothy through to prepare him for his role in God's plan. In Timothy we will see God's purpose and plan for us as well.

📖 Read the following verses, and reflect on what you see to be Timothy's primary role in the book of Acts.

Acts 16:1–3—

_____

_____

Acts 17:14–15—

_____

_____

Acts 18:5—

_____

_____

Acts 19:22—

_____

_____

Acts 20:4—

_____

_____

We see from these passages that Timothy's primary role in his early days with Paul was simply that of observer. In Acts 19:22 we also see that he is used to "minister" to Paul. As mentioned earlier, he was probably with Paul in Philippi but was not involved enough in the ministry to be noticed by those who arrested and beat Paul. An important part of Timothy's preparation was simply to spend time observing the models that God had placed before him—Paul and Silas.

📖 Now read the following verses and identify what commonality they reveal about the preparation process for Timothy.

1 Corinthians 4:17—

_____

_____

1 Corinthians 16:10—

_____

_____

2 Corinthians 1:1, 19—

_____

_____

Philippians 2:19–22—

_____

_____

1 Thessalonians 3:2, 6—

_____

_____

"But you know of his proven worth that he served with me in the furtherance of the gospel like a child serving his father."

Philippians 2:22

In these passages, Timothy has moved beyond being an observer. Paul had begun sending Timothy to fulfill short-term ministry tasks on his behalf. We read in 2 Corinthians 1:19 that Timothy had begun filling some preaching roles as well. Eventually, Paul would refer to Timothy as a *"fellow worker"* (1 Thessalonians 3:2), and it is worth noting what Paul says of Timothy in Philippians 2:20—*"For I have no one else of kindred spirit who will genuinely be concerned for your welfare."* Timothy had become someone Paul could lean on and trust, someone who shared his values and priorities.

📖 Look at the passages below, and record what is revealed there about Paul's training of Timothy.

2 Timothy 2:2:

_____

_____

2 Timothy 3:14:

_____

_____

A key part of Timothy's training was what he had *"seen and heard"* (2:2). What this shows is that there is no substitute for observing ministry as it happens, and that instruction is a key component of equipping. A less obvious truth here is that teaching others is also part of the learning process. Paul knew that Timothy would learn much from teaching others. This learning process was "person to person" (3:14). When you think about it, there is very little in our lives that we did not learn from someone else. Everything from reading, to tying our shoelaces, to prayer and Bible study—someone has taught us things to get us where we are. Those who have taught us the most are those who took the time to build relationships with us. Relationships are the bridges across which truth is often carried.

FOR ME TO FOLLOW GOD

Perhaps the single biggest advancement in ministry is moving beyond ministering **to** people into the realm of ministering **through** people. Sadly, many never get beyond that hurdle and, as a result, their ministry never grows beyond them or outlasts them. Paul's approach was different though. Perhaps he learned it from the way God had used Barnabas in his life, or maybe Paul learned from the disciples that it was Jesus' way. Though our Lord ministered **to** people, most of His time was spent building up the lives of the Twelve so that He could have a ministry **through** them even after He had ascended to heaven. Paul developed a similar type of ministry with the Thessalonian church. Paul writes, *". . . our gospel did not come to you in word only, but also in power and in the Holy Spirit and with full conviction; just as you know what kind of men we proved to be among you for your sake. You also became imitators of us and of the Lord . . . so that you became an example to all the believers in Macedonia and Achaia."* Did you catch the progression there? First we see that Paul and two other companions (Silvanus and Timothy) became examples for the people of Thessalonica. The results of their ministry came as

". . . the things which you have heard from me in the presence of many witnesses, these entrust to faithful men who will be able to teach others also."
2 Timothy 2:2

Timothy DAY FIVE

"You, however, continue in the things you have learned and become convinced of, knowing from whom you have learned them."
2 Timothy 3:14

the people became imitators of those who had led them to the Lord. These new converts then became examples to others. Ministering through people is God's way, for since Christ's ascension, learning to follow Him has come from following others who already follow Him. This is how Timothy progressed from convert to laborer to leader.

Paul invested years in the life of Timothy. He taught him. He took him under his wing and looked after his walk. Paul included him in the tasks of his ministry. Paul sent him to perform tasks he was unable to do himself. And in the end, Paul placed Timothy in charge of one of his most fruitful ministries—the church at Ephesus. Through a process of growth, Timothy moved from being an **object of ministry** to being a **minister**. God desires that same progression to happen in all of our lives.

While a church or a ministry or a spiritual event may be a catalyst in our lives, most of our growth and learning happens "person to person." God brings "Pauls" into our lives who invest spiritual truth in us.

APPLY As you reflect on your own spiritual growth, who have been the "Pauls" in your life who have had the greatest impact on your walk and ministry?

_____

_____

_____

_____

What sort of things did they do with and for you?

_____

_____

_____

📖 Take a look again at 2 Timothy 2:2.

What exactly does Paul instruct Timothy to invest in others?

_____

_____

In whom is Timothy to make these investments?

_____

_____

What is he to expect of those in whom he has made a spiritual investment?

_____

_____

TIMOTHY AND PAUL

At the end of Paul's life, the person he wrote to was Timothy. It was to this faithful disciple that he sent word, *"Make every effort to come to me soon."* We do not know for certain if the apostle Paul ever married—there is some indication he may have had a wife who either had died or left him because of his faith in Christ, although any thought concerning Paul's marital status is pure conjecture. However, it is pretty safe to say that Paul was single for the duration of his ministry to the Church. Yet Paul refers to Timothy as *"my son"* (2 Timothy 2:1) and *"my true child in the faith"* (1 Timothy 1:2). Yet Timothy's biological father was an unbelieving Greek (Acts 16:1). It would seem that Paul became a surrogate father of sorts to his disciple and friend, Timothy.

Paul tells Timothy to take all that he had *"seen and heard"* from Paul and *"entrust"* it to others. The word *"entrust"* speaks of investing wisely. Paul is saying, "Timothy, everything you have seen and heard in me is a valuable treasure. I want you to invest it wisely so it will bring the greatest dividend." Paul exhorts Timothy to *"entrust"* this training and truth into the lives of *"faithful men."* In other words, "don't just give it to anyone, but give it to those who will do something with it." Timothy was to give those truths to people who were faithful or dependable, and who would be able to teach others. Timothy was not to teach those who simply wanted to "sit and soak." He was to expect those whom he taught to in turn teach others.

📖 Our Lord's last words to His earthly disciples before He ascended up to heaven are called the "Great Commission." Look at Matthew 28:19–20.

What were the disciples to do after Jesus left?

_____

_____

What were they to teach to those who became disciples?

_____

_____

Jesus commissioned the eleven to *"make disciples"* of all the nations. In other words, they were to make "followers" of Jesus in all the places He had not been. In so doing, they were to teach these followers to obey all that He had commanded them. What would these followers do with what they had learned? Well, if the disciples were to do their jobs right, they would teach their disciples to make even more disciples, for that was one of the commands Jesus gave them.

🛑 APPLY Who are the "Timothys" in your life—the people in whom God is calling you to "entrust" what you have "seen and heard" from those who have ministered to you?

Make a list of names below:

_____

_____

_____

_____

_____

Are these people who will be faithful to you?

_____

_____

Are they able to teach others (maybe not a congregation of thousands, but someone)?

_____

_____

_____

If you have learned anything from this study, I hope you have learned that even if you know nothing more of the Christian life than what you have studied here, you can start sharing these truths with others.

We must not only take in truth, but give it out as well. Our own spiritual health depends on proclaiming the truth.

Ask God to bring others your way who will teach you His truths, and look to the Lord for those with whom you can share those truths that were taught to you.

When I first became a Christian as a freshman in college, I went through a five-week Bible study with several other new Christians. Since God had saved me from a very worldly, drug-oriented lifestyle, most of my friends were not Christians, but when they saw the changes God worked in me, several came to Christ. They wanted me to teach them the Bible. All I knew of the Bible was this little five-week study I had just finished, but I started a Bible study in my dorm room with them. By the end of that spring we had fifteen guys crammed into my room each week discovering the truths of the Bible. Most of them didn't know the difference between Philippians and Philistines. The most common answer I gave to their questions was "I don't know, but I'll ask someone and tell you next week." Yet God used me in their lives, and He used them in mine.

There is probably already someone in your life who can be a "Paul" to you if you are faithful and teachable. And if so, you can be assured that there are some "Timothys" out there for you to teach what you are learning as well.

Why not take this to the Lord in prayer right now?

Lord, thank You for the "Pauls" you have brought into my life and all You have taught me through what I have seen and heard from them. Bring others my way who will teach me Your truths and challenge me by their example. Never let me be comfortable just sitting on what I am learning. Give me opportunities to apply what I learn. Make me sensitive to the "Timothys" around me who need to learn what little I know. Help me to be a good steward of the truths that You have entrusted to me. Amen.

Prayer of Application . . .

Take a few moments to write down a prayer of application from the things that you have learned this week.

_____

_____

_____

_____

_____

_____

_____

_____

_____

_____

_____

_____

Notes

Notes

The Son of Man

FOLLOWING HIS FATHER

Jesus Christ is **"the Son of Man."** That title carries with it two profound truths. First, it is a title for the Messiah, the One promised throughout the Old Testament and pictured in Daniel 7 as He who is given dominion over an everlasting kingdom. The second truth is found in God becoming a Son of **man**. Our Lord, Jesus Christ is called the Son of Man. He walked on the earth as a man, and as a man He faced all that men face—hunger and plenty, weariness and refreshment, sadness and joy, laughter and weeping, temptation and triumph. Yes, He did this as a man, but, more than that, He did this as the God-Man. Certainly this mystery of the God-Man is one of those truths we cannot fully grasp, but we can receive illumination by His Spirit so that we can truly come to know Him and walk in fellowship with Him—with the Son and with the Father.

> *The Son of Man is worthy to be worshiped and adored. He is worthy to be followed and obeyed.*

JESUS CHRIST: THE SON OF MAN

Prophecy	Ministry	Crucifixion	Resurrection	Coming	Reigning and Judging
Daniel 7:13–14	Matthew 9:1–8; 11:15–19; 16:13–20; Mark 2:23–28; Luke 19:1–10; John 9:1–41	Matthew 16:21; 17:22–23; Mark 10:32–34, 45; Luke 18:31–34; John 3:13–21	Matthew 12:38–41; 17:9; Mark 9:31–32; Luke 9:22; 24:1–49; John 12:23–28; 13:31–33; 20:9	Matthew 13:36–43; 24:3–51 Mark 13:3–37; 14:61–62; Luke 9:23–26; 12:35–40; 21:25–28 John 14:1–3	Matthew 19:28–30; 25:31–46; Mark 13:26–27 Luke 22:67–70 John 5:19–29 Revelation 1:12–19; 14:14–16

As we walk through the Scriptures and the life of the Lord Jesus, we will learn the full meaning of this title "the Son of Man," and in so doing we will discover the Friend who sticks closer than a brother, the One who faced temptation in all its furor, *"yet without sin"* (see Hebrews 4:15). This same Friend can come alongside to encourage, guide, and direct us in whatever we are facing. The Son of Man is worthy to be worshiped and adored, followed and obeyed. Our hope is that in walking through this lesson you will develop a deeper understanding of how to worship and follow Christ, **the Son of Man.**

The Son of Man

THE SON OF MAN IS LORD

What do we discover about the Son of Man in the Scriptures? In the four Gospels, the Lord Jesus referred to Himself as the "Son of Man" over eighty times. In those references He revealed Himself as Lord, as the Messiah, as the Savior of the world, and as the coming King who reigns over all the kingdoms of the world. To see the Son of Man as He is and how we are to follow Him, we must see Him first in the Old Testament.

📖 The key Old Testament passage where the phrase "Son of Man" is used is in the prophecy of Daniel. Read Daniel 7:13–14. What is given to the Son of Man?

_____

_____

_____

What do you learn about Him and His kingdom?

_____

_____

"One like a Son of Man . . . was given dominion, glory and a kingdom, that all the peoples, nations, and men of every language might serve Him."

Daniel 7:13, 14

The Son of Man was given dominion or rulership by the Ancient of Days (God the Father). He was also given glory and a kingdom. As a result, *"all the peoples, nations, and men of every language* [will] *serve Him. His dominion is an everlasting dominion which will not pass away; and His kingdom is one which will not be destroyed."* Christ's kingdom will last forever!

What does this dominion include? When we look at this description of the Son of Man we recognize One who rules over all kings and kingdoms. The New Testament readily applies this to the Lord Jesus. What applications to Him do we discover in the New Testament?

📖 The Gospel of John uses the term "Son of Man" thirteen times. In the first of these, a conversation between Jesus and Nathanael (John 1:45–51), we find some revealing truths about this "Son of Man." What does Philip reveal about Jesus while talking to Nathanael (1:45)?

_____

_____

_____

How did Jesus greet Nathanael (1:47–48)?

_____

_____

What was Nathanael's reply (1:49)? What did he say about Jesus?

_____

_____

_____

Jesus made a promise to Nathanael in John 1:50. What was that promise?

_____

_____

_____

Philip came to Nathanael, telling him they had found the One about whom Moses and the Prophets wrote. In many passages throughout the Pentateuch (Genesis through Deuteronomy), Moses wrote of the Messiah to come. Many prophets also spoke of the coming Messiah. Nathanael honestly questioned if any good thing could come out of Nazareth. When Jesus saw Nathanael, He acknowledged Nathaniel's forthright honesty, _"Behold, an Israelite indeed, in whom is no guile!"_ What did Jesus' statement mean? Nathanael wanted to know how Jesus knew about him. Jesus then revealed that He also knew Nathanael had been under the fig tree well before Philip had found him. To that evident supernatural ability Nathanael responded in awe-inspired faith, _"Rabbi, You are the **Son of God**; You are the **King of Israel.**"_ Nathanael felt that whoever knew what Jesus knew had to be the Son of God, and, if that were true, He had to be the Messiah, the King of Israel. Jesus then promised that he would see even greater things. What did Jesus mean? Let's continue searching the Scriptures.

What word picture did Jesus paint in John 1:51? List the elements of which He spoke.

_____

_____

_____

📖 Now read Genesis 28:10–17, and note the parallels to what Jesus said.

_____

_____

_____

Jesus spoke of the heavens opening and the angels of God ascending and descending on the Son of Man. In Genesis 28 we discover that Jacob had a dream that pictured Jesus' description almost word for word. The angels of God were ascending and descending on a ladder or, more likely, a staircase like that which stood at the entrance of an ancient city. Jacob saw this place as the _"house of God"_ and the _"gate of Heaven"_ (28:17). At the top of the staircase, where a city gate would be located, stood the LORD, the God of Abraham, Isaac, and Jacob. He promised Jacob a land with many descendants (a nation) and a seed in whom all the families of the earth would be

**Did You Know?**

PROPHECIES CONCERNING THE SON OF MAN

Moses and the Prophets penned over 300 prophecies about the Messiah, all fulfilled in the Son of Man, Jesus Christ.

Did You Know?

CAESAREA PHILIPPI

Caesarea Philippi, located at the base of Mount Hermon about 35 miles north of Capernaum and the Sea of Galilee, is known for its abundant waters, rich fields and abundance of trees. During Old Testament times and during the Greek occupation of the area, the city housed many shrines to various false deities. Herod the Great built a white marble temple there in honor of Caesar Augustus. Herod's son Philip ruled from this city (4 BC—AD 34). Philip brought restoration and beauty to the area and named it "Caesarea" after Tiberias Caesar. To distinguish it from the Caesarea on the Mediterranean coast, this Caesarea was called Caesarea Philippi (after Philip). At this location known for its many gods, Peter confessed Jesus as the Christ the Son of the Living God.

Extra Mile

SON OF MAN—
SON OF GOD

The Gospel of John reveals Jesus as the Son of Man and the Son of God. Read John 1:1–18, and list all that you find about Jesus in that passage.

blessed. This promise of a "seed" to Jacob was the same promise of a "seed" that God had given to Abraham. Galatians 3:16 reveals that this "seed" was Christ.

How does the Son of Man fit into this? Who is the Son of Man in John 1:51?

_____

_____

_____

John 1:51 reveals that the Son of Man is the staircase, the connection between earth and heaven. When we look at the context of the conversation between Jesus and Nathanael, we see some other revealing truths. First, when Jesus spoke of Nathanael as one in whom there was no guile or deceit, many believe He was contrasting Nathanael with Jacob, whose name means deceiver. There was no "deceit" or no "Jacob" in Nathanael. Deceit and insincerity marked many in Jesus' day as the Gospels clearly reveal. By revelation, Nathanael saw Jesus for who He is, the Son of God and King of Israel. Jesus revealed Himself as the Son of Man, the One about whom the prophet Daniel spoke, but more than that, He pictured Himself not only as the King who would reign, but also as the bridge (staircase) between earth and heaven, between man and God. He revealed Himself as both Lord and Savior, and the revelation of Himself had just begun.

The events surrounding Nathanael occurred during the first part of Jesus' ministry. As the weeks and months progressed, Jesus revealed more and more of who He was and why He came. In the third year of His ministry, we find Jesus with the Twelve in the city of Caesarea Philippi around the spring of AD 29. Matthew 16 gives the account in which we see a more complete picture of the Son of Man. There Jesus asked His disciples *"Who do men say that I, the Son of Man, am?"* (16:13 NKJV).

📖 Read Matthew 16:14–17, and answer the questions below.

What was their first reply (16:14)?

_____

_____

What was His follow-up question (16:15)?

_____

_____

What do you discover about Jesus in Peter's answer (16:16)?

_____

_____

_____

What does Jesus reveal in response to Peter's answer (16:17)?

_____

_____

_____

Jesus asked His disciples *"Who do men say that I, the Son of Man, am?"* (NKJV). They replied that people thought He was John the Baptist, Elijah, Jeremiah, or some other prophet. To His question *"Who do you say that I am?"* Simon Peter quickly answered, *"Thou art the Christ* [the Messiah], *the Son of the Living God."* Jesus revealed that Peter's confession of Jesus as the promised Messiah **and** the Son of God was by the revelation of His heavenly Father, not by any teaching or skill of men. That matched what God revealed to Nathanael over two years before.

The Son of Man is the Christ, the Messiah. He is Lord. What more can we learn about this Son of Man? We will discover more in Day Two.

THE SON OF MAN CAME TO DIE

Before Jesus was ever born, an angel spoke to Joseph (the husband of Mary, Jesus' mother), and told Him that the child Mary would bear was conceived of the Holy Spirit. He was to give Him the name "Jesus" (the Greek form of the Hebrew word *"Yeshua"* or *"Joshua,"* meaning "Jehovah is salvation"), *"for it is He who will save His people from their sins"* (Matthew 1:21).

As Jesus walked on earth, He knew His mission—*"to seek and to save that which was lost"* (Luke 19:10). From the earliest days He knew the Father had a design for His life (Luke 2:41–52), and He delighted to do His Father's will (Hebrews 10:7–10). Near the beginning of His ministry, Jesus spoke to one of the Jewish leaders, Nicodemus, about the will of the Father and the purpose of the Son of Man. What do we learn from that conversation?

📖 Looking at John 3:13–15, what do you discover about the Son of Man?

_____

_____

_____

Jesus made it clear that He, as the Son of Man who had descended from heaven, *"must . . . be lifted up"* even *"as Moses lifted up the serpent in the wilderness."* The result would be *"that whoever believes may in Him have eternal life"* (John 3:13–15). In that statement we begin to see an unclouded picture of why Jesus came and what He meant by saving the lost. He wanted people to know the forgiveness of their sins and the eternal life that He alone could give.

📖 What do you see about the purpose of God for the Son of Man in the next three verses, John 3:16–18?

_____

_____

_____

Probably one of the most familiar verses in all of Scripture, John 3:16 clearly proclaims the purpose of God in sending His only begotten Son, the Son

Did You Know?
MOSES AND THE BRONZE SERPENT

Numbers 21:6–9 records the incident in which the Lord sent fiery serpents because of the complaints of the people against God and Moses. Many died for their acts of insubordination. When the people came to Moses admitting their sin and asked Moses to intercede, Moses did so. The Lord instructed him to make an image of a fiery serpent made of bronze. Moses set this serpent on a standard and the people were informed that, *"if a serpent bit any man, when he looked to the bronze serpent, he lived"* (21:9). Jesus explained that, as the Son of Man, he too must *"be lifted up"* even *"as Moses lifted up the serpent in the wilderness."* Any person who believes or, in essence, looks to Jesus receives eternal life! Look to Jesus and live!

Doctrine
THE SON OF MAN AND FORGIVENESS OF SINS

Matthew 9:1–8 records that at Capernaum some men brought a paralytic to Jesus who, seeing the man's faith, told him his sins were forgiven. Some of the scribes questioned Him in their minds and even accused Him of blasphemy. Jesus, *"knowing their thoughts,"* rebuked them and then healed the man. He again affirmed that the man's sins were forgiven. Here Jesus, the Son of God and the Son of Man, showed His power by revealing the thoughts of man, by healing the diseases of man, and by bringing healing to the deepest part of man—bringing forgiveness of man's sins. Jesus fulfills all that His name means—Savior.

Doctrine
"MY CHURCH"

The Church belongs to Jesus Christ. He bought it (Acts 20:28) and started it (Acts 1–2). He is building it (Matthew 16:18) and, as His Bride, the Church is being made beautiful by her Bridegroom (Ephesians 5:23–27). He is returning to *"receive"* His own to Himself (John 14:3) so that we will *"always be with the Lord"* (1 Thessalonians 4:14–17).

of Man (as verses 13 and 14 call Him). God loved the world. Therefore, He sent Jesus to be lifted up on a cross for our salvation. The account of the bronze serpent being lifted up in the wilderness to save the people from the deadly bite of the serpent was a prophetic picture of the Son of Man being lifted up (see Numbers 21). We know Jesus went to the cross at the hands of the Jewish and Roman leaders. He died the humiliating death of a Roman cross, *"despising the shame"* as Hebrews 12:2 states. He was sent to die, not to judge the world, but to save the world. The one believing on Him *"is not judged."* As Jesus says in John 5:24, *"Truly, truly, I say to you, he who hears My word, and believes Him who sent Me, has eternal life, and does not come into judgment, but has passed out of death into life."*

 How about you? Do you know the love of the Father and of the Son of Man? Have you come to the place where you know your sins are forgiven and you have passed out of death into life? If not, you may want to read the section at the end of this lesson entitled *How to Follow God.* Make sure you are fitting into God's purpose for your life—God's eternal purpose for you.

How do the truths of John 3 connect to Peter's confession of Jesus as the Christ in Matthew 16? In Matthew 16:18–19, Jesus said that His Church would be built on *"this rock"* (*petra*, a large rock or bedrock), referring to the truth of Peter's confession of the Son of Man as the Christ, the Son of the living God. [Peter is the *petros*, small stone.] The Son of Man, the one to whom all dominion is given, is the Christ or Messiah, the Promised Seed of Abraham and Jacob. He is the one who will be a blessing to all nations by the salvation He brings.

The King of the kingdom of heaven, the Christ, would build His Church, and nothing would stop Him. People would be able to come into the kingdom of heaven through the Lord Jesus, the staircase to heaven. How would that happen? Jesus began explaining to the disciples this very truth immediately after Peter's confession at Caesarea Philippi.

📖 What do you discover in Matthew 16:21?

_____

_____

_____

_____

The Gospels often present Jesus talking about the Son of Man suffering death. At Caesarea Philippi Jesus began revealing that He would go to Jerusalem to be killed at the hands of the religious leaders, but He would rise the third day. Not too many days after the events at Caesarea Philippi—as Jesus and His disciples were moving about in Galilee apart from the crowds—He spoke to His disciples again. In Matthew 17:22–23 Jesus told them that *"the Son of Man"* would be *"delivered* (or *betrayed*) *into the hands of men."* Then those men would kill Him. According to Matthew 20:17–19 the "men" He was referring to included the chief priests, the scribes, and the Gentiles to whom Jesus would be delivered. In each instance Jesus promised that He would rise on the third day, but the disciples didn't seem to hear or understand the words about His resurrection. They could only hear the words about His death, and they were deeply grieved.

📖 Read Philippians 2:5–11, and answer the questions below.

What was the attitude of Jesus as He faced the coming cross? The apostle Paul spoke of Christ's attitude and His mission in Philippians 2:5–11. What was at the heart of all Jesus did according to verses 6–7?

_____

_____

_____

What characterized Jesus according to Philippians 2:8?

_____

_____

_____

What do you discover about the Father's view of Jesus in 2:9–11?

_____

_____

_____

> "And being found in appearance as a man, He humbled Himself by becoming obedient to the point of death, even death on a cross."
> Philippians 2:8

Central in the heart of Jesus was His willingness to empty Himself of His glory to serve as a bondservant. In doing this He did not stop being God. He always existed in the form of God; in His essence He was and is and ever will be God, being equal with God the Father in every way. However, He chose to become a man, and in the likeness of man He walked as a servant. In His outward appearance as man, everyone could see the attitude and the actions of a bondservant. As a man and a servant He humbled Himself, obeying all the Father's will even to the point of willingly giving His life to die on the cross. Obeying the Father's will was why Christ came. The Father has exalted Christ as Lord, revealing to us that the Son of Man indeed lives as Lord and Savior.

The disciples were slow to understand all Jesus was saying. They did not understand the fullness of the purpose of God in the cross, nor did they understand how that cross would impact them. Jesus sought to make it clear to them. We will see that in Day Three.

THE SON OF MAN CALLS US TO COME AND DIE

The Son of Man

DAY THREE

Intermingled with Jesus' words about His cross were words about the resurrection and about being glorified in His resurrection. At one of those times, Jesus illustrated His own surrender to the cross and the glory that would come from that. To glorify someone meant to form a good opinion or view of them. It meant to help reveal his worth and his excellence. How would Jesus be glorified? How would His worth be expressed?

📖 Read John 12:23–24. What is the picture Jesus paints?

_____

_____

_____

How does a grain of wheat show its value? How does one know if a grain of wheat is of good quality?

_____

_____

_____

Jesus was just days before the cross. How did Jesus illustrate this truth about the grain of wheat?

_____

_____

_____

"Truly, truly, I say to you, unless a grain of wheat falls into the earth and dies, it remains by itself alone; but if it dies, it bears much fruit."
John 12:24

Jesus knew that the hour had arrived for the Son of Man to be glorified. He knew that the purpose for which He came into the world was at hand, the hour of His death for the sins of the world. He also knew that in His death He would reveal the heart of the Father as well as His own heart. All the world would clearly see His love, His servant's heart, His purity, and His holiness. He would go to the cross as a sacrificial lamb, the Lamb of God. As a result, many would experience His love and forgiveness. The picture in which He chose to portray this sacrificial love was the story of the grain of wheat. If a grain falls into the earth and dies, it brings forth much fruit for the benefit of many. If it stays out of the ground stored away, protected, and unused, it may look like a beautiful, plump, healthy grain, but it *"remains by itself alone,"* unfruitful, never knowing the life that comes out of death.

📖 How did Jesus apply the truth about the grain of wheat to His disciples in John 12:25–26?

_____

_____

_____

". . . for this purpose I came to this hour."
John 12:27

Jesus readily applied this truth to His followers. He knew He was about to go to the cross to die. Like the grain that dies, Christ's death would mean abundant life for millions, an eternal harvest that would bring rejoicing throughout earth and heaven. If any one of His followers wanted to know that abundant life, he must hate his life in comparison to the life that Jesus offered. We know that Jesus offers a life of forgiveness with His Spirit living within. If a man loves his own life and seeks to protect it and keep it safe, disregarding the call of Jesus, he will lose that life. If he tries to find abundance in his own resources, then he will lose, but if he repents and "dies to his self"—if he surrenders himself to Jesus to obey Him, follow Him, and serve Him—then he will actually keep his life and be honored by the Father forever.

This "death unto life" truth is what Jesus as the Son of Man revealed to Peter in Matthew 16. After Peter's verbal recognition of Jesus as *"the Christ, the Son of the Living God,"* Jesus began to give further revelation of His purposes as the Son of Man. As we have already seen, they included revelation of His betrayal, His crucifixion, and His resurrection. This revelation also included a foreshadowing of the disciples' own dying to self. What explanation did Jesus give His disciples about this matter?

    Read Matthew 16:24–26, and record what Jesus said about cross-bearing. What is the first reason He gives for cross-bearing (16:25)?

_____

_____

_____

What reason does He add in verse 26?

_____

_____

_____

Put Yourself In Their Shoes
CRUCIFIXION

Crucifixion (death on a cross) is one of the cruelest forms of execution ever devised by man. It is a death marked by utter humiliation and shame, extreme agony, and intense pain. The Romans would not execute one of their own citizens in this manner. Jesus asked His followers to take up their crosses daily and follow Him (Luke 9:23). Jesus wants us to take up our cross and die to ourselves at every level so that He can fill us with His life and accomplish His purposes **in** and through **us**.

Jesus cautioned that anyone who tried to save his life would end up losing it, but if anyone would lose his life for His sake, he would find abundant life through Christ. The word for life actually means "soul," referring to the heart of life or, if you will, the very care of who and what we are. One will find true satisfaction when he gives his life away to the Lord for Him to possess, guide, and save. A man who gains the whole world yet loses his soul has lost everything. He profits nothing. There is nothing more valuable than one's soul. No amount of wealth, prestige, or pleasure can fully satisfy a man, nor can these earthly things come close to being worth enough to exchange for one's soul. But there is more to be learned. Jesus goes on to speak of reasons why one should give Him his life.

    Why should one give his life away to Jesus? Why invest in Him? Why should one "lose" his life for the sake of Jesus, the Son of Man? Read Matthew 16:27, and write your insights.

_____

_____

_____

In speaking to His disciples, Jesus introduced a new aspect of the life and work of the Son of Man. He *"is going to come in the glory of His Father with His angels."* He will reveal His exalted position in the splendor of His Father, and He will appear with a multitude of angels. What will He do when He comes? He will *"recompense every man according to his deeds."* Does this refer to some kind of salvation by works? Not at all! Jesus is simply assuring us that we must answer for how we respond to the truth He spoke and the call He made.

Have you given Him your life? Are you trusting in the death and resurrection of Him who is both the Son of Man and the Son of God. Are you depending on His death as payment for your sin? Have you received His righteousness in exchange for your sin? When He comes, He will judge men and women based on their relationship to Him. He will judge whether

A man who gains the whole world yet loses his soul has lost everything. No amount of wealth, prestige, or pleasure can fully satisfy a man, nor can it come close to being worth exchanging for one's soul.

people gave Him their lives or if they kept their lives for self-centered use. He will judge whether people tried to save their lives by keeping and protecting them. If they have tried to preserve their lives rather then surrender them to God, then they will have only their own resources "to bank on" instead of the resources of the Son of Man. Those depending on their own resources will be bankrupt, since none of the currency of self is worth anything in the kingdom of the Son of Man. Only His righteous life accounts for anything.

Just a few days before Jesus and His disciples reached Jerusalem, where He would face the cross, Jesus spoke to His disciples of His approaching death. Near Jericho, He had to deal with James and John, who wanted the two best seats in His kingdom, one on His left and one on His right. (Their mother also joined in the request for her sons.) Remember that this was just days before His crucifixion. James and John certainly were not learning well. However, we should not judge them too quickly. The other ten disciples were *"indignant"* over this request because they too wanted those positions of greatness. How did the Son of Man respond? We find His response in Matthew 20.

📖 What was the Son of Man's view of this world, the Gentile world (Matthew 20:25)?

_____

_____

_____

What did Jesus tell His disciples He expected of them (20:26–27)?

_____

_____

_____

What was His own example to them (20:28)? What do you discover about His purpose in coming?

_____

_____

_____

"[We are] always carrying about in the body the dying of Jesus, that the life of Jesus also may be manifested in our body."
2 Corinthians 4:10

The Gentiles (referring to all those outside the kingdom of God) are known for their seeking to *"lord it over,"* to rule by continually seeking greater authority and more control. Those outside God's kingdom certainly do not seek to give up their lives or to die to self. Jesus said it was to be just the opposite among His followers. They were to outdo one another in serving one another. Greatness in His kingdom came from humility and service. First place went to those who sought to serve as slaves. This serving attitude is the attitude of Christ that we have already studied in Philippians 2. In other words, people who give of themselves wholeheartedly to the benefit of others are living like citizens of His kingdom. Giving yourself involves dying to self, becoming that grain of wheat in the ground, hidden, dying, with the life of God being manifest out of that death to self. That was how the Son of Man saw Himself and His mission. As a matter of fact, He said He came *"to give His life a ransom for many"*—to die for their sins. In doing so He would see many come to know the life only He could give. As He called them to

Himself, to deny themselves, take up their crosses, and follow Him, through their experiences of dying to self, they would come to know the abundance of the life that He freely gives.

What further purpose does the Son of Man have for His people and for this world? We will see some more of His purpose in Day Four.

THE GLORY OF THE SON OF MAN

DAY FOUR

More than once, Jesus spoke of the day when the Son of Man would come in great glory. Just after the incident in Matthew 16:27, Jesus said that some standing there would not taste death until they had seen *"the Son of Man coming in His kingdom"* (Matthew 16:28). To what was Jesus referring? The answer to this question is found in Matthew 17.

📖 Matthew 17:1 follows directly after Matthew 16:28. Read Matthew 17:1–9. What happened in 17:1–2? (You may wish to read Luke 9:28–36 for some additional insights.)

_____

_____

_____

Who appeared with Jesus (v. 3)?

_____

_____

What was Peter's response (v. 4)?

_____

_____

_____

Did You Know?
MOUNT HERMON

Mount Hermon is believed by many to be the location of the Transfiguration since it located near Caesarea Philippi in northern Israel. Mark 9:2 says it was a *"high mountain."* Mount Hermon is 9,232 feet in elevation and would have afforded Jesus and His disciples an undisturbed area for this time of prayer.

Matthew reports that six days after Jesus said that some would see *"His king-dom,"* He took Peter, James, and John on a mountain. Luke adds that He did so in order to pray, and that while He was praying His appearance changed (9:28–29). He was transfigured before their eyes so that *"His face shone like the sun,"* and His clothes were as *"white as light."* Then Moses and Elijah, representative of the Law and the prophets, appeared and began talking to Him about *"His departure which He was about to accomplish at Jerusalem"* (Luke 9:31). Peter suggested that he make three tabernacles for Jesus, Moses, and Elijah. Perhaps he said that because he thought that this would be the perfect place to stay—with the Lord resplendent in kingdom glory and Moses and Elijah there—or perhaps Peter was thinking the king-dom had already come, especially in light of Jesus' statement just days before (Matthew 16:28). He may have been remembering some of the promises of the Old Testament, especially those pictured in the Feasts of Israel. As the Feast of Passover symbolized the crucifixion of Christ our Passover Lamb, and as the Feast of Firstfruits symbolized the Resurrection of Christ, so the Feast of Booths or Tabernacles (celebrated in early October) prophetically symbolized the coming of the Messiah when He would lead His people in a reign of peace.

As Peter spoke, the Father overshadowed them in a cloud and said, *"This is My* **beloved Son***, with whom I am well-pleased; listen to Him,"* and then commanded them to *"listen to Him!"* The frightened disciples were raised to their feet by the Lord Jesus, and then they left the mountain with Him.

What did Jesus tell them as they came down the mountain (17:9)?

_____

_____

_____

Jesus told Peter, James, and John to tell no one what they had seen until *"the Son of Man has risen from the dead."* This experience on the mount of transfiguration in some measure certainly fulfilled Christ's prophetic statement of the disciples seeing a preview of *"the Son of Man coming in His Kingdom."* The prophecy in Matthew 16:28 may also find its fulfillment in John's visions in the book of Revelation. They saw the glory of the Lord and of the Father. They recognized Moses and Elijah and heard their voices as well as the voice of the Father. The phrase *"coming in His Kingdom"* could even be translated "coming in His royal splendor." Later Peter described this event stating, *"we were eyewitnesses of His majesty,"* and spoke of *"when He received honor and glory from God the Father"* (2 Peter 1:16–17).

This incident certainly revealed the glory of the Son of Man, but it did not answer all of the disciples' questions about Him. Another incident as they traveled gave them another glimpse of what it meant to follow the Son of Man. Not long before His crucifixion, Jesus encountered a rich young ruler who was unwilling to sell all and follow Him (Matthew 19:16–26). After that encounter, Peter questioned Jesus about their own stance before Him. They had left all, and he wanted to know what sort of reward awaited them. Jesus did not rebuke Peter for his question. It was a valid question, and Jesus wanted them to understand what awaited them in their relationship with the Son of Man. What did Jesus tell them?

📖 Looking at Matthew 19:27–29, what will occur in the *"regeneration"*?

_____

_____

_____

What is the reward for the disciples who *"followed"* Jesus (19:28)?

_____

_____

_____

What is the reward for anyone who follows Jesus (19:29)?

_____

_____

_____

Did You Know?

CLOUDS

The Lord often manifested Himself in a bright cloud sometimes called the "cloud of glory" or the *"Shekinah,"* related to the Hebrew word meaning "to reside or dwell." The Father manifested Himself in a bright cloud at the Transfiguration, and Jesus often spoke of returning in the clouds of heaven with power. Acts 1:9 says Jesus ascended in *"a cloud,"* and the angels who stood there told the disciples Jesus would *"come in just the same way"* as He left. Revelation 1:7 speaks of Jesus *"coming with the clouds,"* and Revelation 14:14 pictures *"One like the Son of Man,"* (NKJV) sitting on a white cloud and crowned with a golden victor's crown.

Jesus assured Peter and His other disciples that a time was coming *"when the Son of Man will sit on His* **glorious** *throne"* (or, "the throne of His **glory**" [emphasis mine]). This particular event is referred to as the *"regeneration,"* a time when the Lord will reign on the earth and all will be restored. Acts 3:21 speaks of *"the period of restoration of all things,"* a time prophesied and anticipated by the prophets and the people of God for ages. In that time the disciples will sit on thrones judging or governing the twelve tribes of Israel. All those who have given their lives to Jesus Christ will additionally be rewarded many times over and experience the blessing of eternal life.

The Son of Man is spoken of in many passages. His glory is revealed in many ways. Matthew 24:29–31 speaks of the end times when *"all the tribes of the earth . . . will see the* SON OF MAN COMING ON THE CLOUDS OF THE SKY *with power and great glory."* Matthew 25:31–46 shows us that when the Son of Man comes in His glory He will judge the nations as sheep and goats. Even before Caiaphas and the Jewish leaders on the night before His crucifixion, when asked if He was *"the Christ, the Son of God,"* Jesus testified, *"It is as you said"* (NKJV). Then He added, *"Nevertheless, I tell you, hereafter you shall see* THE SON OF MAN SITTING AT THE RIGHT HAND OF THE POWER, *and* COMING ON THE CLOUDS OF HEAVEN" (Matthew 26:63–64). Are you ready for His coming? In Day Five we will explore how we can be better prepared for Christ's coming.

FOR ME TO FOLLOW GOD

The Son of Man DAY FIVE

W hat does it mean to follow the Son of Man? We have seen that He is Lord. Following Him as Lord means surrender to His will His way. We have seen Him as the Savior who died for our sins, offering us forgiveness and eternal life. Following Him as Savior means receiving His death for us, His Life within us, and receiving His righteousness in place of our unrighteousness. We have seen that the Son of Man will come in His glory to reign over all. Following Him means being ready for His return. How do we do that day by day?

📖 The first question each of us must ask is "Do I have a right relationship with God?" Read 1 Timothy 2:4–6. What is the first priority on God's heart according to verse 4?

_____

_____

_____

According to verses 5 and 6, what has God done to make sure we come to know Him in truth?

_____

_____

_____

_____

> *"For there is one God, and one mediator also between God and men, the man Christ Jesus."*
>
> *I Timothy 2:5*

APPLY Do you know Jesus Christ as **your mediator**? This is the question of **salvation**. Are you rightly related to Him through His salvation? (See the section "How to Follow God" at the end of this lesson if you are not sure.)

📖 Jesus said that the grain of wheat does one of two things. It either remains by itself intact and alone, or it falls into the ground and dies, producing more life. What kind of grain are you? Read James 4:13–16. What does James say your life is like on this earth?

_____

_____

What is James' counsel to you?

_____

_____

_____

APPLY Your life is like a vapor, like a morning fog that will soon be gone. Are you living for the moment, for what you can get for yourself right now? Are you living your life for the temporal or the eternal? Are you giving yourself for the ongoing, ever-growing kingdom? These are questions of **surrender**. James says the daily cry of our hearts should be *"If the Lord wills, we shall live and also do this or that."* Is that the cry of your heart today?

📖 Read 1 Timothy 6:17–19. What is the counsel of the apostle Paul in verses 17 and 18?

_____

_____

What is the promise of verses 17 and 19?

_____

_____

What are we to *"take hold of"*?

_____

_____

Paul knew from experience what it meant to give His life to the Lord Jesus, to fall into the ground and die as a grain of wheat. He knew what it meant to die to self and what it meant to begin to see eternal fruit in the lives of those in whom he invested. His instructions to those *"who are rich in this present world"* cover a broad range of the *"rich."* His definition of "rich" is not just those with millions of dollars, but refers to those who have more than they need. His counsel is very wise; never rest in the things you have. Riches are never a certainty, but God's love is always certain. Rest your life in His hands. What should we do with our riches? We should look to the Lord to guide us in doing good, in being generous, making sure we are ready to share. In this way our "riches" can be an eternal investment. Giving our lives and our "riches" to the Lord is taking hold of *"that which is life indeed."*

Think of this truth as a question about our investments. How are we investing our lives? The events of life, especially death, continually speak a message about **eternity**—this life is not all there is. There is something beyond the present. Life's events also convey meaning concerning our **destiny**—we are all headed toward one of two destinations. We will either be with the Lord in heaven, in His wonderful presence forever, or we will be separated from Him forever in hell.

There is also a word about **opportunity**—we have a choice to make. Will we surrender our lives and rest our hope of salvation on Jesus Christ? Or will we "keep" our lives and try to "save" our lives ourselves? That is the question about our eternal destiny. With that we then have the opportunity to invest our lives in what lasts forever—knowing and following. We have the opportunity to invest our lives in Christ and in getting the Word of God to the lives of people. That means helping them know His Word in order to know Him and His love more fully and thus come to follow and obey Him more completely. In these choices we and those who follow His Word can have a glorious destiny and a wonderful eternity with the Son of Man!

In 1 Corinthians 3:9–15, the apostle Paul paints a vivid picture of how we can invest our lives. Read those verses. What are the materials with which we can build?

_____

_____

_____

What materials pass the test of God's fire (3:12–13)?

_____

_____

What are the two possibilities for each man (3:14–15)?

_____

_____

In building *"God's building,"* believers can use *"gold, silver, precious stones, wood, hay, straw,"* two categories of materials that face fire in totally different ways. The first three pass through the fire unharmed. If anything, only the dross is burned. The precious metal remains. In the second three, everything is burned up. Only ashes remain. God's fiery gaze will test the **quality** of each man's work, not the quantity. More is not necessarily better. Those believers who have built with lasting materials will receive a reward, and those who have used the inferior materials will suffer loss of reward, though they themselves will be saved.

How do we assure ourselves that we are building with the gold, silver, and precious stones? We must surrender our lives to the Lord and let Him guide us in the building process. As we walk by faith, we are building with "gold." As we depend on His Spirit we are putting "precious stones" in place. As we follow Christ we are seeing "silver" placed where He wants it. Every time we walk by sight instead of faith, carry out the desires of the flesh, or follow "self" instead of Christ, we have stored up wood, hay, and straw.

> *"Take hold of that which is life indeed."*
> I Timothy 6:19

> We must surrender our lives to the Lord and let Him guide in the building process.

APPLY How about you? How are you building? Stop for a moment, and spend some time in prayer. Ask the Lord to give you His perspective and His evaluation of where you are. Ask Him to show you how to follow the Son of Man as He followed His Father.

 Lord, thank You for coming as the Son of Man. Thank You for showing me that You are indeed a gracious Lord and Savior. Thank You for being born a man and living as a man and the God-Man on this earth. I know You know all that I go through. You *"sympathize with* [my] *weaknesses"* (Hebrews 4:15). You know how I feel and what I face since You have been *"tempted in all things as* [I am tempted]*, yet without sin."* Thank You that I can draw near to Your throne of grace and speak with confidence, telling You all that is on my heart. I know You won't send me away but will give me *"grace to help in time of need"*—well-timed for **my** exact need (Hebrews 4:15–16). Thank You for Your compassion and mercy. Give me ears to hear You so that I listen carefully to all that You say. Then help me fully obey You. May I walk in such a way that I build with gold, silver, and precious stones, not the wood, hay, and straw of self-centeredness. I want to be ready for Your return, not ashamed at Your coming, but glad over the joy of seeing Your face, the face of the Son of Man. In Jesus' Name, Amen.

In light of all you have seen about the Son of Man and knowing His coming approaches, write your own prayer to Him in the space provided.

_____

_____

_____

_____

_____

_____

_____

_____

_____

_____

_____

Notes

Notes

How to Follow God

STARTING THE JOURNEY

D id you know that you have been on God's heart and mind for a long, long time? Even before time existed you were on His mind. He has always wanted you to know Him in a personal, purposeful relationship. He has a purpose for your life and it is founded upon His great love for you. You can be assured it is a good purpose and it lasts forever. Our time on this earth is only the beginning. God has a grand design that goes back into eternity past and reaches into eternity future. What is that design?

The Scriptures are clear about God's design for man—God created man to live and walk in oneness with Himself. Oneness with God means being in a relationship that is totally unselfish, totally satisfying, totally secure, righteous and pure in every way. That's what we were created for. If we walked in that kind of relationship with God we would glorify Him and bring pleasure to Him. Life would be right! Man was meant to live that way—pleasing to God and glorifying Him (giving a true estimate of who God is). Adam sinned and shattered his oneness with God. Ever since, man has come short of the glory of God: man does not and cannot please God or give a true estimate of God. Life is not right until a person is right with God. That is very clear as we look at the many people who walked across the pages of Scripture, both Old and New Testaments.

JESUS CHRIST came as the solution for this dilemma. Jesus Christ is the glory of God—the true estimate of who God is in every way. He pleased His Father in everything He did and said, and He came to restore oneness with God. He came to give man His power and grace to walk in oneness with God, to follow Him day by day enjoying the relationship for which he was created. In the process, man could begin to present a true picture of Who God is and experience knowing Him personally. You may be asking, "How do these facts impact my life today? How does this become real to me now? How can I begin the journey of following God in this way?" To come to know God personally means you must choose to receive Jesus Christ as your personal Savior and Lord.

- First of all, you must admit that you have sinned, that you are not walking in oneness with God, not pleasing Him or glorifying Him in your life (Romans 3:23; 6:23; 8:5-8).

- It means repenting of that sin—changing your mind, turning to God and turning away from sin—and by faith receiving His forgiveness based on His death on the Cross for you (Romans 3:21-26; 1 Peter 3:18).

- It means opening your life to receive Him as your living, resurrected Lord and Savior (John 1:12). He has promised to come and indwell you by His Spirit and live in you as the Savior and Master of your life (John 14:16-21; Romans 14:7-9).

- He wants to live His life through you—conforming you to His image, bearing His fruit through you and giving you power to reign in life (John 15:1,4-8; Romans 5:17; 7:4; 8:29, 37).

You can come to Him now. In your own words, simply tell Him you want to know Him personally and you willingly repent of your sin and receive His forgiveness and His life. Tell Him you want to follow Him forever (Romans 10:9-10, 13). Welcome to the Family of God and to the greatest journey of all!!!

WALKING ON THE JOURNEY

How do we follow Him day by day? Remember, Christ has given those who believe in Him everything pertaining to life and godliness, so that we no longer have to be slaves to our "flesh" and its corruption (2 Peter 1:3-4). Day by day He wants to empower us to live a life of love and joy, pleasing to Him and rewarding to us. That's why Ephesians 5:18 tells us to *"be filled with the Spirit"*—keep on being controlled by the Spirit who lives in you. He knows exactly what we need each day and we can trust Him to lead us (Proverbs 3:5-6). So how can we cooperate with Him in this journey together?

To walk with Him *day by day* means ...
- reading and listening to His Word day by day (Luke 10:39, 42; Colossians 3:16; Psalm 19:7-14; 119:9).

- spending time talking to Him in prayer (Philippians 4:6-7).

- realizing that God is God and you are not, and the role that means He has in your life.

This allows Him to work through your life as you fellowship, worship, pray and learn with other believers (Acts 2:42), and serve in the good works He has prepared for us to do—telling others who Jesus is and what His Word says, teaching and encouraging others, giving to help meet needs, helping others, etc. (Ephesians 2:10).

God's goal for each of us is that we be conformed to the image of His Son, Jesus Christ (Romans 8:29). But none of us will reach that goal of perfection until we are with Him in Heaven, for then "we shall be like Him, because we shall see Him just as He is" (1 John 3:2). For now, He wants us to follow

Him faithfully, learning more each day. Every turn in the road, every trial and every blessing, is designed to bring us to a new depth of surrender to the Lord and His ways. He not only wants us to do His will, He desires that we surrender to His will His way. That takes trust—trust in His character, His plan and His goals (Proverbs 3:5-6).

As you continue this journey, and perhaps you've been following Him for a while, you must continue to listen carefully and follow closely. We never graduate from that. That sensitivity to God takes moment-by-moment surrender, dying to the impulses of our flesh to go our own way, saying no to the temptations of Satan to doubt God and His Word, and refusing the lures of the world to be unfaithful to the Lord who gave His life for us.

God desires that each of us come to maturity as sons and daughters: to that point where we are fully satisfied in Him and His ways, fully secure in His sovereign love, and walking in the full measure of His purity and holiness. If we are to clearly present the image of Christ for all to see, it will take daily surrender and daily seeking to follow Him wherever He leads, however He gets there (Luke 9:23-25). It's a faithful walk of trust through time into eternity. And it is worth everything. Trust Him. Listen carefully. Follow closely.

Notes

61032991R00117

Made in the USA
Middletown, DE
18 August 2019